PENGUIN BOOKS

LINGUISTICS

David Crystal was born in 1941 and spent the early years of his life in Holyhead, North Wales. He went to St Mary's College, Liverpool, and University College London, where he read English and obtained his Ph.D. in 1966. He became lecturer in linguistics at University College, Bangor, and from 1965 to 1985 was at the University of Reading, where he was Professor of Linguistic Science for several years. He is currently an Honorary Professor at University College, Bangor. His research interests are mainly in English language studies, and in the clinical and remedial applications of linguistics in the study of language handicap.

David Crystal has published numerous articles and reviews, and his books include *Linguistics* (Penguin 1971, second edition 1985), *Child Language Learning and Linguistics*, *Introduction to Language Pathology*, *A Dictionary of Linguistics and Phonetics*, *Clinical Linguistics*, *Profiling Linguistic Disability*, *Who Cares about English Usage?* (Penguin 1984), *Listen to Your Child* (Penguin 1986), *Rediscover Grammar*, *The English Language* (Penguin 1988), *The Cambridge Encyclopedia of Language*, *Pilgrimage*, *The Cambridge Encyclopedia of the English Language* and *An Encyclopedic Dictionary of Language and Languages* (Penguin 1994). He is also the editor of the Cambridge family of general encyclopedias, and the editor of *Linguistics Abstracts* and *Child Language Teaching and Therapy*.

David Crystal now lives in Holyhead, where he works as a writer, lecturer and consultant on language and linguistics, and reference books editor. He is also a frequent radio broadcaster. In June 1995 he was awarded the OBE.

David Crystal

Linguistics

Second Edition

Penguin Books

PENGUIN BOOKS

Published by the Penguin Group
Penguin Books Ltd, 27 Wrights Lane, London W8 5TZ, England
Penguin Books USA Inc., 375 Hudson Street, New York, New York 10014, USA
Penguin Books Australia Ltd, Ringwood, Victoria, Australia
Penguin Books Canada Ltd, 10 Alcorn Avenue, Toronto, Ontario, Canada M4V 3B2
Penguin Books (NZ) Ltd, 182–190 Wairau Road, Auckland 10, New Zealand

Penguin Books Ltd, Registered Offices: Harmondsworth, Middlesex, England

First published in Pelican Books 1971
Reprinted with revisions 1981
Second edition 1985
Reprinted in Penguin Books 1990
10 9 8 7 6 5 4

Printed in England by Clays Ltd, St Ives plc
Filmset in Sabon

Contents

Preface

There are many excellent introductions to linguistics already available; but it seems to me that they all presuppose a great deal of understanding on the part of a reader – and I mean 'understanding' both in the sense of 'sympathy' and of 'prior knowledge'. Many questions of a pragmatic, historical and philosophical nature are taken for granted. I have therefore tried in this book, especially in Chapters 1–3, to look rather more thoroughly at these preliminary questions than is usually the case in short introductions. In a paperback introduction, also, it is inevitable that certain topics will be dealt with summarily which really deserve more space. In particular, I have had to avoid entering into details of controversial issues, relying on the existence of the many textbooks on more restricted topics to develop the positions sketched out here. I have also avoided any unnecessary duplication with the Pelicans on *Grammar* and *Phonetics*, which were being written simultaneously with this one. But I hope that the preliminary topics covered in the first three chapters will be able to make good my partial coverage, and provide a satisfactory general foundation for the interrelating of more specialist issues. Chapter 4 is the main chapter, presenting the various branches and current trends of the subject in a largely historical perspective. Chapter 5 looks at the overlap between the subject-matter of linguistics and that of other fields, and attempts to suggest points of contact between the theoretical emphasis of Chapter 4 and the practical demands of Chapter 1. And I have incorporated an extended illustration of one kind of linguistic reasoning as an interlude between the more 'academic' ruminations of Chapters 3 and 4.

My thanks are due to John Lyons, Frank Palmer, and Ron Brasington, for much-needed advice while this book was in preparation.

Preface to Second Edition

For this edition, several parts of Chapter 4 have been updated in order to take account of recent developments in the field of syntax and semantics. A new section, on pragmatics, has been added. And there have been numerous minor revisions, to both text and references, to make the book a more accurate reflection of emphases within linguistics in the 1980s.

D. C.   July 1984

1. Why Study Language?

Introductory books and courses on linguistics invariably try to get away from their rather complex-sounding titles as soon as they can, by producing a thumb-nail definition which (it is hoped) will provide a more familiar starting-point. This is usually something like 'Linguistics is the scientific study of language'. The authors then proceed to explain exactly why it is important to emphasize that linguistics is language studied *scientifically*, and follow this up by analysing the object of study, language, in some detail. All of which assumes a considerable amount of prior interest and commitment on the part of the reader. It is, after all, no small task to embark on a thorough introduction to linguistics; some books of this kind have four hundred pages or more! And it would be naïve of an author to expect anyone to work systematically through so many pages of text, notes, and (often) exercises without there being some advance interest or special reason for doing so.

Until recently, of course, an author could rely on the existence of this prior commitment. Most people who have read an introduction to linguistics over the past twenty years or so (for it was only in the late fifties that introductions to linguistics really began to increase and multiply) have had a vested interest in getting into the subject. They were students of English or modern languages, teachers of various languages (particularly of English to foreigners), translators, academics in related disciplines (such as sociology or psychology), and other 'professionals'. Their introductory reading implied a serious involvement: it would be followed up or accompanied by further reading; and, for the majority, their linguistic knowledge would be made use of later in life, though perhaps in some watered-down form.

It is only recently that the climate has changed, and to some extent this is a sign that the subject has 'come of age'. It now seems that linguistics is of interest to a much wider audience. It is coming to be on a par with a number of other subjects that people would like to read up – not because such subjects have any particular relevance to their own work, but simply because they 'sound interesting'. The aim is to get a clear general picture of a subject, not at all a specialist introduction. To have read a paperback review of such fields as psychiatry, holography, cryptanalysis – or linguistics – is to obtain a kind of 'bird's eye view' of the field, which might never be followed up in any way. And consequently, a rather different way of introducing and covering these fields has to be found than is seen in the more 'academic' publications. If the subject is at all unfamiliar – as is surely the case with linguistics – then the reasons for studying it have to be gone into in greater depth than would otherwise be necessary. In a sense, the author has to don the guise of a missionary, and take nothing for granted. Thus, in the present case, as I implied above, the first question that has to be asked is not 'What is the scientific study of language?' or even 'What is language?' but rather 'Why bother to study language at all?'

There is no single, simple answer. Most people, after all, do *not* bother. A fairly common argument runs, 'Why should we bother? We can all use language, can't we? It grew naturally along with the rest of us. I understand my friends and they understand me. So why have a course of study about something which can be taken so much for granted?' This reasoning is attractive enough, at first sight; but it can be answered, and in a powerful way. One approach – perhaps that of the polished debater – would be to ask a parallel question. 'Why study the brain? We use it without difficulty. It developed naturally . . .' Or again 'Why study vision? We can all see without analysing our eyes . . .' But for these subjects, I do not think anyone would seriously begin to ask such questions, and it is instructive to examine the kinds of answer that might be given in order to see why. 'If we never studied vision' (one might run), 'how could we perform eye-surgery, or fit people with spectacles? How could we develop telescopes and microscopes?' Such rhetorical answers in turn suggest important general principles which can be applied to the less obvious case of language study. One principle states that it is important to study such aspects of human behaviour, because when things start to go wrong, we would otherwise have no knowledge of how to effect a cure. The other principle states that there are always a number of practical applications arising from such studies – other areas of experience which our analyses can help illuminate. So our question must now be, 'How can language go wrong? And what other areas could language study influence in this way?'

Before answering these questions, I have to stress one basic point. I am not suggesting that people will only begin to investigate the nature of language if they have an 'applied' interest in their study. All the applications I shall discuss below are largely dependent for their information on a body of knowledge about language which is available for them to tap and make use of in their own way. There can be – indeed, there has to be, and always has been – a 'pure' interest in language study also; and it is this interest in accumulating information about language as an end in itself which is the primary justification for having a separate discipline of study, linguistics. I shall be going into this issue in greater detail in Chapter 3. Here I would simply emphasize that for many people, the question 'Why bother to study language?' would be as pointless, irrational and insulting as asking a philatelist 'Why bother to collect stamps?' The ultimate answer in both cases is that it is a question of personal taste, and no amount of reasoning about applications can get round this. Some people find language a fascinating aspect of human behaviour, and they take a great delight in prodding it from various points of view – where does language come from? why do people speak differently? how do words change their meaning? could we think without language? how many languages are there? which is the oldest language? could an artificial language work? are the different languages of the world basically the same? Topics such as these are regularly discussed – with varying degrees of informedness – in everyday conversation. (There is at least one teachers' common-room, in my experience, where problems of etymology (the history of words) provide the normal, lunch-time gossip.) Some of these questions are naïve, some are complex (and there are of course many more that could be added to the list); but all are interesting, and require careful answers. The answers, however, will do no more than satisfy a curiosity, settle an argument, or add to someone's 'store of knowledge about the world'. There is no serious intention to apply the knowledge in further work, and why should there be?

But while I do not wish for one moment to deny the pure interest in language which exists in many people's minds, it is far out-weighed by the interest of those concerned with the applied side of language study. Most of us begin to notice language, and to worry about it, and to ask questions about it, when it starts to break down, to cause problems. How, then, does it do this?

Perhaps the most obvious case, which brings people up against the importance and complexity of language with a shock, is when language suddenly disappears, or fails to develop at all. Brain damage in an accident, a stroke, and various other catastrophes of this kind can effectively remove our language abilities. People may begin to speak unintelligibly, lose control over their speech, or even lose their ability to speak at all, quite literally, overnight. Can anything be done? It depends. In many cases of this kind, therapy has had some success. But successful therapy requires, at the very least, detailed knowledge of the nature of the skill which has been lost, and in what ways this skill can be broken down into teachable units. Language analysis is obviously prerequisite in this case. And similarly with the various kinds of impaired or delayed language acquisition. A child in its first year may begin to worry its parents by not producing the range of noises which they were expecting – its cry might be unduly shrill, to their ears, or its babbling odd, in some way. Is this an indication of something wrong? Is the child's brain damaged? Is there cardiac disease? Is the child deaf, possibly? Or is it just imagination? And again, when eighteen months comes round, and there is still no sign of a clear 'first word', is there mental retardation, or psychiatric disturbance, or is it simply a case of late development? In all these cases, the issue is the same. People begin by noting, rightly or wrongly, what they think is an abnor-mality in language use (or, in the case of the baby, 'pre-language' use), and inevitably, they worry. Of course in many cases there may be nothing wrong at all: language does not develop at the same speed or in identical ways for all children. But parents, being parents, want their worry confirmed or discredited; and so they go to a paediatrician, or an audiologist, or a speech therapist, or a specialist in some related field. If there *is* something wrong, then a diagnosis may be made, and a course of treatment prescribed. The story is familiar enough, and sounds simple.

But how do you diagnose a language disorder? Is it so simple? Can it be done without specialist, linguistic training? How valid is the argument I referred to earlier ('I know my own language, don't I?') in this context? I would argue that it has no validity at all. Imagine going to a doctor with something wrong with your heart: the extent to which he will effect a cure will depend primarily on how much he knows about hearts – in particular, about how hearts work normally. The doctor who begins by searching for a heartbeat on the right-hand side will hardly convince the patient that he will be able to help him. In a similar way, in order to diagnose a language disorder, you have to know a great deal about how language works normally. You have to know its structure, its development, and how it normally functions, in detail. Without this knowledge, there is little chance of getting a diagnosis right or developing successful treatment. Such situations often arise. The heart example may seem rather bizarre, but I have come across many cases of specialists whose ignorance of normal language development (through no fault of their own) has been as marked as this example suggests. And one can see how ludicrous the argument 'I know my own language; I've been speaking it for years' is in this context. I have had a heart for years, but I would not know whether anyone else had a hole in theirs, or how I would go about demonstrating it. The structure of language is in many ways as complicated and difficult to study as the structure of the human body – and in some ways more so, because it involves some extremely abstract reasoning. But this will become clear in due course.

In other words, to understand, let alone provide therapy for language disorders – for linguistic abnormality – one has to have had some grounding in linguistic normality. Whether it is pronunciation, grammar, vocabulary, or some combination of all three that is deficient, this principle is the same. Unfortunately, as we shall see, many people's knowledge of normal language is very shaky; and their ability to describe what it is they know is shakier still. Most of us have had no training in language study at all – apart from a few dimly and uncharitably remembered days in grammar classes at school.

But this field, language pathology, is perhaps a rather specialist justification for language study. Problems of speech disability are relatively few and far between, and do not affect many of us. There are, however, a number of other, more everyday areas of experience where some knowledge of language's structure and use can be invaluable to avoid linguistic breakdowns. We may introduce them by considering the more general, and much more familiar concept of *communication*.

When two people claim to be 'talking the same language', they mean a great deal more than that they are using the same pronunciation, grammar and vocabulary. The phrase usually implies that they have begun to understand each other; they are 'on the same wavelength'; they have begun to communicate. These days the term 'communication' has something of a vogue status. We are continually being urged to pay attention to it, in all walks of life. If this book had been called *Communication*, it would have had a much more attractive ring about it! But it would have been dishonest to call it that, for while it is true that language is the most important method we have of communicating, it is manifestly not the only method. (We can communicate by gestures, facial expressions, or touch, for instance, and these are not language, as will be made clear in Chapter 4.) But despite the considerable difference between the concepts of communication and language, it is still generally agreed that the main purpose of language is to communicate; hence much of the discussion over the last few years about the importance of studying ways and means of improving communication techniques is relevant to the study of language.

Problems of communication affect us all in many aspects of day-to-day living, and can cause serious trouble. It is incredibly easy to be unintentionally misunderstood, or to speak ambiguously, or vaguely. An excellent example of difficult communication is in the doctor–patient relationship, where most patients (particularly those in the lower social groups) find it very difficult to get the right words to describe their symptoms – even fairly general terms, like 'ache', are vague, and used differently by different patients. The problem affects doctors too, who often have a job to formulate a diagnosis in words which the patient will understand, and which will not have any unexpected repercussions. They may use a term which has 'loaded' associations for the patient, for instance, and this could cause unfortunate side-effects. There is no necessary connection between the terms 'growth' and 'cancer', for example, but for many people there is a strong feeling that the two *are* associated, and a casual description of a physical state as a 'growth' can easily lead to considerable unnecessary worry.

Any terms which try to describe our sensations are liable to cause problems, of course: it is not easy to describe our reactions to a painting, or a symphony; nor is it easy to convince others about the merits or demerits of an artistic work when the main tools we have to work with are words with inherently vague, subjective meanings. (We can very often sympathize with the newspaper critic who finds it necessary to lapse into extended and vivid metaphors in order to get his reactions across without sounding too banal.) 'I gotta use words when I talk to you,' complained T. S. Eliot's Sweeney, perhaps rather bitterly. In these cases, the communication problem is not normally comparable in importance to the doctor–patient problem ; but there are other areas where the implications are, quite literally, of world importance. The Iron Curtain, it has been said, is also a 'semantic' curtain – a curtain through which meanings find it difficult to pass. And it is certainly true that many of the political and philosophical terms which describe Western ideals and norms of behaviour have different meanings when these same terms are used in Eastern countries. The meaning of a term like 'freedom' is very relative; terms like 'progressive', 'communist' and 'democratic' have good or bad or neutral overtones depending very much on which part of the world you were brought up in. And on a lesser scale, we can point to large- and small-scale vocabulary differences between any two social groups within a community.

This last point could be illustrated by the problems facing people in many areas: the fostering of an ecumenical dialogue between different religious groups is one case beset with communicational difficulties of this kind; and the problems facing the bureaucrat attempting to formulate rules and regulations in language that will be comprehensible to *all* sections of the community is another. But perhaps the clearest example of this point is in industry, where business management has been gradually becoming aware that many of the difficulties which cause strikes, lose orders, and create ill feeling are really due to breakdowns in communication. Managers are discovering that an absence of effective communication between employers and staff must lead to trouble and lack of confidence; and, what is more important, they are finding out that to remedy this lack they must use modern educational methods, and not just rely on a 'grape-vine' around the factory floor. American management has already gone in for this in a big way, and now pays a great deal of attention to the means whereby communication takes place at every level in industry. Courses in communications and management are widespread. 'Are your executives BLIND to the communication effects of their decisions and actions?' queries one college brochure, inviting enrolment. 'Do they have communication awareness?' demands another. The economist Sir Geoffrey Vickers once defined management as 'largely consisting of directing what other people do by means of signals given and received – and that is communication'. This coordinating role of the manager is well illustrated by the (possibly apocryphal) story of the managing director who said to his visitor, while showing him round his plant: 'I'm not too sure what happens; but here at this end we put in metal, and down there it comes out as refrigerators'!

As suggested above, communication covers much more than language, and this is true of business management too. Vickers also makes this point: 'It is not surprising that in the literature of business management, "communications" has virtually ceased to imply the exchange of information as such. It has become a term of art to include every form of human contact which may help to get cooperation within the organization and a good Press outside.' It thus includes the study of different media of communication (such as posters, journals, loudspeaker systems, discussion groups – what is generally referred to as 'Works Information'), the relevance of traditional attitudes and the study of a large variety of social prejudices ('My father always taught me, if the manager talks civil to you, watch out, he's trying to put one over'). But linguistic problems are in many ways more fundamental than this. To begin with, there is the pressure on managers to ensure not only that language is used, but that it is used in quantity. In business management, it is speech which is golden; silence is anathema, for it leads to ignorance – and that leads to lack of confidence, which in turn leads to trouble. A Ministry of (at that time) Labour pamphlet on this subject stresses the point over and over: 'Without communications, particularly in big industries, people don't know what they're doing, or they don't know why they are doing whatever it is that they are doing. The result is that they jump to conclusions which are often wide of the mark – they say the management or the Government is mad, or that nobody cares.'

But to initiate communication is one thing: to make it successful is another. There are many traps for the unwary. Industrial vogue words can all too easily be used as a smoke-screen (whether intentionally generated or not) behind which there is little content: 'efficiency', 'incentives', 'morale', 'motivation', 'productivity', 'standards', 'development', 'continuity', 'partnership' . . . Getting agreement as to what these terms mean, and how they are to be interpreted in specific cases – for they are all fundamental in the language of negotiation – is a major problem. Another linguistic barrier to successful communication is the use of unnecessary technical phraseology (usually labelled as 'jargon'), or the highly artificial formulae of much business correspondence – though this is much on the wane these days, according to most current handbooks providing instructions about the writing of business letters. A third problem – and a well-recognized one – underlies the frequent demand for brevity and clarity in writing reports and directives. One firm has on its wall: 'Remember the Ten Commandments!' – the point being that of the 284 words used (in one translation) 217 are of one syllable, and only 10 of more than two. 'Think clean – avoid double meanings' says another poster, presumably getting at the tendency to use such ambiguous constructions as the so-called 'clothed imperative', which implies an order without actually stating it (e.g. 'The materials which we expected yesterday have not yet arrived', i.e. 'Do something about it!' – though without explicitness, who can be blamed for errors of judgement?). And, as a final example, managers have to be very much aware of the different connotations words have. Connotations are the individual feelings we have about words, the associations they arouse in our minds; and, as the Iron Curtain cases above indicated, there are many words which have good connotations for one group and bad connotations for another. So for the management to talk blithely about 'automation' and 'work-study', in the firm belief that these concepts connote efficiency and productivity, is naïve; for to so many people on the shop-floor, such terms regularly have connotations of redundancy (in the first case) and slave-driving (in the second). A word can set off a strike. Business managers, as all communicating human beings, have to take the receiver's point of view into account. It is financially important for them to remember that the test of a successful communication is what happens at the receiving end.

In this field, as in many others, prevention is more important than cure. While it is never going to be possible to get absolutely perfect communication between disparate social groups, at least the main hindrances can be anticipated and avoided; but this requires a prior awareness of the general nature of the problem. Of course, most experienced businessmen and women do develop a kind of intuitive awareness of such problems; but it takes many years to become experienced, and meanwhile these problems face the younger manager. It would presumably be ideal if one could provide all new managerial staff with a manual of linguistic principles and procedures recommended to deal with the language troublespots; and perhaps such material will one day appear. The point I want to emphasize here, however, is that the initial study of these matters which has to be carried out prior to any manual-writing is a full-time and complicated job in its own right. It is not easy to collect representative and accurate information about language use and abuse. Nor is it easy to devise a clear and precise way of defining the problems in order to teach them. (Even the communications analyst is beset by problems of communication!)

And so once again there would seem to be a strong case for a separate, systematic study of language habits – another answer to the question which introduced this chapter.

The benefits which might come from increased language awareness in management are largely hypothetical at the present time: very little has actually been done. There are however a number of other fields where the application of linguistic methods and data has been producing helpful results for many years. The most important field to cite is the teaching of foreign languages. Foreign language teaching is nowadays a major industry in most countries. As more and more people travel abroad, both for business and pleasure, the demand for foreign languages steadily increases. This is especially so in the field of international trade, where an earlier 'imperialistic' view ('If they really want our products, they'll learn English') is now being replaced by an awareness that it pays far more to learn the language of the customer. But more people than ever before are taking up learning a foreign language for quite uncommercial reasons – usually because they are planning a visit abroad, but sometimes for no more specific reason than that they wish to 'broaden their education'. The evidence for this lies in the remarkable increase in the number and nature of language teaching courses in the past few years: institutes and colleges specializing in languages, summer schools, records, radio and television programmes. And not only has this increase affected the so-called 'popular' languages – French, German, Spanish, and Italian; there is a growing demand for less familiar tongues, such as Portuguese, Greek, Swedish, Chinese, Arabic, Japanese, and Russian. The biggest language-teaching industry of all, however, involves English. More people learn English as a foreign language every year than any other language. There are still many parts of the world where English is the official language of a country, though not the native language (in West Africa, for example), and English is still a major language for international communication in many scientific and technical fields (the language of air traffic control, for instance, is largely English).

Behind all this intense activity there lies one fundamental principle, whose full implications are sometimes forgotten; namely, that in order to teach a foreign language successfully – any foreign language – it is first of all necessary to know about it. This is not so obvious a statement as it sounds. The complication lies in the word 'about'. To 'know about' a language is by no means the same thing as to 'know' a language. Everyone reading this book 'knows' English, in the sense that they can read it, write it, and, probably, speak it. But fluency in a language (whether it be our mother-tongue or any other) does not carry with it any honorary qualifications to teach it. Being able to speak a language fluently is no guarantee that we are able to explain its structure to others in a systematic and precise way, and organize a course of studies so that it will become relatively easy to learn. Amateur language teaching is rarely useful and regularly detrimental. There are too many cases of people having been taught the wrong facts about a language, because a teacher has had inadequate training, or who have given up learning a language because they 'couldn't follow the book', the information being presented in an obscure or un-intelligible way. Even with professional teaching, there are difficulties: schoolchildren can still make their first visit to a foreign country, whose language they have been learning for some years, and find that they are unable to understand the language, or make themselves understood. 'They speak French differently from the way we did at school,' runs the complaint. Nowadays, the situation is rapidly improving, due to the development of new approaches to language teaching, but there is still a long way to go.

It is not difficult to see why such a sad state of affairs has arisen in language teaching. It is partly a question of people approaching a language with a falsely preconceived idea as to what it is like, assuming that they will find in it all the concepts and structures that they remember from their days of studying English or Latin in school. And when they find that the language does *not* have the same structure as English, reactions range from incredulity to contempt. 'No definite article in Russian?' I remember hearing one student say at a beginner's evening class – 'but it *must* have!' What this student would have said had he been learning a language with only one tense, or with no prepositions, I shudder to think! Another example of this kind is when people learning a language automatic ally assume that the language displays the characteristics of Latin, so that they say, in such a sentence as 'A girl saw a girl', that the first 'a girl' is nominative, and the second is accusative, even though there is no distinctive 'case-ending' for the second, as there would have been for most nouns in this position in Latin. The fact that English uses word-order to indicate the relationships of meaning between words, whereas Latin used a system of case-endings at the end of words, is a difference that is regularly overlooked. I shall be discussing these matters further in Chapter 2. Here, the general point has to be made that there is no reason to expect a foreign language to be the same as our mother-tongue, in pronunciation, grammar, or vocabulary. There will always be *some* similarities between different languages, of course – universal design-characteristics of a particular type (see Chapter 4). But there are also major differences, and these have to be studied and learned, not ignored. To teach one language as if it were another – to see English through Latin spectacles, or Russian through English ones – may seem an attractive way to go about things at first sight, but teachers who work in this way will only end up by confusing the issue and making their task more difficult. 'Where *is* the accusative case?' a child might plaintively ask, concerning *A girl saw a girl*. And it is difficult to find a convincing answer, because there is none there.

Another reason for the unsatisfactory state of much language teaching often lies in the nature of the language which is selected to be taught. All too often the language taught is of a rather restricted kind. It is very often a written kind of language, and not a spoken kind. In English, for example, foreigners are often taught the grammatical rules and vocabulary that are more characteristic of written English, and are given very little training in the spoken varieties. To take but one example, it is still normal for foreigners learning English to be taught to say *I shall* not *I will*, and to observe the differences in meaning which it is claimed exist between the two whenever they are both used; all of which ignores the fact that the normal way of expressing future time in the verb system in speech is to use neither of them, but to say *I'll*. In French, some forms of the verb (the 'subjunctive', and the so-called 'historic present' tense) are rarely used in speech. In German, and in English too, there are major differences in word-order between speech and writing. These differences are illustrated further in Chapter 2, but a hint of the extent of the difference between connected speech and writing can be provided by transcribing a stretch of the former. This is part of a lecture, and I choose it because it shows that even a professional speaker uses structures that would rarely if ever occur in written English, and displays a 'disjointedness' of speech which would be altogether lacking there. (Everyday conversation provides even more striking differences.) The dot indicates a short pause, the dash a longer pause, and the *erm* is an attempt to represent the noises the speaker made when he was audibly hesitating.

well now. I'd like to turn now to assessment – and I hope you won't mind if I use this opportunity to try to give some indication . of . erm – a . more modern – more recent . approach to the assessment problem . than perhaps I myself was brought . brought up on – and I want . very arbitrarily if I may to divide this into three headings – and to ask . erm . three . three questions . assessment why – assessment of what – and assessment how . so this really . means I want to talk about . first of all the purposes of assessment – why we are assessing at all – erm secondly the kind of functions and processes that are being assessed – and thirdly I want to talk about techniques –

It should be clear from this that the spoken and written forms of a language are very different things (try marking sentence boundaries in the above extract, for instance), and that to teach the latter only is to produce a very artificial and stilted form of speech. If we all spoke as we wrote (BBC newsreader style, perhaps), it would be a strange linguistic world indeed. But when learning a foreign language, we still often find that, perhaps unintentionally, it is the written language that is being taught.

It is not particularly surprising that this situation should have developed. Before techniques for making a permanent record of speech were invented – and, in particular, before the invention of the tape-recorder in the 1940s – it was well-nigh impossible to find out what speech was really like. It was easy enough to get a general impression just from listening; but to get a detailed account of the syntax of everyday speech, to catch all the nuances and complexities that it contains in its structure, required a degree of training and systematic observation and analysis that has been but recently developed. We still in fact know relatively little about the syntax of spoken English – or any language; but what we do know suggests that the differences between speech and writing are going to be more, not less, than was at first suspected. There is clearly a lot to be done, and linguistics has a central role to play in identifying and describing these differences, and in getting rid of the misconceptions that are still with us. An advertisement for a language course once ran: 'Russian course of 20 lessons, to teach *speaking* – so there's not much grammar.' A fallacy as fundamental as this is indeed serious.

Ignoring the complex distinctiveness of spoken language has been a major factor contributing to the tendency to teach language of a rather restricted kind. Another factor concerns the formality of the language being taught. Very often a language is taught in its most formal guise only – the more informal, colloquial styles of the language being neglected, or even castigated as incorrect. English again provides good examples of this. Traditional grammar books still teach us that sentences should never be ended with prepositions, even though to do so is quite normal in the spoken usage of educated people. What is being forgotten here is that very often in English speakers have a choice as to whether they end their sentences with the preposition or not. It is largely a question of formality. *Do you see that man John was talking to?* is a far more informal way of speaking than *Do you see that man to whom John was talking?* * The former is the one we should most of us use on the majority of occasions; the latter would sound artificial and pompous in everyday conversation. But it is the latter which is still taught as the 'correct' form in many textbooks. Similarly, when English people learn French or German, they are all too often provided with a formal, literary style of these languages to model themselves on – a style which no self-respecting French or German person would ever think of using in everyday, friendly conversation.

* Language examples cited for purposes of illustration or discussion will be given in italics throughout the book.

These are just some examples of what 'knowing about' a language involves. It also involves much more. It means being able to analyse the structures of the language and to describe them in a reasonably precise terminology; it means knowing the areas of uncertainty in usage (do we recommend the pronunciation CON*troversy* or *con*TRO*versy*, for instance?); it means being up to date with research into the language, and with changes taking place in the modern state of the language (many rules to be found in grammar books and pronunciation manuals are based on nineteenth-century usages); in particular it means having a thorough knowledge of the structural differences between the language learners already know and the one they are trying to learn, as these differences will be to a very great extent the areas of greatest difficulty they have. Perhaps the most remarkable fact of all about language teaching is the great gaps which language teachers (and linguistic scholars, for that matter) have in their knowledge about the structure of these languages. Far from having a complete knowledge of all aspects of English grammar, for instance, there are many areas about which next to nothing is known (see Chapter 2), and in the absence of these facts, poor learners have to be left to fill out their language fluency as best they may. Linguistics, by providing a systematic method for analysing and describing languages, is of value in that it aims to plug these gaps, and provide a well-defined basis for attacking these problems. It has in fact already proved its worth. During the Second World War, for example, many African and Oriental languages were analysed and taught intensively using linguistic ideas – languages, that is, which were relatively unfamiliar to Western traditions of language study and which displayed considerable divergences from European languages. Some of these languages had hardly ever been studied intensively before, from the point of view of foreign language teaching. In such cases, then, linguistic techniques were the only means of 'getting the language down on paper' – and these are the techniques which are still widely used, in fields as far removed as commercial advertising and Bible translation. Only a minority of the world's languages have been written down and studied, and there are a number of organizations which spend a great deal of time finding and describing hitherto unknown languages. But linguistic ideas have an equally important role to play in the teaching of familiar languages too – namely, the removal of misconceptions about these languages, and the development of a more comprehensive and precise account of them than is available. Language teaching is probably the most widespread application linguistics has these days: to some people, indeed, language teaching and the phrase 'applied linguistics' are synonymous.

This discussion of language study in relation to foreign language teaching naturally suggests the parallel question of whether linguistic ideas and techniques could be of any value in teaching the native language, or mother-tongue. Is it the case that teaching about English to people who already speak it as a mother-tongue will have any effect on their ability to use the language? Would courses on the English language, done linguistically, make them more fluent and aware? These are controversial questions at the present time, for there is little evidence to point to, and the answers depend very much on which aspects of language study we are thinking of. It is generally agreed, for instance, that a long and detailed course on clause-analysis and parsing is unlikely to have any lasting effect on spoken English (though it does seem to be of greater relevance for improving written composition). But there are other aspects of our 'command' of the mother-tongue which do not develop naturally, and in which most of us could usefully receive some training. These aspects do not so much concern our ability to speak and write English ourselves, as our ability to understand the spoken or written language of other people, particularly on complex matters. How many people, when they finish their formal education, are at home with the English language as it is found in legal documents, hire-purchase forms, or income-tax forms? Very, very few. For most, this language is obscure, or even impenetrable. They do not know how to go about 'making sense' of it – that is, analysing it. And while sometimes the obscurity is due to some inadequacy on the part of the authors, they cannot be blamed on all occasions. The complex structure and 'jargon' of legal documents, for instance, is to a very great extent an essential characteristic of these texts, being largely a reflection of the need for a precise, unambiguous formulation of legal issues. It would be perfectly possible to write legal documents in a loose, colloquial style, but this would soon play havoc with justice. There was once a plea in the House of Commons that legislation should not be drafted in obscure language. The Prime Minister at the time was sympathetic, but, as he said in reply, 'The difficulty about legislation is that the courts have to interpret litigation based upon it, and it is, therefore, essential it should be not so much simple as precise.' Less seriously, we might bear in mind the anxiety of Mr Tulliver about his son (in George Eliot's *The Mill on the Floss*): 'I want him to know figures and see into things quick, and know what folks mean, and how to wrap things up in words that aren't actionable. It's an uncommon fine thing, that is, when you can let a man know what you think of him without having to pay for it.'

So it would seem that some training in the techniques of understanding legal English, and other complex varieties of this kind, would indeed be beneficial for the language user. And a similar argument could be constructed for other varieties, or 'styles' of a language. The analysis of advertising language, or political speechmaking, or of other 'persuasive' styles, has an obvious relevance for education. The detection of logical flaws in argument, of omitted premisses, of loaded terms, of speaker bias: this is a skill which can be taught, but only with a certain amount of linguistic knowledge acquired first. The analysis of *any* use of language, for whatever reason, has to be based on some general principles and techniques. The bits of language that propagandists use to make their points have to be described somehow if teachers hope to communicate them to a class; and the more precise the language the teacher can devise for doing this, the easier the job of understanding what is going on will be.

A related difficulty in the teaching of the native language arises in connection with the linguistic demands made by society on school-leavers. There is probably no job these days which does not demand some kind of language awareness. Even the most menial of occupations requires employees to be aware of safety and health regulations; and the lowliest shop assistant or mechanic needs to be communicative if impressions of surliness are to be avoided.

The greater complexity of human relationships in a work situation brings with it the need for the new employee to develop fresh language habits, to begin to 'speak a new language' – not merely in the sense of learning to use technical terms, but also in the sense of having to interact linguistically on everyday matters with work-mates or colleagues who may come from very different social backgrounds. The change from school to employment is for many people a linguistic trauma. It is often under-estimated just how precisely language is used in school: teachers tend to speak with care, and if they have not communicated a point, will rephrase it and try again. In the harsh outside world, however, there is no time to instruct gently and repeatedly; employers do not make com-munication allowances of this kind. And the flow of language which can hit school-leavers when they are given a set of instruc-tions to carry out is sometimes far in excess of what they are used to, with the result that they can look blank, or, worse, attempt to carry them out without having understood. In either case, they will be criticized as stupid, though what has happened is in fact nothing to do with intelligence: it is essentially a deficit in language educa-tion which could and should have been remedied in school or in some intermediate course. In a different way, the same problem affects the new secretary, who finds that 80 words a minute dicta-tion speed in the controlled atmosphere of the secretarial college does not mean the same as 80 in the busy office, where hesitations, false starts, telephones and other distractions abound.

Language problems do not start with the difficulties of the first few weeks of employment, of course; nor do they stop there. Before school-leavers get a job, they have to compete, and these days more and more concerns are setting or raising language requirements as conditions of entry. Either they expect passes in certain examina-tions (the English language examinations that most British students take around the age of 15, for instance), or they set their own tests of written and spoken English. Some organizations make their applicants phone in for interviews to get some indication of their ability and confidence in using spoken English in advance. Lan-guage is the important index for many employers who want to know 'How will he/she fit in with my staff?' And all jobs require an initial stage of letter-writing or form-filling, which regularly poses unfamiliar and sometimes intractable linguistic problems for the school-leaver (at whatever level) who has not been given some training to cope with them. Getting a job also means coming to grips with such things as conditions of employment, insurance regulations, indentures of apprenticeship, and the like, most of which are not presented in 'easy stages'. And lastly – in case it is felt that the assimilation and production of language is a problem for school-leavers only – there are the difficulties of the many business people who come to evening classes for courses in remedial spelling, public speaking, or remedial (rapid) reading. The higher up they go, the more they find that public speaking, fast reading, and other such abilities, are highly desirable. All these can presumably be taught; but it is rare to find anything being done about them while children are at school or in higher education. More and more educationalists are becoming aware of the problem these days; but it is difficult to know what to do to remedy the situation, either in theory or in practice. Many people expect linguistics to be able to help – for instance, by establishing the exact nature of the linguistic demands being made, and suggesting ways of drawing together remedial material. It would be premature to expect too much of the subject in this field at present; but if a solution *can* be found, I do not doubt that linguistic techniques will be playing a large part in it.

A further aspect of educating people in the use of their own language arises out of the point just made concerning 'establishing the nature of linguistic demands'. Let us take such questions as 'What makes a successful newspaper report, or speech, or sports commentary?' 'What is the best way of writing a scientific report, or narrating an event?' Many schoolteachers automatically bring this kind of information in to their classes, but it is usually done in a rather sporadic kind of way, and its value is reduced by the elementary fact that most teachers have never been trained in handling language material of this kind – nor do they have the time themselves to do the necessary homework. For homework there is, and much of it. These questions are not easy to answer. Scientific English, for example, is a much more complex phenomenon than it may appear at first sight. Whether or not scientists have anything of importance to say about their subjects, their way of saying it is to a very great extent laid down – sometimes in style-books, sometimes simply in unconscious awareness of 'how scientific writers write'. A scientific journal will not accept an article unless it is written in what the editorial board believes is an appropriate style; and this in the end comes down to following a large number of specific rules about grammar, vocabulary and general lay-out. For students of scientific English, of course, it is not just a matter of getting to know what makes scientific English distinctive; they have to know *why* it is distinctive in the way that it is. To take just one example, scientific English makes use of an abnormally high proportion of impersonal, passive constructions (*The mixture was poured into the test-tube*) as opposed to personal, active ones (*I poured the mixture into the test-tube*). The student should have some ideas about why this is the preferred style – or, at least, should be aware of the difference in overall effect which would be the result of a scientific report written in this personal way. And a similar procedure is required for the analysis of *any* varieties of a language. What are the distinctive linguistic characteristics of a television advertisement? Or a set of instructions? Are they matters of pronunciation, grammar, vocabulary, lay-out, or all of these? And if grammar is involved, which grammatical structures does the variety tend to rely on, and which does it not use at all? To answer these questions accurately involves a great deal of work. It involves studying typical pieces of a use of language, to determine its salient characteristics, then describing these features, and then interpreting this description in terms of 'effectiveness', 'success', and so on. But very little information of this kind is available at present. Ideally, there ought to be a compendium of data about the various styles, spoken and written, which make up the totality of 'the English language' – a dictionary of stylistics, which teachers, and others, could turn to for assistance when faced with the need to train people in any of these matters. But no such dictionary exists as yet, for research into these questions is of fairly recent origin. Writing it will keep scholars in business for some years.

This use of the word 'stylistics' suggests yet another area in which language study could be of value – the study of literature. Literary language is generally taken to be the most powerful and complex language developed by a community. It is characteristically evocative. It seems to be impossible to define the 'meaning' of a literary work in its entirety. The range of its subject-matter comprehends and transcends the whole of human experience. The language of literature is a very difficult thing to study, because of its ambivalent status: on the one hand, the language of a work is central, in that it is the 'medium of the message', and the only means the author has of communicating his or her ideas; and yet it is not central, in that it is but a means to the more important end of understanding the author's intention. But if it were possible to devise techniques of language study which, when used sensitively, could illuminate the meaning of a literary work, then this would indeed be a justification for the subject of this book. Linguistically orientated techniques and principles of literary stylistic analysis have in fact been suggested, though not, at the present time, thoroughly tested and evaluated. It is by no means clear, for instance, whether the qualitative differences between literary language and other varieties of a language require a separate study to be made of the former, in its own terms. Personally, I do not think we should overestimate the difference. Literary language *is* a heightened, and more sensitive, use of language, but it nonetheless has to use the same basic range of devices as any other use of language. An English author is first and foremost a user of the English language *as a whole*: his or her originality in manipulating the language to say things in a more meaningful or novel way is something which is only really comprehensible within the context of this normal background. As Robert Graves said, 'The poet has got to master the rules of English grammar, before he attempts to bend or break them.' So too have literary critics to know these rules, before they attempt to explain an author's original use of them to their audience. The mastery of systematic techniques of language study could thus provide the critic with a highly useful tool, and these techniques would be no different from those which are required for the study of the other varieties of a language, referred to above.

(I must point out, however, that the question is a source of dispute between some linguists and literary critics, and has been for some time.)

But this chapter was not called 'Why study languages?' or 'Why study the English language (in any of its forms, literary or otherwise)?', but 'Why study language?' Such a question should really be, 'Language?' For once again I must emphasize that the main task of linguistic scholars is not to improve the language teaching situation, nor to study the English language as an end in itself, nor to improve their appreciation of literature or general understanding of other complex styles – though they will, in the course of their training, sensitize themselves to language sufficiently to develop many or all of these skills: their task is basically to study and understand the *general* principles upon which all languages are built. What are the 'design features' of human language? This is their prime concern. How far can we define universal characteristics of language? Or, putting this another way, 'What are the differences between languages? how can we describe and classify these? and how far are they fundamental? What concepts do we have to develop before we can begin to talk about language at all?' Of course to study such questions, we have to start somewhere, with the speech of a specific person speaking a specific language on a specific occasion. But it does not matter whether this language is English, or Yoruba, or Chinese. In much the same way, an apprentice car mechanic may start training with a Vauxhall; but his or her aims are to find out about the structure and function of cars in general. Linguistic scholars want to get as precise and as comprehensive an idea as possible about the general principles underlying human language. Once they know this, their knowledge will certainly help them to be better students of any one language (given sufficient motivation to learn it); and they may then teach it better; but in the first instance, the applications of language teaching are not their concern.

In a short chapter such as this it is not possible to cover all the areas of human behaviour into which language study enters and where its furtherance could be of value. For other examples, I could point to contemporary interest in the nature of language by philosophers and theologians, by professional translators and interpreters and people in the field of machine translation, by people interested in improving standards of literacy, by people concerned with the transmission of language over long distances (such as the telephone companies, who in fact finance much of the research into phonetics, described in Chapter 4), and so on. But these specialist interests are far outweighed by the interest of the general public in matters linguistic. In a sense, the best answer to the question 'Why study language?' is simply, 'Because so many people seem to get so worked up over it!' Our language does indeed seem to be the most sensitive side of our characters. 'Sticks and stones may break my bones . . .' runs the refrain; but we all know that names *do* hurt, sometimes much more. And as adults, we have not lost this touchiness. The letter columns of the national press are full of comments bearing witness to this point. 'What has happened to the letter *a* as pronounced by the younger generation in such words as *hat, flat, happy*?' begins one writer. 'It is quite the ugliest sound I have ever heard. If you do not know what I mean, ask Mrs Freeman (of Dale fame!) to say *The fat cat sat happily on my lap* and then ask Gwen and Jennie to repeat the same sentence. The former, I venture to think, will give you pleasure; the latter, if you are like me, intense pain.' Another paper recently had half a page devoted to people's sensitivity about their accents. The lead story was extreme, but significant. 'Blacksmith X died a victim of dialect snobbery. He killed himself at 70 because he was ashamed of his Yorkshire accent when he went to live in the South, it was said at the inquest.' Another news report, talking about Harold Wilson, began as follows: 'The Prime Minister, when it suits him, may speak the broadest Huddersfield he can manage. But woe betide the humble receptionist, secretarial agencies agreed yesterday, whose accent would put off or confuse a firm's clients. Yesterday's report that a Scots girl, Miss X, receptionist for an estate agent in Y, had been dismissed after a month because her employer said that people could not understand her, caused mixed feelings in the secretarial business . . .'

These stories are by no means atypical. The BBC in particular is attacked from all quarters over the pronunciation its announcers use, though only a tiny minority of the letters it receives are ever printed in its journals. People sometimes get so worked up about this that they form societies to preserve what they consider to be the purity of the language (though different groups usually have different ideas as to what this 'purity' consists of). There is for example a Society for the Protection of the Letter R, whose members have to promise to complain to the BBC whenever they hear an announcer sound an intrusive 'r', as in 'I sawr a man') or fail to sound a linking 'r' (as in 'Theata organ'). And firms have been quick to see the commercial potential in this situation. 'Your friends *can't* tell you and your business associates *won't* . . .' runs a banner headline on one brochure, and it continues, '. . . what hampering speech mannerisms may be interfering with your social and financial success.' They then go on to outline an elocution course on records which will enable the user 'to speak correctly and pleasingly', and impart to them 'without affectation, the proper accent that is the mark of a cultivated individual'.

I shall be suggesting a healthy approach to this kind of problem in Chapter 2. It is certainly undeniable that some accents and dialects carry more social standing than others in a community. Educated people in Great Britain for instance will be more likely to speak with a fairly neutral accent than with one dominated by regional overtones. The mark of an educated person, it has been said – and this is true to a very considerable extent still – is that by listening to them you cannot tell which part of the country they come from. And it would be very unlikely that anyone with a very broad regional accent would make a success of a job as a High Court judge. But it does not follow from all this that, just because one accent used in Britain carries more social prestige than others, the socially restricted accents are in any absolute sense 'undesirable'. There are no absolute standards of this kind. An accent is not *intrinsically* ugly, or beautiful. It depends on what we are used to, what our tastes are. To a Northerner, Southern accents may sound 'posh' and 'affected'; to a Southerner, Northern accents may sound 'harsh' or 'crude'. But of course Southerners do not consider their accents to be affected, nor do Northerners think they speak harshly. Too many people have been given a guilt complex about the way they speak because they have been led to believe that there is something necessarily inferior in their accent or dialect. Too many people try to insist that everyone else should speak as they do. Too many people think that all words have a pristine, perfect pronunciation which must be used, and that any variations on this are wrong. But these principles are fallacious, as Chapter 2 makes clear. 'Live and let live' is a good working motto for this aspect of language study: if it were practised and preached, a great deal of everyday worry might well be avoided.

Sometimes, concern over a language becomes so marked that it achieves the status of a national problem. When a minority community wishes to preserve its identity in a changing society, one of the lines it invariably takes is to set up its language as a symbol of national identity. This, of course, can cause major problems, when equal status is demanded for the language (as in the case of Welsh today, for instance). Language riots in Belgium or India or Canada over the relative prestige and status of conflicting language-groups typify what is unfortunately a common phenomenon in the world. Perhaps, it could be argued, if the study of language were placed on a more widespread and objective footing, and more people knew about its principles and vagaries, less trouble would develop. This may be a pipe-dream, but there could be some possibilities in it. To take one small example, much of the concern over preserving a 'pure' kind of English would surely disappear if people were more aware of the inevitability of language change – of the fact that languages do not and cannot stand still over the years. Or again, if people learned to recognize the independent existence of many divergent kinds of English in all parts of the world, each with its own prestige, then many pointless letters to the *Radio Times* might never get written. It comes as a shock to some to realize that in some parts of the world, the 'Queen's English', as it is rather misleadingly called, far from being spoken, is positively scorned. The correlate of 'Americanism' is 'Britishism'.

If reasons are required for the study of language, then, it would be necessary to point to such problems and applications as are reviewed in this chapter. I am not of course saying that a formal course of study in language will help in all these fields – still less, be a panacea; but it is bound to be of some value, in that it will make people more aware that there are problems of this kind, and that they are widespread and complex. 'Language sensitization' is the immediate practical need. From the academic viewpoint, the important thing to realize is that *all* the areas covered in this chapter involve essentially the same kind of problem – the same linguistic issues are involved, and the same principles and techniques can be brought to bear to analyse them. But, as I emphasized at the beginning, the potential applications of linguistic study provide but a small part of its justification – though perhaps the obvious part. Ultimately more important, it seems to me, is the need to study language because it is the key to the understanding of so much of human behaviour, both of ourselves and of our interaction with others. It is impossible to conceive of a rational being, or of a society, without implying the existence of language. Language and thinking are so closely related that any study of the former is bound to be a contribution to our understanding of the human mind – a point made with special force by Noam Chomsky; and this understanding is unarguably worth pursuing as an end in itself. It is perhaps subordinate only to the grander aim of understanding ourselves in relation to others in society; and here too language is prerequisite.

It is not particularly surprising, then, in view of the great complexity of language, and of its permeating role in society, that there should have developed an independent field of study to try to put its analysis on a sound footing. Linguistics is the usual name of this discipline; its students are called 'linguists' (sometimes 'linguisticians' – a rather self-conscious title which linguistics scholars themselves never use, but which is sometimes useful to help avoid confusing the two senses of 'linguist', namely 'student of language', which is the sense intended here, and 'speaker of many languages', which is what is popularly meant by the word). The discipline is sometimes called general linguistics, to emphasize the fact that its principles and techniques are for all languages, and not just for the analysis of English, or French. It is also sometimes called linguistic science, to emphasize the fact that its methods are rather different from traditional methods of language study. The purpose of this book is to explain what is involved in a linguistic approach to

35

language study. However, before we can do this, we need to look at some of the unsatisfactory methods which have been and still are used to study language – many of which have been the actual stimuli for the development of linguistic thought. Linguistics is still a very new discipline, and it still arouses controversy, particularly when it comes into conflict with traditionally held ideas. But much of the controversy is due to misunderstanding. One way of trying to avoid this is by putting the new in the context of the old.

2. Traditional Approaches to Language Study

If my arguments in Chapter 1 are valid, it seems that as a rule people are unaware of the powerful implications of the skill they have mastered, language. I have suggested that this lack of awareness is particularly unfortunate, since language's effects enter into so many areas of our professional and everyday lives, and that something ought to be done about it. But what? I shall argue in the rest of this book that some basic knowledge of the principles of general linguistics, the academic, scientific study of language, while not a panacea for all linguistic ills, is still of definite value in our dealings with practical language matters, and provides a subject whose intellectual and aesthetic intricacies are a fascination in themselves.

However, it might be argued: Why do you need a new, academic, scientific discipline in order to find out about language? Has not language been studied for centuries – indeed, thousands of years? Are there not many treatises, with titles like 'On the nature of language', dating back to Classical Greek and Roman times? Are there not also many grammatical manuals of English, French, and other languages, dating back to the Middle Ages? And do we not learn the basic facts about our language – about its structure, its use, and its development – in school? Why cannot this accumulation of 'traditional' data about language and languages suffice as a basis for attacking the kinds of problem outlined in Chapter 1? These questions are all very relevant, and there is some truth underlying each of them. We shall see below that the study of language has indeed a respectable – though at times a rather chequered – history. But these earlier traditions of study cannot, for the most part, provide the kind of information we need to satisfy the demands of Chapter 1. The main reason for developing a new discipline, linguistics, is that on the whole people have found the earlier approaches unsatisfactory – sometimes stimulating, more frequently tantalizingly unhelpful, and all too often wrong. The reasons for this, and what to do about it, are the subject-matter of the present chapter.

It is, of course, easy to be critical in retrospect. It has for some time been standard practice amongst linguists to introduce their subject by pointing to the inadequacies of traditional approaches to language study, and then building up (what they hope is) a more adequate approach by contrast. It is so standard a practice, in fact, that many lecturers and authors on linguistics, when starting completely from scratch, find themselves psychologically unable to talk about the subject in any other way – and I am no exception. I think, however, that this is quite justifiable: it seems to be partly a reflection of the way in which linguistics actually developed in the early part of this century, and partly an inevitable reaction to the intellectual climate of the present, where the dominant attitude is to look critically at the emergence of new 'disciplines' of study, particularly in the arts and social sciences, and to ask them to justify their existence in plain language as well as in the language of journals. Linguistics, however, has perhaps an even more pressing need to evaluate previous work than other candidates cited for potential academic status, such as ethology. The problem which linguistics has to face is not that of having to teach people a completely new subject – for if there were any such background of total popular ignorance (as perhaps existed in the case of ethology), this would provide an admirable foundation for a new subject. Rather, the problem is that, having such a powerful tradition of study behind it, and being on everyone's minds, as it were, because of its pervasiveness and relevance to everyday living, people think they know it all already. It was this complacency, and an atmosphere of fallacious dogma, which linguistics had to combat in its early days – and which to a very great extent it still does. Perhaps the main achievement of the subject so far this century has been to make one thing clear to people who care to look, that language is complicated! And that to face up to the task of describing and explaining its complexity requires new concepts, new methods of analysis, new questions. But an essential preliminary to the construction of new buildings is the demolition – or at least the evaluation – of anything built on the same site hitherto.

Before going any further, it is wise to sound a note of caution. In contrasting a new approach with an old, it is all too easy to paint a picture in black and white, whereas the reality of the situation is many shades of grey. It is true that many features of traditional theories and descriptions of language have proved to be unhelpful or positively misleading, and one of the main stimuli for the development of linguistics was a reaction against this. On the other hand, it is equally true that many of the principles and procedures of modern linguistics are foreshadowed – sometimes only implicitly, but sometimes in chasteningly explicit detail – in the work of earlier scholars. As a matter of fact, many linguists have gone through a kind of academic Telemachus complex in recent years, trying to demonstrate their recognition of lines of intellectual ancestry within their research. In the late sixties, it became fashionable – and certainly it would be a point in your favour – to show that your thinking was not original, but had been anticipated by scholars of some hundreds of years previously. And this emphasis, even if exaggerated at times, has indeed redressed the balance after the linguistic attitudes of the fifties and earlier, where the keynote was to point to differences from earlier scholarship, not similarities. As usual, a compromise provides the least misleading picture. When linguistics began to develop in the early decades of this century, there was a natural and reasonable reaction against much of traditional study. This, however, led to many of the valuable insights of this study being ignored or their importance minimized. Nowadays, many of the early scholars have been 'reassessed', usually for the better. In this sense, linguistics has come of age; it is beginning to recognize its debt to the past, as well as to plan its contribution to the future.

Who, then, were these earlier scholars? And what are the traditional approaches to language study? We have to be very careful not to be over-simple here. One sometimes hears people say, 'The trouble with traditional grammar is . . .' But such a comment is meaningless, without careful prior qualification. For there is no such thing as a single, homogeneous, traditional approach – either to grammar, or to anything else in language study. The phrase 'traditional grammar', if it means anything, attempts to summarize a state of mind, a spectrum of methods and principles which appear in various combinations and emphases over the years, associated with many schools of thought. There are ideas about sentence structure deriving from Aristotle and Plato, ideas about parts of speech deriving from the Stoic grammarians, ideas about the nature of meaning stemming from the scholastic debates of the Middle Ages, ideas about the relationship between language and mind deriving from the seventeenth-century philosophical controversies between rationalists and empiricists, ideas about correctness in language coming from eighteenth-century grammars of English, and ideas about the history of language deriving from the nineteenth-century emphasis on comparative philology. We shall be looking further at these areas of influence below. Each of them – and there are many others – had strong and weak points. But there was never any one traditional grammar which enshrined all the fallacies linguists like to cite as illustration of how not to study language. The picture one paints of traditional grammar is kaleidoscopic – a stereotype – but one which has some value for teaching purposes nonetheless.

In my view it is particularly important for people to have some historical perspective in linguistics. It helps the researcher or teacher to avoid unreal generalizations or silly claims about modern developments and 'innovations'. It can also provide a source of salutary examples, suggesting which lines of investigation are likely to be profitable, which fruitless. At a time when postgraduate theses seem to be increasing in almost geometrical progression, it is especially important for researchers to be as aware as they can be of what has already been done, or at least attempted. For the general reader, too, a historical perspective for linguistics is useful, because it explains to a very great extent why the modern subject has developed in the way it has, and relates the subject to other areas which may be more familiar, thus in a way re-presenting – though from a different angle – the argument of Chapter 1 concerning the integral relationship of language to other areas of experience. This book is hardly the place to go into this perspective in any detail (for those interested, R. H. Robins' *Short History of Linguistics*, published in 1967, provides an admirable treatment), but some hint of what has happened will be a useful background for later chapters, as well as being of some interest in its own right.

It is not too difficult to find evidence of the main themes and issues which indicate the respectable ancestry and variegated history of language study. Language has always been so closely tied in with such fields as philosophy, logic, rhetoric, language teaching, literary criticism, and religion that it is rare to find great thinkers of any period who do not at some point in their work comment on the role of language in relation to their ideas. But before we go into the more technical matters arising from such links, it is worth pointing out that early ideas about language are to be found in a much broader context than that normally associated with the development of Western – specifically European – thought. There has always been a considerable body of tradition and myth in many cultures concerning the nature and origins of language. It is important for linguists to be at least aware of this in formulating their own approaches, even though they may find little here of direct relevance to their practical problems. Research in cultural anthropology has shown quite clearly that most primitive cultures (and, indeed, some of the not so primitive) were sure that a divinity had been involved with language from the very start. It is God who gives Adam the power of naming, as described in the Book of Genesis ('And the Lord God having formed out of the ground all the beasts of the earth, and all the fowls of the air, brought them to Adam to see what he would call them; for whatsoever Adam called any living creature the same is its name'); and similar stories are not hard to find in other cultures. The god Thoth was the originator of speech and writing to the Egyptians. The Babylonians attributed it to their god, Nabû. A heaven-sent water-turtle with marks on its back brought writing to the Chinese, it is said. According to Icelandic saga, Odin was the inventor of runic script. And Brahma is reputed to have given the knowledge of writing to the Hindu race.

It should not be surprising to see such a widespread and deep-rooted connection between divinity and language. We can see this if we look at the superstitious and mystical ideas about the nature of language which affect many primitive societies, or – at another level – children. To take the latter case first, the apparently miraculous power of language is early appreciated by children: a cry produces comfort, makes food materialize, in a sense 'controls' objects. Children look at language with respect: strict adherence is expected for any language rules used in a game; there is a clear awareness of word taboos; name-calling is a standard and highly effective insult. For the primitive also, it is not difficult to see why language should seem to control objects. Writing, for instance, would be regarded as omniscient: it could tell a person things though many miles away from the writer; it could even provide information about the actual message-carrier. There are regular tales in the anthropological literature of natives stealing an object in a parcel, but delivering the message which accompanied it, only to be found out! They felt that the writing had a voice, a life of its own – or maybe that a god lived in the letters. From such ideas, that messages 'spoke', came many beliefs and theories. In some cultures, alphabets began to be interpreted mystically, as a proof of the existence of God, or as a way of predicting the future. Names were seen as embodying the power of their owners. According to Scripture, one way the true God was to be distinguished from idols was through his voice: he would answer when called upon; they could not.

It was only a short step from the belief that words were somehow connected with things to the notion that words *were* things, and had a separate existence in reality. The concept of word-souls is found in places as far apart as Ancient Egypt, modern Greenland, and the pages of Plato. Words were held to embody the nature of things – a belief still fairly common, even in parts of the 'civilized' world (cf. p. 50). But a more important step was to see words as all-powerful, and then to use them deliberately to control or influence events. Runes were originally charms, and the power of a charm or an amulet depended largely on the writing upon it – the more spiritual the subject-matter, the better the charm. We find this kind of belief in Jewish phylacteries, and in the occasional

Christian custom, such as that of fanning a sick person with pages of the Bible, or making him eat paper with a prayer on it. Again, if words control things, then their power could be intensified by saying them over and over: as the anthropologist Malinowski put it, 'The repetitive statement of certain words is believed to produce the reality stated.' Magic formulae, incantations, rhythmical listing of proper names, and many other rites exemplify the intensifying power of words – and even, at times, word hysteria. Devils, or people, can be controlled by language in these traditions too – it is not simply a question of physical objects. There are many examples in folklore of forbidden names which, when discovered, break the evil spell of their owners – Tom-tit-tot, Vargaluska, Rumpelstiltz-kin. Many primitive peoples do not like to hear their name used, for a personal name is a supreme, unique attribute, wherein resides the whole of one's being. A characteristic situation would be for a tribal chief to take a new name, let us say the name 'life' – then a new word for 'life' would have to be found in the language, so that his name would not be used in inauspicious circumstances. Nor is it usual for the names of the dead to be uttered: while a name endures, a dead person does also, and those who utter the name bring the evil of death upon themselves. If the name involved was one's 'secret' or 'special' name, then, of course, concern was doubled. Many Australian and New Zealand tribes have this belief; and every ancient Egyptian had two names – one for the world, and one for God, which was never divulged. To know a person's secret name was really to have power over them. Only a god could acceptably know people and use their names so freely. In some cultures, if a child died, the next by the same mother would be called by some evil name, to show the death spirit that the child was not worth bothering about. In the Roman levies, too, the authorities took good care to enrol first men with auspicious names – Victor, Felix, and the like. From another point of view, once the billion names of God have been intoned (goes the legend) the world will end, because its *raison d'être* will have ceased to exist. (Recently, someone has wanted to test this, using a prayer-wheel attached to an electronic speech synthesizer!)

Examples of this kind abound in the history of cultures. But

43

primitive logophobia and logophilia (one might call it) have little specific importance for understanding the history of language study. They simply indicate how deeply ideas about language can come to be ingrained within the individual or group psyche, and testify to the existence of a language awareness which exercised considerable influence in the development of particular issues later. One way in which this latter point can be illustrated is by reference to the kind of language which was to be used for the worship of God. The language of worship is invariably the product of particular care and attention on the part of a community, and this motivation sometimes produced detailed studies of language which were great achievements, even when viewed by modern standards. In ancient India, for example, the Hindu priests had begun to realize (around the fifth century B.C.) that the language of their oldest hymns, Vedic Sanskrit, was no longer the same, either in pronunciation or grammar, as the contemporary language. Now this is a common enough linguistic fact, that languages are continually though gradually changing (see Chapter 4), but it had particular point for the priests and scholars of the time; for an important part of their belief was that certain religious ceremonies, to be successful, needed to reproduce accurately the *original* pronunciation and text of the hymns used. The solution adopted in order to preserve the early states of the language from the effects of time was to determine exactly what the salient features of Vedic Sanskrit were, and to write them down as a set of rules – in other words, describe the grammar and pronunciation of the old language. In this way, there would be an authoritative text, one not bound down by the vagaries of individual oral tradition. The earliest evidence we have of this feat is the work carried out by Pāṇini in the fourth century B.C., in the form of a set of around 4,000 aphoristic statements about the language's structure, known as *sutras*. This was, in fact, a grammar of Sanskrit, and its effect went far beyond the original intentions of the authors. For in producing this work, a great number of phonetic and grammatical minutiae were presented, and methodological and theoretical principles and ideas developed, some of which are still used in modern linguistics. A similar, though less influential development took place later (around the seventh century A.D.), in connection with the Koran and Arabic studies. The fact that the Koran was not to be translated, and was to receive a very literal interpretation, promoted considerable study of Arabic, both as a native and as a foreign language, and there were developments in lexicography (dictionary-making), the study of pronunciation, and language-history in subsequent centuries which stemmed directly from this essentially religious stimulus.

There were many other ways in which religious studies and goals promoted language study. Missionaries have often written the first grammars of languages, introduced writing, or developed methods of language teaching. Bishop Wulfila's Gothic translation of the Bible dates from the fourth century, and indeed provides almost all the information we have about that language. Buddhist missionaries contributed to Chinese linguistic study from as early as the fifth century A.D. Around 1000 A.D. in England, Abbot Aelfric of Eynsham wrote a kind of 'conversation-reader' for the purpose of introducing everyday Latin to Anglo-Saxon pupils; his 'colloquy', as it is called, is of particular interest to the student of English history, because of the picture it paints of the contemporary social scene, but such dialogues had long been a normal instructional method in the monastic schools of Western Europe. The period labelled the Renaissance had a number of linguistic side-effects, and many of these were the product of religious activities. Geographical exploration brought more languages to the notice of the world, especially in Africa, south-east Asia, and the Far East; and with this came missionary activity. The department *De Propaganda Fide* of the Roman Catholic Church was of particular importance in promoting missionary work, and several languages in these areas were first given a written form and grammar by Jesuit missionaries, as part of the general concern for translating the Scriptures. One such alphabet, made for Vietnamese in 1651, is the basis of Vietnamese orthography still, and other parts of Asia benefited in a similar way. Printing had matured sufficiently to make word-lists, strange alphabets, dictionaries, and early grammars available to the interested scholar, and there were many comparative surveys and collections of bits of language – a collection of the

Lord's Prayer in as many languages as possible, for example. In particular, there was a renewed interest in Greek, Arabic, and Hebrew, the latter largely in connection with biblical studies: in the early Middle Ages, almost all Western textual analysis had been based on the Latin Vulgate version of the Bible; but after the fall of Constantinople, older texts and commentaries (and, incidentally, different traditions of grammar) became available.

This fresh contact with older traditions brought fresh contact with older controversies, of course. In particular, the questions of the origins of language and the world's oldest language returned. These questions had been to the fore in early Greek speculation, as we shall see below, but they were raised in various forms by other civilizations too, such as the Indian, Arabic, and Egyptian. One indication of this, which all histories of linguistics like to quote, is recorded in the writings of Herodotus, the Greek historian. In his second book he tells of what may well have been the first psycholinguistic experiment (for psycholinguistics, see Chapter 5, p. 262). Apparently Psammetichus, an Egyptian king of about the seventh century B.C., wanted to find out which of all the peoples of the world was the most ancient. His way of determining this was to discover the oldest language, which, he thought, would be sure evidence of the oldest race. To do this, he placed two newly-born children of poor parentage in solitary confinement, but for the care of a shepherd, with strict orders that no one should utter a word in their presence. He assumed that, when the time came for them to speak, having received no external stimulation from contemporary language, they would revert naturally to the world's first. After two years, the children began to repeat constantly an utterance (recorded as 'bekos') in the presence of the shepherd, who immediately reported this to the Pharaoh. Psammetichus, upon making inquiries, discovered that this was the word for 'bread' in Phrygian, a neighbouring language. The unavoidable conclusion for him, therefore, was that this language *must* have been the world's original tongue, and that the Phrygian race was more primeval than his own.

This 'experiment' makes a fine story, and it is easy to be contemptuous of the Pharaoh's naïvety. His experiment has, as we shall see, no validity; and the importance of imitation for the development of spoken language is by no means disproved, particularly if we consider the close similarity of the sounds of 'bekos' to the only sounds the children would have consistently heard – the sheep! But it would be wrong to ridicule, for Psammetichus' curiosity on this issue is by no means an isolated case; in a way he illustrates a question which has since developed an almost archetypal significance. There are several other experiments of a similar kind on record. James IV of Scotland is reputed to have carried out an identical investigation (probably in 1493), and it is reported that at the end the children spoke very good Hebrew! Some years previously, the Holy Roman Emperor, Frederick II of Hohenstaufen (d. 1250) also experimented along these lines – though in this case the children unfortunately died. Interest of a similar kind survives in legend, sacred book, folk-tale and ancient document in many other countries, and it takes very little to make people start wondering along these lines. For example, when a wild boy was discovered in the woods near Aveyron in France in 1797, and it became known that he had had no contact with humanity, there was considerable expectation that he would emerge into civilization with a fair command of Hebrew, or perhaps some other ancient language. As it happened, he did no such thing: he could make animal noises, but had no human language. The intrinsic interest of this issue is undeniable, and in the sixteenth and seventeenth centuries, speculation about the oldest language reached a new pitch. Because of its prestigious position for religious studies, Hebrew was a firm favourite. There were many elaborate 'proofs' proposed for this, for if Hebrew was the oldest language, then it had to be demonstrated that all living languages were descendants of, or variations of it. This led to the working-out of many complex permutations of letters between words of similar meaning in different languages, to try to demonstrate such a causal relationship. One justification for this letter-juggling (as it is sometimes called) was that Hebrew had been written from right to left, whereas other languages went from left to right. Later, Voltaire was one who voiced his scepticism of such deductions: he defined etymology (the study of word-history) as a science in which the vowels count for nothing and the consonants for very little!

There were, however, others at this time who proposed other languages as the world's original. The Swede Andreas Kempe presented the view that in Paradise Adam spoke Danish, the serpent French, and God Swedish – though probably this was partly a satire on contemporary clerical attitudes. J. G. Becanus (1518–72) is also regularly cited in histories of language study. He argued the position of German as the primeval tongue. The first language must have been the most perfect, it was argued, and as German was superior to other languages, then it must have been first! (Historically, German was the language Adam spoke in Eden. It missed Babel, because the early Germans (the Cimbrians) did not assist in the construction of the Tower. God later caused the Old Testament to be translated from the original German, no longer extant, into Hebrew.) Later, more esoteric languages were suggested as primeval, such as Chinese. And in the eighteenth century, the influence of romanticism fostered further interest in the origins of language question: essays by such scholars as Rousseau and Condillac proved highly influential in creating a general intellectual curiosity about the subject which has lasted right down to the present day.

The modern linguistic view, on the whole, is that of the early linguist Whitney who condemned most of what had been said in connection with this topic as being 'mere wordy talk'. By the turn of this century, the Linguistic Society of Paris had a standing order barring papers on the origin of language from its meetings. This was partly a reaction to the previous century of vague theorizing on the subject, but it was also an expression of an awareness that the question of the world's oldest language, and the more general question of the origins of language, were not questions of a scientific nature. There was no evidence, no experimental test, which could be brought to bear on the matter. Rhetoric aside, there was no way of evaluating contradictory speculations. What evidence there was about language-history (see Chapter 4) militated against acceptance of even the most basic assumptions used in the arguments about primevalness. The studies of comparative philology in the nineteenth century had shown no signs of a primitiveness that could be taken as a hallmark of an early or original tongue, though this had been frequently taken for granted in debate ('the first language must have been a simple one'). Indeed, the opposite was the case: the further back one traced a language in time, the more complex it seemed to become; and the earliest extant remains of language (e.g. the inscriptions of early Egyptian) were clearly many thousands of years later than the time when language may well have developed in man. Scholars like Edward Sapir constantly emphasized the view that to call languages primitive was in any case a misunderstanding. 'We know of no people that is not possessed of a fully developed language,' he said in his book *Language* (published in 1921). 'The lowliest South African bushman speaks in the forms of a rich symbolic system that is in essence perfectly comparable to the speech of the cultivated Frenchman.' I shall have more to say on this point below (p. 71). The problem, however, remains a fascinating one, and scholars have searched for better ways of approaching it. Recently there has been an attempt by some linguists to re-open the question, but this time from the viewpoint of comparative biology. Can the comparison of animals and human beings, from the point of view of communication, shed any light on the development of language in the latter? If there are anatomical and other antecedents of man in the higher primates, might there not be linguistic ones there also? The research is too recent for any clear conclusion to have emerged.

This discussion indicates very nicely how impossible it is to impose any neat classification of themes on the history of a subject. I began by discussing the religious orientation of much of traditional language study, and have ended with the introduction of a far more general theme. But enough has been said, I think, to show that the history of ideas in linguistics is remarkably bound up with the history of religious thought, in its widest sense. More fundamental and far-reaching than this, however, is the activity which was stimulated by a primarily philosophical motivation. To understand this, we have once again to go back to the beginning of Western thought. Questions to do with the nature of language were a major concern of early Greek and Roman scholarship. The Greeks seem to have initiated many lines of thought about language, as about so much else. There was a keen awareness of the identity of the Greek language, and of its dialects, and especially of the need to see it in the light of the early, classical language of the Homeric poems, to which, from as early as the sixth century B.C., they devoted considerable study. They developed an alphabet different in principle from the writing systems previously known, and one which was to be the forerunner of most subsequent alphabets. (Their permanent contribution in this area is nicely indicated by the history of the term 'grammar' (*grammatikē*), which in this early period implied understanding the use of letters – that is, having the skill of reading and writing.) The Greek propensity for speculation on language matters is, however, really apparent in Plato, whose dialogue *Cratylus* is standard reading for anyone wishing to trace the history of ideas in linguistics. It is the earliest surviving linguistic debate: a wide-ranging discussion about the origins of language and the nature of meaning, in which considerable attention is paid to the study of the origins of words (etymology). One central question was: Are words somehow tied by nature to the things they refer to, or is the relationship quite arbitrary, a matter of convention? This question is one which continued to be discussed for centuries and still underlies many contemporary misunderstandings of language (cf. p. 63). And there were other speculations. Was there any general principle of regularity underlying language's form and structure, or was there in the essence of language a force always tending to produce irregularity in its structure? What standards could be devised in order to preserve the original forms of the Greek language (as preserved in Homeric poetry) from decay?

Plato, Aristotle, and the Stoics devoted a great deal of time to the development of sometimes quite specific ideas about language. Plato was called by a later Greek writer 'the first to discover the potentialities of grammar', and his conception of speech (*logos*) as being basically composed of the logically determined categories of noun and verb (the thing predicated and its predicator) produced a dichotomous sentence-analysis which has fathered most grammatical analyses since, whether the parentage has been acknowledged openly or not. Aristotle, and later the Stoics, examined the structure of Greek very carefully indeed, producing definitions of much of what people feel grammatical analysis is concerned with –

definitions of the parts of speech, in particular, but also of many of the so-called 'categories' of grammar, e.g. case, number, gender, and tense. This fairly detailed study of the language, part of the more general study of 'dialectic', was of major influence on subsequent grammatical thinking. It was taken over by the Romans with very little change in general principle, and, through the influence of Latin on Europe (see below), was introduced, in various degrees, into every grammatical handbook written before the twentieth century. Many of the features of modern linguistic theory too (for example, the idea of levels of grammatical structure, see Chapter 4) can be traced back to this early period. But so, unfortunately, can most of the fallacies.

We can see this if we look at some facets of the subsequent influence of Greek and Latin scholarship in Europe. Latin, largely under the aegis of the Church, became the medium of educated discourse and communication throughout Europe by the end of the first millennium. Largely as a result of this, the emphasis in language study was for a while almost exclusively concerned with the description of the Latin language in the context of language teaching. The massive codification of Latin grammar by Varro, and the subsequent grammars of Aelius Donatus (fourth century) and Priscian (sixth century) are the outstanding examples of this approach. Donatus' grammar was used right into the Middle Ages – and a popular grammar it was too, being the first to be printed using wooden type, and providing a shorter edition for children. Throughout this period, a high standard of correctness in learning was maintained, especially in pronunciation. The Benedictine Rule, for example, heavily punished the mistakes of children in Latin classes, and the historian G. G. Coulton tells us there was even a devil, Tutivillius, 'especially deputed to collect the fragments of speech which drop from dangling, leaping, dragging, mumbling, foreskipping, fore-running, and overleaping monks'. By the Middle Ages, when it had come to be recognized that Latin was no longer a native language for the majority of its prospective users, the grammar books became less sets of facts and more sets of rules, and the concept of correctness became even more dominant. One popular definition of grammar was *ars bene dicendi et bene scribendi* – 'the art of speaking and writing well'. Later, in the age of humanism, it was common to hear people identify the aim of learning grammar with the ideal of being able to write Latin like Cicero. A similar attitude had characterized much Greek language teaching also: especially after the Alexandrian school (third century B.C.) the language of the best literature was held up as a guide to the desired standard of speech and writing for all. The Greek language had to be preserved as far as possible from decadence. As with Latin, all change was for the worse.

The effect of these attitudes to language on later thought was considerable. The teaching of Latin grammar and the study of Latin literature were perhaps the two most important aspects in the history of language study for promoting the development of misleading principles of analysis in traditional grammars. The pride of place given to Latin was clear in the classical orientation given to grammar and rhetorical studies, which formed two thirds of the scholastic *trivium*. Grammar to many was the basis of all arts and all education (as the phrase 'grammar school' reflects – the term 'latinskole' in Danish being an even more interesting formation). The sixteenth century provided the peak period of prestige for Latin, and other languages suffered accordingly. The preservation of the Classical tongues was felt to be the main task of the literate. A very apposite comment in Roger Ascham's *The Scholemaster* (1570) summarizes this state of mind: 'the providence of God hath left unto us in no other tongue save only in the Greek and Latin tongue, the true precepts, and perfect examples of eloquence'. The vernaculars were thus clearly inferior. Spanish and French were seen simply as examples of much-decayed languages. The favourite adjectives for English in the sixteenth century were such as 'base', 'barbarous', 'rude', 'gross', 'vile', and 'uneloquent'. Languages, it was felt, were corrupted by commoners and preserved by the educated. Dictionaries, moreover, were only to define the words used by the best authors. It is not difficult to see the long-term effects of attitudes such as these. Grammars came to be considered as preserving a language's purity. Their role was to tell people authoritatively how to speak and write. The Latin grammars were to be used as models for the description of all new languages. Only the best authors, the literary giants, were to be studied as examples of what a language was like. And when English grammars came to be written, especially in the eighteenth century, the authors, steeped in these Latinate and literary traditions, regularly produced rules of 'correct' usage ('normative' rules, as they are sometimes called) which bore little relation to the facts of everyday speech, and rules derived from Latin into which the features of English structure were forced (such as the use of a case system for nouns, mentioned in Chapter 1). Dryden, for example, seems to have introduced into English the 'rule' about not putting prepositions at the end of a sentence, taking his idea from the grammatical situation that existed in Latin; and his influence was so great that it has appeared in most grammar books since – though it is doubtful whether there has ever been a time in English when prepositions were so restricted in their placement in a sentence. Similar standards of correctness were imposed upon other languages too, sometimes being formalized in a more extreme way, as in the establishment by Cardinal Richelieu of an *Académie* in 1635 to preserve the purity of French. The attempt failed, as it was bound to do: the language continued to change with the years; and in France, as in England, the prescriptions of the grammarians simply became more and more removed from the majority usage (i.e. the reality) of the times. I shall take up this point again below (p. 57).

In a way, much of the concern over language teaching, literary standards, speculation about the origins of language, and so on, was superficial, though influential. There was, however, throughout this whole period a more serious movement of philosophical thought which stemmed from early Greek speculation, and which was later to interpret most of these ideas in its own terms. It is important to realize that almost all of the discussion about language which went on in the early Greek period was continued with a more general, philosophical purpose in mind. People were not interested in language phenomena as such. The discussions about meaning were largely part of a general debate as to the nature of reality; the subject/predicate distinction, along with subsequent developments, was the linguistic reflex of a fundamental distinction in logic; the debate over regularity in language structure was part of a wider issue as to whether proportionality was a principle for all things; and so on. On the whole, it was a philosophical awareness of the nature of language – of language as part of a more general study of behaviour and knowledge ('philosophia') – that the Graeco-Roman scholars produced. In saying this, I do not wish to underestimate the importance of their thinking in providing a working grammatical apparatus for describing sentence structure; their apparatus was to be used, with very little modification, until the twentieth century (apart from those parts of the world which had developed their own traditions, such as the Arabic and Indian). But the apparatus was itself motivated to a very great extent by a desire to classify experience and knowledge. And when the twentieth-century subject developed, it proved necessary to filter out much of the philosophical content, and redefine many of the categories, in order to make them applicable to the task of language description as an end in itself. (We shall be seeing why later in this chapter, and also in Chapter 3.)

The philosophical motivation of the early period persisted through the Middle Ages until well after the Renaissance. The influence of scholastic philosophy was of particular importance. Grammar, along with rhetoric and dialectic, constituted the scholastic *trivium*. But this was no longer the language teacher's interest in grammar. Scholars were primarily interested in establishing philosophical explanations for the rules of grammar. Could an examination of behaviour and knowledge account for the nature and development of language, explain patterns of syntax, word structure (morphology) and meaning? 'As is the fool to the wise man, so is a grammarian ignorant of logic to one skilled in logic,' it was said. Such terrible ignorance would presumably make a man fit only for language teaching! To the group of philosophers known as the Modistae (thirteenth century), only the philosopher was entitled to decide on grammatical judgements (a common maxim was *philosophus grammaticam invenit* – 'it is the philosopher who discovers grammar'). The assumption (or 'insight', as it would nowadays be called) was that there was one common, or universal, grammar underlying the structure of all languages, which was based, not on language form, but on the laws of reason. The search to determine the shape of this grammar, to find a general explanatory set of principles for language, was on. To begin with, the question was discussed almost exclusively in relation to Latin, which was held to embody any such universal laws of thought. Later, in the seventeenth century, the scope of the discussion widened, as part of the general debate between the two philosophical positions of rationalism (which broadly speaking claimed that all human knowledge comes from the mind, or 'reason') and empiricism (that all human knowledge derives from experience). A number of 'philosophical grammars' came to be written, and these went far beyond the Latinate restrictions. One such grammar, the 'Port-Royal' grammar of 1660, has achieved a certain notoriety due to its having been cited by various influential present-day theorists (Chomsky, in particular) as embodying some striking anticipations of current linguistic thinking. But there were many others, not only in France, which attempted to expound a general theory of grammar – one not based solely on the features of a single language, like Latin. In order to do this, contemporary philosophical distinctions were introduced into the linguistic analysis, such as a two-level view of the nature of meaning (language has an 'outer' expression and an 'inner' or 'deeper' meaning), which was a clear product of the body–mind dichotomy propounded by Descartes and others. A little later, Leibniz, amongst others, concerned himself with the development of a new symbolic system in which *all* knowledge could be expressed; and once again the question had to be asked whether all languages could not be reduced to a single set of rules. The real complexity of this problem increased with the advent of romanticism in the eighteenth century, which brought with it a high regard for the languages of primitive societies, local dialects, and 'vernaculars' of any kind; and in the face of an embarrassing wealth of linguistic diversity, it is not surprising that people lost sight of the philosophical issue. There were certainly many alternative ideas which seemed to provide practical solutions to a number of problems – the development of artificial languages (like the later creation, Esperanto), systems of spelling reform, shorthands, and international alphabets. These attracted a great deal of attention in the seventeenth century and later. But their usefulness was limited, and contemporary linguistics has for the most part ignored these relatively superficial movements, and devoted its attention to investigating the central question of whether a universal grammar is feasible or not. The position of Chomsky and some of his associates in this has been largely influenced by rationalism: their view, that linguistics is essentially a theory and set of techniques to improve our understanding of the human mind, leads them to talk of linguistics as a branch of cognitive psychology. I shall be returning to this issue in Chapter 3. Here it need only be emphasized that a very large number of what many linguists feel to be the central questions of current linguistic theory in fact originated in the philosophies of the seventeenth century. This is one of the more beneficial legacies linguistics has received from its past.

Now that we have seen a little of the historical background of modern linguistics, and despite all the simplification and omission which the past few pages have inevitably produced, we are in a much better position to appreciate some of the reasons for the emergence of the new subject, and to be more specific about the misconceptions and difficulties inherent in traditional approaches to language study. We may therefore return to the questions raised at the beginning of this chapter. It is clear that a lot of intelligent people have spent a great deal of time and effort studying language. Why, then, cannot this accumulation of information suffice or be extended to provide the answers to the intellectual and practical problems raised in Chapter 1? There is no simple answer: there are many reasons. All I can do, I think, is to classify these reasons under a number of distinct headings, and hope that the simplification necessarily involved will not distort our understanding of the real-life complexity of the situation.

Firstly, while it is indeed possible to find examples of linguistic investigation which had a permanent value (for example, the Indian phoneticians), and to read into early movements striking anticipations of modern ideas (for example, the seventeenth-century general grammars), it is nonetheless the case that by far the greater proportion of the work which went on under the heading of language study had very little relevance to a real understanding of the structure and function of language, and hence, very little applicability to the kinds of problem presented in Chapter 1. For the most part, people were not interested in the study of language for its own sake, as an isolatable, complex, highly distinctive, and essentially human characteristic. Language, with very few exceptions, was studied in relation to other disciplines, of which philosophy, religion, logic, rhetoric, history, literary style, and language teaching have all been mentioned; and this lack of intrinsic interest naturally led to the development of partial accounts of language, certain features being selected for study at the expense of others because of their relevance for the elucidation of a particular (e.g. philosophical) problem. It is not in fact so much what traditional grammars actually tell us about language that is the real worrying factor, as what they do *not* tell us. As was suggested in Chapter 1, many of the rules of traditional grammar apply only to the written language, and cannot be made meaningful in terms of the spoken language, without much qualification and addition. A simple example is the rule which tells us that the regular plural of an English noun is formed by 'adding an *s*': as it stands, this has no clear counterpart in speech, where this *s* has three distinct pronunciations, depending on the nature of the sound a noun ends with – listen to the endings of the words *boats*, *trains* and *horses*, for instance, where the first sounds like the *s* of *soap*, the second like the *z* of *zoo*, and the third like the word *is*. There are simple rules to account for this, but they are never made explicit in traditional approaches. A more complex example is the use of the word *only*. In traditional grammars, it is said that *only* should come as close to the word it modifies as possible: thus *I only saw John* would be called incorrect, and *I saw only John* recommended instead. The reason given is that the first version is ambiguous – it could read 'I only SAW John (I didn't speak to him)'. But this ambiguity is present only in the written language (and even there it is by no means frequent, as common-sense knowledge of the context can tell us what the intended meaning will be). In speech, the stress-pattern of the sentence (that is, the pattern of loudness which makes some words stand out at the expense of others) tells us how to interpret it. If I put the louder words in capitals, in speech the first sentence above would go

I ONLY *saw* JOHN, and this can *only* mean 'It was John alone whom I saw'. To obtain the second interpretation, we would have to say *I* ONLY SAW *John*. From a consideration of large numbers of examples such as this, it is clear that there is no general restriction for *only* in speech as grammars suggest, but that it *is* important to be aware that ambiguity can exist in writing, and that sometimes the rule may need to be applied.

There are many examples of this kind – features of the spoken language which are either assumed to work in the same way as in the written language (in other words, they get described in a false perspective and become distorted), or which are ignored, because they did not happen to be in the written materials analysed by early grammarians. Large areas of syntax are not covered at all, such as the 'elliptical' sentence-types illustrated by *Who, me?*, *Many thanks*, *In the morning* (in answer to the question *When are you going?*). There is little attention paid to the complexity and flexibility of word-order in language: adverbs are said to modify verbs, for example, but apart from a few words like *only* their very flexible positioning in sentences in relation to the verb is rarely discussed (cf. *Quickly John came in*, *John came quickly in*, *John quickly came in*, *John came in quickly*, and the kind of problem raised by adverbs which do not admit the same kind of flexibility, such as *frankly*, *rarely*, or *interestingly*). In traditional grammar the ways in which sentences follow each other in a dialogue (or indeed in a written paragraph) are not made clear either. Most authors do not even realize that this is a problem. But it *is*, as indicated by such words as *however* and *nonetheless*, which if they begin a sentence require a preceding sentence to have been uttered. I shall be looking at other cases of this kind below (p. 126, ff.). In addition, areas of language structure other than grammar were disregarded in most traditional accounts: the pronunciation system of languages is treated very scrappily, usually only in connection with the formulation of spelling-rules or rules for elocution; and the 'prosodic' side of language (the melody, stress, rhythm, and general 'quality' of speech) is also usually discussed only in relation to speech-correction. I find that something like nine-tenths of the problems which have to be faced in teaching a language to foreign students, or in teaching about style, cannot be answered by reference to the traditional literature. Indeed, there is usually no mention of these problems at all in the books.

It should be quite clear from these examples that in traditional grammars there was very little recognition of the extent of the difference between spoken and written forms of language. Many grammarians and lexicographers, particularly in the seventeenth century, were aware of the existence of such a difference, but did little to analyse it. And most authors paid only lip-service to the existence of the spoken language. In a way, this is not surprising. It is partly due to the way in which Latin was taught, almost solely as a *written* language (with the bizarre result that in the sixteenth century – and of course since – scholars of different nationalities were often unable to follow each other's spoken Latin). But more important than this, the neglect is due to the fact that it is extremely difficult to study speech without some mechanical aids to make the speech permanent, and therefore more precisely analysable. Early attempts to overcome this difficulty come to mind. There is, for example, the research of the early phonetician, Joshua Steele, into the melody of speech (in the mid eighteenth century). He used a bass viol, on which he played notes to try to match the pitch of his voice as he spoke – a highly complicated, and, of course, artificial exercise. Daniel Jones, the greatest phonetician of the present century, used to wear out phonograph recordings by trying to place the needle at a particular spot so as to be able to listen repeatedly to a piece of speech. But it was only with the development of the tape-recorder in the 1940s, and, more recently, of the tape-repeater (a machine which repeats over and over a short section of speech on a loop of tape), that there has been any breakthrough in this field. It is difficult to imagine now what research into spoken language could be like without such mechanical aids; so it is hardly surprising that earlier scholars paid so little attention to it. But having said this, it is important to appreciate that the rules of the written language must not be forced on to speech, as they so often are. We need not consider the nature of language for long to see that this is so. Writing is a later and more sophisticated process than speech. Speech is the primary medium of linguistic expression:

59

we begin to speak before we write, most of us speak far more than we write in everyday life, all natural languages were spoken before they were written, and there are many languages in the world today which have never been written down. To base our statements about language on writing rather than on speech is therefore a reversal of linguistic priorities, and leads to all kinds of confused thinking. I do not want to exaggerate the differences between the two media – spoken and written English are, after all, both forms of *English*; but it is prudent for a linguist, even if only for a short while, to consider the two media as separate systems of communication, so as to avoid falling into the trap of always looking at one through the eyes of the other.

A distinct but related aspect of the partial account of language given in traditional studies is that the material presented does not even cover the whole range of a language's written forms, but is restricted to specific kinds of writing – the more formal styles, in particular. Anything which smacks of informality tends to be carefully avoided, or if mentioned, castigated as 'slang' and labelled 'Bad Grammar' – even though the informality may be in regular and widespread use among educated people. We do not, after all, use the same kind of formal language when at home or writing a letter to friends as we do when we are giving a speech or applying in writing for a job. A language can be used at many levels of formality, and it should be one of the tasks of a linguistic description to take account of these differences, and not to select some levels as 'right' and others as 'wrong'. For example, we are all familiar with the 'rule' in English which tells us that we should use *whom* and not *who* as the relative pronoun in a sentence like *the man — you were talking to was a foreigner*. But such rules simply distort the reality of English. It is not a question of *whom* being correct usage, and *who* being incorrect: each is appropriate (a less loaded word than 'correct') in certain circumstances and inappropriate in others. The difference is essentially one of formality: *whom* in the above sentence tends to be a more formal way of making the point than *who*, which is more colloquial. It would be as inappropriate to introduce formality into an informal, chatty conversation, as it would be to introduce an informality on an official occasion.

This is yet another way in which traditional grammar gives a distorted view of the proportions and function of language forms. The grammar books imply that the language they describe is normal, general usage, whereas in fact it is frequently a specialized variety. There is rarely any explicit reference to the simultaneous existence of different styles of usage in language, or any suggestion that the way in which we speak or write in one situation may be very different from the way we might in another. In language description, absolute standards are by no means as common as we are sometimes led to believe. What we normally refer to as '*the* English (or French, etc.) language' is in reality not a single, homogeneous entity, about which we can speak absolutely; it is rather a conglomeration of regional and social dialects, personal and group styles, all of which are different from each other in various degrees. I shall be looking at these factors in greater detail in Chapter 5; but from just a brief and general mention, it is clear that ignorance of stylistic variation can produce a picture of language that is over-simplified to the point of distortion.

A specific aspect of this point can be traced right back to early Greek attitudes to language, namely, that there is a strong tendency in many traditional grammars and dictionaries to cite the usage of only the 'best' authors. Most of the quotations illustrating grammatical rules in even fairly modern grammatical handbooks are taken from famous novelists or non-fiction writers. Clearly, the result of applying such standards is to produce a description of a very specialized, literary language. If we all spoke like Austen or Thackeray or Trollope, as many grammar books would have us do, the result would be bizarre indeed. But it is not only the grammarian or lexicographer who takes this line. We frequently find in popular discussion slogans like 'Preserve the tongue which Shakespeare spoke!' – this particular one coming from a newspaper article written a few years ago. The English language is held to have 'decayed' (the writer of the article uses the word) since this period of literary excellence – though the mind boggles at the thought of a community all speaking in iambic pentameters!

Another aspect of the restrictions traditionally imposed on the idea of a language derives from the expression of a general conception of the nature of language in essentially aesthetic terms. A language, structure, word, or sound is said to be more 'beautiful', 'ugly', 'affected', and so on, than another. This was a very common attitude in older times, when beauty was frequently associated with eloquence and the Classics – particularly, as we have seen, in the sixteenth and seventeenth centuries. These days, aesthetic judgements about language are particularly common when talking about people's accents, and again it is an unrealistic standard. No one sound is intrinsically better or more beautiful than any other. We respond to other people's language in terms of our own social background and familiarity with their speech. If we are from Liverpool, then Liverpudlian speech will sound more pleasant than it will if we are not. This is simply one of the socio-linguistic facts of life. If we insist on criticizing someone else's accent as 'affected' or 'ugly', or whatever, or praising it as 'musical' or 'lilting', then we are simply trying to impose our own standards of beauty on others, and judging other people in terms of our own particular linguistic preferences. We usually forget that we probably sound just as odd to the person we are criticizing. Of course, some accents are, from the point of view of their value to society, more useful or influential than others. As we have seen in Chapter 1, a strong rural accent is frequently not acceptable in many city jobs, and a city accent equally unacceptable in the country. But this is a different matter: it is a problem of social standards, and not a purely linguistic question of aesthetics or intelligibility at all.

These attitudes probably have their roots in a deeper psychological premise about language, which also can be traced back to Classical Greek times, that the older states of a language are in some way more 'real', more 'pure', than the contemporary language. Perhaps this is partly tied up with views about the divine origins of language, partly a residue of the at times fanatical concern to discover the oldest language, and partly a regard for the prestige attached to the work of literary giants of the past – but mainly, I think, it is a reflex of the strong and natural tendency in people (particularly older people) to preserve the status quo. This linguistic nostalgia has, however, a number of specific effects, ideas which are widespread but fallacious. One popular view is that the 'true' or 'correct' meaning of a word is its oldest one. Thus, the 'real' meaning of *history*, it might be argued, is 'investigation', because this was the meaning of *historia* in Greek; or the real meaning of *nice* is 'fastidious', as this was one of the senses it had in Shakespeare's time. Frequently, indeed, people go so far as to call a word 'meaningless' because it no longer has a particular earlier meaning – *nice* being a case in point. But the ultra-conservative viewpoint of this 'etymological fallacy' (that is, the oldest meaning of the word is the correct one) is reducible to absurdity, as is clearly shown in many introductions to linguistics, if we follow its reasoning to its logical conclusion. For what is the oldest meaning of a word? Presumably the meaning it had in the language in which it was first used. But which was the language which first used a word like *nice*? It can be traced back through Old French to Latin (where *nescius* had the meaning of 'ignorant'), and ultimately to the ancestor-language of Latin about which very little is known. And as this ancestor-language presumably had an ancestor itself, about which we know nothing at all, it would follow, if the etymological argument were correct, that we just do not know what the correct meaning of a modern word is. But if we never know the meaning of words, then how is it that we use them perfectly well to talk to each other? The absurdity of the argument should be transparent. It arises, clearly, from a confusion between two sets of criteria which should be kept apart. This time the confusion is not between speech and writing, but between the historical and non-historical dimensions of study. The meaning of a modern English word is to be found (and can only be found) by studying the way in which the word is used in *modern* English – the kinds of object or idea currently being referred to. The meanings a word may have had years ago are irrelevant to this. We do not criticize modern English clothing for failing to live up to Greek or Elizabethan standards. Why then should we criticize our modern linguistic habits for not living up to older ideals?

A particular aspect of this confusion of historical and non-historical criteria is quite common in traditional grammars, as well as in everyday arguments about the meaning of words. This is the way in which grammarians spend time explaining the older states of a language as a preliminary to their description of the modern language, implying that the older information will be useful in understanding the modern state of affairs. But usually quite the reverse takes place. The older state of the language, being different in many ways from the modern, simply sets up ideas which then have to be modified, or disregarded, when we move on to the latter. An example of the confusion that can be caused is when a grammarian insists on describing the auxiliary verb *ought* as if it were the past tense of the verb *owe*. This used to be the case, but is no longer: we do not say *I ought you fifty pence*. Such reasoning is irrelevant to the study of modern English: there is enough to be said about the modern use of *ought* without going into the uses it once had. We do not need past information to study the present state of a language. (And, incidentally, the reverse is also true: to read modern English structure into a study of Anglo-Saxon can be equally distorting.)

A further aspect of the partial account of language structure so often implicit in traditional grammar lies in what (for want of a better word) could be called 'linguistic complacency'. The so-called 'armchair grammarians' sat back and dealt only with those aspects of grammar which came to mind as they thought – a highly subjective impressionism which was ultimately distorting, because awareness of the patterns of language and of our own usage is in many cases unclear or mistaken, and rules based on this are therefore bound to be unsatisfactory. To put it briefly, we just do not know what is going on in the whole of the language, or what our normal usage is on all points. And very often the language itself is indeterminate: our usage systematically differs noticeably from that of the person next to us. This does not normally matter. In everyday speech, particularly of an informal kind, we can and do tolerate these differences, as they rarely impede intelligibility. But as soon as we try to write a grammar book, these differences and uncertainties become a major problem – or at least they *should* become one. Grammarians have to realize that they are human, and have uncertainties about language like everyone else (though perhaps of a more sophisticated kind).

I am not here talking of some of the fairly obvious patterns, such as the article going before the noun, or the subject going before the verb in English, about which there would be no disagreement over usage. It is the less obvious features of pronunciation, grammar or vocabulary which cause the problems, and there are a sufficiently large number of these to make the issue important. For instance, most people, if asked, would say that their normal pronunciation of words like *him* and *her* had a *h* sound at the beginning, and would get most upset if anyone accused them of 'dropping their *h*s'. But in point of fact, these words *rarely* have a *h* at the beginning of them in the normal, colloquial speech of educated people. If we say, *I gave it to her mother yesterday*, at normal speed, without hesitating, there is no *h* sound in the word *her* (compare the way in which we drop the *f* in the phrase *cup of coffee*). Putting these sounds in would make us sound disjointed, foreign, or over-precise, and people in fact never do. The *h* is regularly used only when the word is spoken in isolation (*Who did you see? Her mother*) or with extra stress (*I gave it to* HER *mother, not his*). Another example of uncertainty in pronunciation is the word *controversy*. In this (as in many similar cases), a person may feel absolutely certain that they pronounce this word with the main stress on the first syllable, as CON*troversy*, and then a few days or minutes later, they (or someone else) may catch themselves saying *con*TRO*versy*, with the stress on the second. Examples of grammatical indeterminacy are also not hard to think up. If a group of people were asked if they would say, or find acceptable (i.e. allow into a grammar of English) the following sentences, they would not all agree on the answer: *He is regarded insane* (as opposed to *He is regarded as insane*); *I was sat opposite to by a stranger* (as opposed to *I was sat opposite by a stranger*); or, *John and Mary aren't very loved*. The point is that sentences of this kind are used frequently every day, but we do not have a clear intuition about them. They sound odd, in some way, but not in a way which is easy to define. Language is filled with questions of acceptability of this type, and grammarians cannot, therefore, rely solely on their own feelings about such matters, as they cannot guarantee that their own intuition is somehow an infallible guide to the usage of the majority, which is what the grammar book should contain. What they have to do is test each statement (even some of the apparently more obvious ones, for even here they may be being fooled by their own upbringing) by supplementing their own intuition with information derived from other people's intuitions about their language (see Chapter 3). And if it is the case that fifty people say one thing and fifty another, then this division of usage must be reflected in the rules the grammarian writes. It is not a question of one being right and another wrong: as we have seen, both are, to a certain degree, acceptable. Unfortunately, there was rarely any attempt made by armchair grammarians to check their assertions about usage by referring to the usage of the educated majority: if they had, many artificial prescriptions (such as not ending sentences with prepositions) might have been avoided.

Here, then, we have another example of an account of language distorted by an artificial over-restriction of the scope of linguistic investigation. To the linguist, these matters are central: many of the problems of language learning and teaching, for instance, reduce to stylistic issues of the kind discussed in this chapter; many communication problems arise from one person giving a term an older meaning than another – appeals to the 'real' meaning of a word in an argument are common enough, and can be highly misleading. But to most of the scholars referred to in the brief historical review at the beginning of this chapter, these matters would be considered unimportant, if they were noticed at all. It is a very striking characteristic of the history of language study that a great deal of time has been spent discussing and investigating a very small range of issues; there were certain preoccupations which, because of the philosophical or religious motivation of the authors, were considered central. Aspects of language which were not considered central to these broader themes were, as we have seen, ignored, e.g. those aspects of sentence structure which could not be thought of as having any bearing on the expression of logical relationships, 'laws of thought', and so on. And speculation was rife on such matters as the origins of language, which, as already suggested (p. 46), would have little place in modern linguistics. I am not saying that such speculations are necessarily trivial or uninteresting, for they are not; only that the lack of any kind of scientific basis for their pursuance makes them largely irrelevant as far as developing a sound theory of language is concerned, and that there is nothing here which could meet the intellectual and practical demands of students of language, as suggested by the range of topics referred to in Chapter 1.

Much of the irrelevance arose, as we have seen, from the lack of autonomy for the subject of language study. This concept of autonomy for linguistics is sometimes misinterpreted. It should not be construed as meaning that linguistics should have nothing to do with other subjects. The study of language cannot and should not be divorced from the study of other aspects of human behaviour, psychology and sociology in particular. This point was made long ago by Edward Sapir, one of the founders of modern linguistics, and it is just as relevant now as then. Linguistics needs to extract information from other subjects for its own theoretical development – biology, mathematics, psychology, and many others; and it also contributes information itself to them. But the point is that any contribution it makes must be formulated in terms independent of, and not subservient to or derived from, those other disciplines – otherwise all that is achieved is a theoretically complacent, ingrowing, unscientific school of thought. Every science needs a period of autonomy, of internal development independent of the pressures and principles of other, well-established disciplines, if it is to produce any principled framework for the analysis of phenomena. Linguistics never got this autonomy until the nineteenth century (for historical studies) and the twentieth century (for general linguistic studies). It may well be that, after some fifty years of autonomous development, linguistics is now at a point where it is no longer necessary to emphasize this concern for autonomy, and where it can once again become an integrated component of a more general discipline – on its own terms. There are signs of this happening in at least two areas: for some scholars, linguistics is becoming one branch of the science of the human mind, an aspect of cognitive psychology (see more in Chapter 3); for others, linguistics is one branch of the more general study of human communication (*semiotics*, of which I shall have more to say in Chapter 4). Here I only wish to emphasize that the integration of language

67

study and other fields now envisaged is of a totally different kind from that conceived of in earlier centuries. The linguistics which contributes to psychological research now has a body of independently derived techniques and theory at its disposal which was never available before. This is essentially what is meant when we talk of the study of language 'as an end in itself'.

So far I have been discussing a set of weaknesses inherent in the traditional 'heritage' of language study which all in some way relate to the subordinate role it had in early scholarship. To complete the critical assessment of the background to the modern subject, however, I need also to refer to certain other kinds of misconception which were particularly prevalent, and which had a formative influence on the development of early linguists. There is, for example, a different side to the uncritical spirit of complacency which we have already noted in many earlier approaches. Often grammarians would take over and work within a traditional frame of reference, assuming that it was satisfactory for their purposes, whereas a more conscious awareness of linguistic principles would have shown that it was not. The best example of this, the attempt to describe modern languages as if they were variants of Latin, has already been mentioned in Chapter 1. Not all grammars did this: some were at pains to point out differences between Latin and their own language; but for the most part they accepted Latin categories and ideals in matters of syntax, vocabulary and style. This was not particularly surprising, in view of the millennium of concentration on Latin studies to the exclusion of almost everything else. But, as a result, we can still find textbooks which do such things as prescribe half a dozen cases in order to talk about English nouns. Now if we examine this situation really carefully, we can see that it is just an attempt to treat English as if it were Latin; and English is *not* Latin. By 'case', grammarians normally refer to a kind of variation in the actual form, or shape, of the noun, which shows the noun's relationship to other parts of speech, or its function in a sentence. So if some noun is in the accusative case, we know that it must be directly governed by a verb, or a preposition. This variation in the form of a noun is called *inflection*, and a language which displays it is called an *inflected* language. English has hardly any inflectional endings for its nouns: it has the genitive case (as in *cat's*, *cats'*) and a general case which is used everywhere else (*cat*, *cats*). To call *cat* in *The cat came* and *I kicked the cat* different cases, is simply to misuse the word 'case', for there are clearly no differences between the endings of the two nouns. In examples like these, we know the difference between the doer and the receiver of the action by the position of the noun in relation to the verb: before the verb (the 'subject' position), one 'does' the action; after the verb (the 'object' position), one 'receives' the action. Other cases would be expressed in English through the use of prepositions (*for the cat*, *by the cat*, etc.). The general point to be made here is that the description of a language must not be carried out using the descriptive framework originally devised for the specific study of some other language – even if there are strong cultural affiliations with this other language. English is a complex enough language without trying to force the complexities of Latin into it. This is not, of course, to deny the existence of genuine points of similarity between any two languages; but such points must always be taken as hypotheses which have to be carefully tested. I shall take up this point again in Chapter 4 (p. 228), where a different sense of the term 'case' is discussed.

In traditional grammars, then, there is a tendency to treat Latin as a kind of authority to turn to when doubts arise about grammar. There are, however, other authorities expressly or implicitly involved in grammars of this kind, or in everyday conversation about language, which produce equally unrealistic results. I have already mentioned the literary, aesthetic and historical 'authorities' which are sometimes used in this way. Equally fallacious is the argument from *logic*, which is used a great deal in everyday casual talk, and which can often be found underlying traditional prescriptions. Statements like 'English is a more logical language than French' or 'It's more logical to say *spoonfuls* than *spoonsful*' confuse two standards of usage which should be kept apart: the standard of linguistic usage, and that of logical usage. Human language is not a logical construct, beautifully regular, though some people would have it so (and have wanted to have it so from at least Classical Greek times). Usage is as diverse, irregular and changeable as the society of which it is a part. We cannot apply logical reasoning to it. For example, to insist that 'two negatives make a positive' in an English sentence leads to all kinds of difficulties. *I am not uninterested* does not mean exactly the same as *I am interested* – there is a tentativeness in the former which implies a qualified assent. More obviously, the little boy who says *I've not done nothing* certainly does not mean that he has done something. We may not like his way of putting it, and call it 'sub-standard' usage, or 'bad' grammar; but the source of any objection is that we do not like the dialect he is using – it is not a logical question at all. In short, it is best in language matters not to mention the word 'logic', but to talk instead in terms of regular and irregular forms, showing how there is always a tendency for the irregular forms in language to be made to conform to the pattern of the regular ones – a process called *analogy*, which is at work in the *spoonful* example above.

There is no 'most logical' language, or 'more logical' structure. The fact that people still talk in these terms is probably another result of the philosophical search for laws of thought underlying language forms, which we can trace back to the Greeks. There may well be such laws. The point is that it is the underlying meanings or relationships of meaning which can be discussed in terms of logic; and not the form of the language in which these various relationships have received syntactic and lexical expression. Reality may or may not work logically; language does not. Nor, similarly, is there a 'most complex' language – where complexity means 'difficult to learn'. Standards of difficulty are relative: a thing is more difficult to do depending on how much practice we have had at doing it, and how used we are to doing similar things. If someone says that 'Chinese must be an awfully difficult language to learn', this may be true, for that person, but we must be careful not to draw the conclusion from this that 'Chinese is therefore a difficult language'. Whether it is really hard to learn depends in particular on whether we speak a language in the first place which is at all similar to Chinese in its sounds, writing system, grammar and vocabulary. On the whole, all else (e.g. our motivation) being equal, the greater the grammatical and other differences between our own language and any other, the more difficult (or 'complex') will that language turn out to be. But Chinese is not, absolutely speaking, a more difficult language than English: a Chinese, after all, must find learning English just as difficult.

Complexity is sometimes opposed to primitiveness in language study, but to talk about 'primitive' languages is, as we have already seen (p. 49), a misconception also. Just because a community happens to be, anthropologically speaking, primitive (that is, low on a scale of cultural development), is no reason for arguing that its language is primitive also – for it never is. Every language, as Sapir said, has enough sounds, structure and vocabulary to cope with its own needs. A language may not have as many words as English, let us say, but it does not follow from this that it is 'more primitive' than English. It has no need of so many words, that is all (for example, the vast numbers of technical terms which constitute two thirds of English vocabulary). It has enough words for its own purposes, and may indeed have more words than English has to talk about some areas of experience (the number of Eskimo words for kinds of snow is one example which readers will constantly come across in linguistic literature). We should be able to see from this that such old arguments as 'the French have a word for it' (implying, presumably, that in this respect French is a better language than one's own) are not valid. It might take the English language a dozen words to talk about a notion that French expresses in one, but we can still talk about this notion to our own satisfaction – and if we cannot, and the concept is needed, then the language will 'borrow' the word, and it will in due course become a part of English vocabulary (as with *restaurant*, *coup de grâce*, and thousands of others). Languages are not better or worse; only different. But people do continue to talk as though there were a perennial linguistic Derby which they had a vested interest in!

It will be clear from what has been said that much of the unsatisfactoriness of traditional approaches to language is due to their prescriptive attitude towards their data: writers were concerned to make rules about how people *ought* to speak and write, in conformity with some standard, or set of standards, which they considered primary. They were not concerned so much with ascertaining how people actually *did* speak and write. Some grammarians, it is true, were more enlightened, and made it clear in their work that they did not think it was the job of the grammarian to legislate about language; but their voices were a minority. The older approaches were typically prescriptive, and it is in opposition to this general attitude that many of the themes of early twentieth-century linguistics were developed. Modern linguists, as we have seen, do not want to gear their descriptions to non-linguistic standards of correctness. Linguists are aware that the grammarians of a language do not 'make' the rules of that language. Grammarians cannot do this, and they should not. They should restrict their ambitions to codifying and explaining what is already there, the usage of the people who speak the language. If grammarians attempt to overreach themselves, they will lose: their rules will be overruled by the weight of majority usage, if this differs from what they prescribe, and people will ignore their prescriptions when using the language unselfconsciously. This situation has in fact developed in English. People do not speak in accordance with the rules of the traditional grammar books, and are aware of this. The unfortunate thing, of course, is that many people who perceive this difference allow themselves to be worried by it. They very often try to speak or write 'grammatically', or tell their children to, on the grounds that if they do not there will be some social sanction. What they are attempting to do, of course, is to conform to rules which no longer have any general force in English. They do not realize that they speak grammatically already, and that their usage has in fact a greater authority than the old grammars' rules because it is alive whereas that of the grammar books and dictionaries is fossilized. They have forgotten (if they ever knew) the fact of language change.

For linguists, then, considering two alternative usages, one is not 'right' and the other 'wrong' – the two are merely different. They must describe both in their studies, and leave others to decide which is socially more appropriate to which situations (and thus to be used in teaching, translating and so on, where prescriptions are essential). They are not advocating irresponsibility in language use: they are not saying to teachers, 'It doesn't matter. Anything goes!'

On the contrary, the whole point is that anything *doesn't* go – that different uses of language are geared very tightly to different occasions (as in the *whom–who* example already discussed), and that people ought to be aware of this correlation between language and social use, and build this awareness into their teaching, translating, or whatever. As we have seen in Chapter 1, a great deal of time and money can be wasted in maintaining the naïve, egocentric purism which colours so many judgements about language. One of the main tasks of the linguist is to combat these attitudes. But this is sometimes difficult, for often it is not at all clear on what grounds these attitudes are based.

This last point needs separate comment. In order to present an alternative approach, the linguist must first thoroughly understand the inadequacies of the approaches already available, and sometimes these are very explicit. One illustration of this is the vagueness of definition which surrounds many of the central categories of the older models. The parts of speech, for instance, are sometimes defined in a very unhelpful way. These categories were set up in order to explain how the grammar of a language 'worked'; but many of the definitions seemed to have nothing to do with grammar. A standard example is the noun, regularly defined as 'the name of a person, place or thing'. But this definition tells us nothing about the *grammar* of nouns at all; it merely gives us a rather vague indication of what nouns are used to refer to in the outside world (which is part of what we mean by the 'meaning' of nouns). A grammatical definition of noun ought to provide grammatical information – information about their function in a sentence, about their inflectional characteristics, and so on. The above definition gives us none of this. Moreover, the information which it does give, apart from its irrelevance, is so inexplicit as to be almost useless. Are abstract nouns like 'beauty' included in this definition? If so, under what heading? Can we reasonably say that 'beauty' is a 'thing'? And what about those nouns which refer to actions (supposedly, in traditional grammar, a feature of verbs), such as *kick* (as in *I gave him a kick*)? Metaphysical questions of this kind are surely not the province of grammarians, and they ought to steer well clear of them.

It is easy to get the impression from traditional grammars that parts of speech are almost god-given – neat pigeon-holes into which the words of the language can be sorted. There is plenty of historical excuse for this feeling, of course, as people have adopted this attitude, with few exceptions, since the time of the Stoics. But it is a misleading attitude, and in a linguistic approach we should try to avoid the distortions that an inflexible grid of this kind can provide. We can see the limitations of the method by taking some words which do not fit very well. Is *asleep* an adjective, or an adverb, or something else? Is *garden* (as in *garden chair*) an adjective or a noun, or some kind of mysterious combination? Should *three* be called an adjective? Should *John* be called a noun? Is *this* a pronoun or an adjective? And what are *yes*, and *not*, and *very*? Is *the* an adverb (as in *the more the merrier* – most dictionaries say 'yes')? And what about all the other words that are called adverbs, such as *however*, *there* (as in *there was a man . . .*), *better* (as in *I'd better not*), *so* (as in *so he said*), and *well* (as in *well, yes*)? It is not for nothing that the adverb was referred to (in early Greek grammatical thinking) as a 'dustbin' class. It is almost as if someone had said: 'If you don't know what part of speech a word belongs to, call it an adverb!' I shall suggest a way of answering questions such as these in Chapter 3, when I talk about the need for explicitness in language study. Here I want only to say that any classification of words which raises so many problems is clearly suspect, and it behoves us to try to find a better. A zoologist who could not fit so many animals into a classification would surely want to change it – and so it is with the linguist.

As I said at the beginning of this chapter, it is easy to paint a picture in black and white in discussing traditional approaches to language study. At the moment, the black has certainly been stressed, for the purposes of the argument. But we must not forget that linguistics has a great deal to be grateful for in the work of many early scholars, and I shall bear witness to this often in the rest of the book. Any emphasis on weaknesses is, however, a useful one, in an introductory book, as it has an appropriately chastening effect. It is easy to be smug about language, to rely on our school grammar for all occasions, and when it does not work, to pass it off on the assumption that '*it's* all right, it's just me that doesn't understand'. The purpose of this chapter has been to suggest how inadequate school grammar and lay beliefs can be as a source of information about language capable of facing up to the tasks outlined in Chapter 1. It has, I hope, emphasized how complex the reality of language is. From now on, we shall be speaking more positively and constructively, by outlining the main tenets and techniques of the only alternative approach to language study that has been developed, linguistics. The first point to make, I suppose, bearing in mind our definition on page 9, is that it is a science. But what does *this* mean?

3. Linguistic *Science*

Much of the information and state of mind which I have tried to characterize in Chapter 2 can be summarized in a word: it was unscientific. Linguistics, indeed, usually defines itself with reference to this criterion: it is the scientific study of language. But this is a deceptively simple statement; and understanding exactly what people are committed to once they decide to do linguistics is an important step, an essential preliminary to any insight into the essence of the subject. What *are* the scientific characteristics that make the modern approach to language study what it is? A few years ago, it would have been possible to give a straightforward and generally agreed answer to this question, with almost everyone who called themselves a linguist (in the sense of this book, i.e. a student of linguistics) replying in terms that scientists from other disciplines would have no objection to. Recently, however, a conception of scientific investigation different in certain basic respects from the standard approach has come to be advocated, especially within the school of linguistic thought usually referred to as 'transformational-generative theory'; and the dominant influence exercised by this theory on everyday linguistic thinking these days makes it necessary to examine its claims thoroughly. But before looking at the reaction to earlier views which this approach embodies, it is necessary – and I think prudent in an introductory book – to present the older and still widely used approach first. The first part of this chapter, then, presents an account of the 'scientificness' of linguistics which stems largely from the influential behaviourist climate of a few years ago, and which derives primarily from the stated attitudes of scientists from other disciplines and philosophers of science. Later in the chapter I shall indicate the difference between this and the more recent, mentalistic (or 'rationalist') approach to linguistics. The two positions are sometimes presented as theoretical extremes; but as we shall see, there is a fair amount of similarity between them.

I return, then, to the question: What are the scientific characteristics of a linguistic approach to language study? To begin negatively, these characteristics are not simply reducible to electronic machinery and the use of abstract symbols and formulae, though these are very much in evidence when one begins to study certain branches of linguistics. Open a textbook on grammar these days, and the odds are you will be faced with symbols that might make you think you had wandered into the algebra section of a bookshop. Walk into the phonetics section of a university department of linguistics, and you could be forgiven for imagining yourself in a corner of an applied physical sciences laboratory. But these are the more superficial sides of the 'scientificness' of linguistics. The symbols and machines are means to a further end, and not ends in themselves, as we shall see in due course (pp. 120–21); and it would be both a grave misunderstanding and highly misleading to think of the science of language purely in these terms. Far more important than these is the way linguistics relies on scientific procedures in its study – for want of a better phrase, on a 'scientific method'. But what does *this* mean?

It seems to be generally agreed outside linguistics (and for many linguists too, of course) that for any enterprise to qualify as scientific, in the usual sense, it should display at least three major characteristics – characteristics which should be in evidence regardless of whether we see linguistics related more to the scientificness of the natural and physical sciences, or to that of the social sciences. Terminology varies somewhat, but I shall label these three *explicitness*, *systematicness*, and *objectivity*. What do these concepts involve? We shall begin with explicitness, as unless this is part of a linguist's state of mind from the very beginning, it is doubtful whether much progress would ever be achieved under the other two headings. Much of what follows will be old hat for anyone who has had anything at all to do with scientific analysis in other fields; but the way in which linguistics illustrates the application of these concepts may not be so familiar; and for potential students of the subject (especially those with a predominantly arts background) the perspective is essential.

The requirement of explicitness in language study can be interpreted in relation to a number of different issues. Many of these are, of course, considerations which would affect any subject approached scientifically, such as being clear about the assumptions on which a study is based, or making the intermediate stages of an argument clear, particularly if further assumptions are involved, or defining terms clearly and consistently. But linguistics has some peculiarities of its own in regard to the need for explicitness, and even in relation to the fairly standard requirements just mentioned, it is sometimes by no means obvious how inexplicit reasoning in language study might best be guarded against.

We may take terminological problems as an initial illustration of this last point. The last chapter has shown how easy it is to take linguistic terminology – usually referred to as a 'meta-language' – for granted, and how confusing this can be. Even supposedly basic terms, like 'vowel', 'syllable', 'noun' and 'sentence', have a multitude of definitions; and it is dangerous to assume that your own particular view of a term will be clear, without explanation, to your audience. The term 'adverb' is a very good example of the need for some explicit definition if there is to be any meaningfulness about its use (see p. 74). The term 'sentence', with over 200 definitions, is another. Grammar is an area where the counter-argument 'Well, it all depends what you mean by . . .' is particularly common. But all branches of linguistics are affected; and the danger of ambiguity becomes even more insidious when the terms used do not seem on the surface to be technical at all. Words such as 'situation' and 'feature' have a highly technical status in some corners of the subject, where they have a very specific place within whole systems of concepts; and to avoid the looseness associated with their everyday, 'domestic' senses, it is clearly important to keep the need for definition firmly in the forefront of our minds.

It is probably the long history of thinking about grammar which accounts for the variety of definitions of grammatical concepts in both traditional grammar and linguistics. The lack of standardization is certainly a problem – and it is a clear sign of the immaturity of linguistics that an agreed terminology has not yet developed. But the effects of this lack can be minimized, if individual linguists use terms consistently. At least then we know where we are with a specific piece of work, and are in a position to compare different approaches more precisely. However, a prerequisite for consistency is that linguists are fully aware of the basis of their terminology, of how they arrived at the terms they use; and to develop this awareness, it is probably wise for them to err on the side of caution, and adopt a critical attitude to *all* terms, at least at the present time. How can they do this? One way is to make explicit their criteria for identifying (that is, labelling) a particular feature of language. What things have to be present in order to permit a particular feature to be called an 'X'? We may illustrate this attitude with the label 'noun'. Let us imagine a group of linguists who want to find out what nouns are in English. They know that there are words in a language which 'name' objects, and the like, and they want to establish whether there is any more precise way of identifying these words when they occur than to try and guess at them on the rather vague grounds of their meanings (cf. p. 73). In order to do this as unambiguously as possible, they will set up various criteria for identifying a word as belonging to the class 'noun'. Some of these criteria will be fairly obvious; some will be less so. For example, they may say: 'We will call a noun any word which can act as the subject of a sentence' (as in *cats smell*); 'We will call a noun any word which can be preceded by the definite article' (as in *the cat*); 'We will call a noun any word which can be used in both singular and plural forms' (as in *cats/cat*); 'We will call a noun any word which can have a case-ending that shows possession' (as in *cats'*); and 'We will call a noun any word which can be preceded by a preposition which governs it' (as in *behind cats*). At this point they may stop, thinking that these five criteria are enough to provide a clear-cut basis for identifying words as nouns. It is certainly a start, for most of the words in the language which they may feel intuitively ought to be nouns do all the things these criteria say. And whether they try to define some other criteria or not, they are at least now in a very good position to handle any awkward cases which arise. There are, of course, a number of such cases – words which in some traditional accounts of English would be called

Linguistics

nouns, in others would be called something else. For example, some scholars prefer to call words like *John* and *London* 'proper names', treating them as if they were a distinct part of speech; others call them 'proper nouns', treating them as nouns, though of a rather different kind from the general 'common' type. The question is, are they nouns or aren't they? The choice of labels for such words reflects two quite differing opinions.

It is impossible to decide this question without having thought about criteria of the kind illustrated above. Just how similar *are* the two types of word? Do they work in the grammar in the same kind of way? If they do, then they can validly be referred to using the label 'noun'; if not, then to call them nouns would be an inconsistent use of the term, and this would be confusing. Now if we compare words like *John* with words like *cat*, using the above criteria, the reason for the traditional divergence of opinion immediately becomes clear – they are not the same, but they are not completely different either. The structural differences are in the second and third criteria: we cannot say *the John is here*, or *Johns are here*. (The asterisk indicates an unacceptable utterance.) But the other criteria all apply (*John's, John smells, behind John*). In a complete study, on the basis of these and other criteria (which I have not gone into here), it would emerge that words like *John* have far more in common with words like *boy* than differentiates them, and that, consequently, they might legitimately be called a type (more strictly, a 'sub-class') of noun, without this being unduly misleading; and in the course of the study, the precise extent of the structural difference (i.e. the extent to which we might be misled by treating them as nouns) would be determined. But in a case of this kind, where we find partial similarity in two (or more) directions, there is obviously room for disagreement. To take a colour analogy, is orange nearer to red than to yellow? Indeed, much of the interest of doing grammar lies precisely in problems of analysis of this kind: is structure X more like structure Y than Z? Should one relate structure X to structure V as well as to W? And (to take the argument underlying the need for explicitness a stage further, though it is not something we can go into here), on what grounds were the criteria for identification selected in the first place? Why choose the above five criteria and not others? If others had been chosen, would the results have been different? Here I wish only to point out that discussion of this kind can never even begin without some attempt being made to bring the problem out into the open through the use of some criterion or other – and this is one facet of what explicitness means.

Any attempt to classify or sub-classify patterns in a language ultimately forces us to have recourse to criteria. A neat classification of sentences in a language into ten types, let us say, is of no value unless we know on what grounds the typology was based – for otherwise how can we evaluate an alternative and comparably neat classification of these same sentences into *nine* types by someone else? But this, like the above example, is a particularly complex case. It does not follow that all cases are so complex, or that we have to press for the definition and evaluation of *every* conceivable general term in a linguistic study, for otherwise we should make no empirical headway at all; we should always be defining, and the more single-minded of us would be off chasing criteria for criteria into an infinite regress. Terms which are of no direct theoretical relevance to the main line of an investigation may, of course, be taken for granted, if they have a reasonably standard use in the literature on linguistics – or at least if any debate about their meaning does not affect the point under consideration. For example, in a project about number in English, it would obviously be necessary to describe how nouns form their plurals. Here we would point out, amongst other things, that the -s ending has different pronunciations, depending on the nature of the sound with which the noun ends (cf. p. 57). In order to explain this difference, we would have to say that in words like *cats* the -s is 'voiceless', whereas in *dogs* it is 'voiced'. Now the terms 'voiced' and 'voiceless' have standard definitions in phonetics (see p. 168), referring to the way in which the vocal cords are functioning during the articulation of the sounds; but there would be no point in making these definitions clear here, as the phonetic details of the alternation are of restricted interest, and do not affect our general understanding of the nature of number in nouns at all. (On the other hand, if we were investigating the way in which the voice cords worked, it would be important to make it absolutely clear what we intended the terms 'voiced' and 'voiceless' to mean, as there are many examples in language where the distinction is blurred.) Having said this, however, it is worth reiterating the importance, as a rule of thumb, of cultivating a critical approach to terminology. We can never be sure in advance which concepts are going to be of direct relevance to our own study and which not; without this critical awareness, it is all too easy to take for granted a concept whose evaluation (we later realize) was crucial for guaranteeing an objective basis for our research.

The problem of terminology and the need for criteria perhaps affect linguistics more than other subjects. For linguists, language is both the end and means of their investigation: they have to analyse language, using language. There are other issues too in linguistics where the need for explicitness is paramount, and where the problem is unlikely to turn up to the same degree in other subjects. One of these is in relation to the use of transcription. Before we can analyse spoken language, it has to be written down, and, if we are unhappy with ready-made systems of orthography, this involves using some system of phonetic transcription (see p. 165). But every system of transcription that has been invented is very selective: certain features of the sounds used are given a symbolic notation, and others are ignored. The [p] symbol at the beginning of the word [pit], in the system of transcription known as the International Phonetic Alphabet, refers to a sound made by the sudden release of closed lips, the vocal cords not vibrating (or 'buzzing') at the time – technically, a 'voiceless bilabial plosive'. Here we have three features of the way in which this sound is articulated; but there are other features of a [p] articulation not given in this definition. For instance, the muscles of the lips are very tense for the production of a [p] sound, especially when compared with a [b] (as in *bit*); there is a puff of air released after the sound ('aspiration', which can easily be felt if the hand is raised close to the lips while the word is uttered), whereas in a word like *bit* this is negligible; and so on. Other systems of transcription might define the [p] symbol in such a way as to take account of these features of articulation (though no transcriptional system would

ever try to define its symbols with reference to *every* feature underlying the articulation of a sound – the transcription would become
so cumbersome as to defeat its purpose). I shall have more to say on
this point in due course (p. 120). Here, the important thing to note
is that the way in which symbols are used can sometimes reflect the
theoretical intentions of the author – that is, the selection of which
symbol to use is dictated by the author's opinion as to which feature
of a sound (or combination of features) is the central, defining one.

We can illustrate this very easily from British English. Here,
words like *beat* and *bit* are quite distinct: they mean different
things. But what is the phonetic basis of the difference? There seem
to be two important factors involved: there is clearly a quantity
difference (i.e. a difference in length, the first vowel being longer
than the second), and there is also a quality difference (i.e. the
position of the tongue is higher in the mouth in the case of the first
word). Now if analysts think that the length difference is the important one – the real reason why we can tell these words apart –
then they will want to show this in their transcriptions of the
words, for example by transcribing [bi:t] and [bit] respectively (the
: indicating the extra length). If other analysts were to feel that the
tongue height difference was the crucial one, then they might well
transcribe the pair using different vowel symbols, to try and emphasize this point (as in [bit] and [bɪt] respectively, there being no
length symbol used this time). And if yet other analysts felt that
both length and height were equally involved in the difference (that
is, you could not tell the two words apart unless your tongue was
higher *and* the vowel longer in the first word), then they might
transcribe them as [bi:t] and [bɪt] respectively – in other words,
conflating the two transcriptions above. Here, then, are three different transcriptions of the same pair of words, but it is important to
see that the reasons for the differences are bound up with a more
general matter concerning analysts' views about which feature is
more important in the identification of words by native speakers.
The choice is based on a theoretical position: is length of vowel or
height of vowel a more valid explanation of the patterning of the
English sound system in this respect? This is a fairly trivial example,
and one which can be tested easily enough by experiment; but it

indicates how important it is not to take a transcription for granted. The choice of a particular symbol (or, more usually, set of symbols) can have a number of far-reaching theoretical implications, and these ought to be made clear by researchers when they present their transcribed data for analysis. The basis of their transcriptions should be made explicit.

A final example of the need for explicitness arises out of the nature of the data linguistics is for the most part concerned with. While the main aim of the subject is to establish general, theoretical principles which will explain the structure of particular languages and ultimately language as a whole, in order to even begin moving towards this goal, we must, in the nature of things, start with the study of individual language users. We start with the speech of one person, and move on from there. It very quickly emerges, however, that there are sometimes very many differences between the speech patterns of one person and those of another. People speak differently, and have different feelings about what is normal, correct, acceptable, and so on, in their language, as we have seen in our first two chapters. And a linguistic theory, if it is to explain *all* about language – the permissible idiosyncratic variations as well as the general patterns – has therefore to try to establish principles which will account for these differences. Much of the research into sociolinguistics and psycholinguistics, as we shall see in Chapter 5, is along these lines. But if we are engaged in investigating a point of disputed usage, let us say – for instance, whether people say CON-*troversy* or *con*T R O V*ersy* – we must be quite explicit about all the factors which are relevant to the question, and which could influence any statistical account. If we decide to take a sample of the population, for example, and ask them how they say the word, at least two kinds of factor have to be borne in mind.

First, we must take care to present the issue in a way which does not prejudice the answer, using a wide range of possible contexts. (By 'contexts' here I mean the types of linguistic structure in which the word could be used.) If we ask someone, baldly, how they pronounce the word 'controversy' (showing them it written on a piece of paper), then they will reply boldly (though sometimes not at all); but give them a sentence to read in which the word appears, and they may very well give a different pronunciation of it. On its own, CONt*roversy* sounds all right, and this is the answer most people would give. But put it in such a sentence as *There was a controversy over the introduction of the use of the cane* ..., and the interesting fact is that many of the people who say CONt*roversy* in isolation switch to *con*TROV*ersy* in connected speech. There could be a number of reasons for this. One possible reason is that it provides a better rhythm to the sentence if the stress is on *trov*, as the number of unstressed syllables on either side of this syllable are in a better balance. But whatever the reasons for the change, it should be clear that, if our results are going to be able to be scientifically evaluated, we must make quite explicit what range of structures we examined – or did not examine, as the case may be.

The second factor is also basic if our research is to be evaluated properly: it concerns our selection of people to ask about the pronunciation of the word. Who should we choose as a sample of 'informants'? Do we simply go out in the street and pick the first thousand speakers? We might end up with figures of seventy per cent to thirty per cent in favour of *con*TROV*ersy*, but what would this prove? Very little, in fact. For is there any pattern in either of these figures? How do we explain the minority use? Are they all old people? upper-class people? women? foreigners? Northerners? linguists? and so on. People are not items to be sampled like apples on a conveyor belt. We can be reasonably sure that every fifth apple sampled, say, will provide a reasonably homogeneous sample at the end; but every fifth person may not, for there is no guaranteed homogeneity in any two people's linguistic background. The number of variables which makes one person's speech habits different from another's is large and relatively unstudied. But whenever we investigate language it is important to be aware of the kind of factor which could affect our analysis of a problem, and to make explicit those factors which we do pay attention to, in order to make precise comparative study possible. For only by a careful comparative statement can we ultimately build up a more complete picture of the language as a whole, and thus approximate to the general account which it is the aim of linguistics to establish. I have more on this point below, p. 135, ff.

Explicitness, then, is a major concern of linguistics, particularly since the development of generative grammar (see pp. 216, ff.). It is – or should be – part of the 'state of mind' of linguists when they approach their subject. If they remember that all their meta-language is man-made, subject to error, then they may avoid many procedural and terminological pitfalls, such as characterized traditional grammars. One of the main weaknesses underlying traditional approaches was that criteria for analysis, data-selection, and so on, were rarely made explicit. It does not, of course, follow from this that these grammars made mis-statements about language; but it does mean that many of the statements they did make could not be given any consistent or clear interpretation. Often we simply cannot see why a sentence was parsed in the way it was, or why one word was called an adverb while another was not. And the smart child who raised a hand in a grammar class and asked 'But *why* is that word an adverb?' was voicing a perfectly legitimate criticism. The frustration which many children felt after doing grammar in school, stemmed largely from the fact that there was never any answer given to such questions apart from 'Because it is'. Intelligent people want reasons for things, in grammar as in anything else.

The second main characteristic of a scientific study of language referred to above is its systematicness. I do not mean to imply by this that it is a totally different question from explicitness, however – to a certain extent the difference between systematicness and explicitness is one of emphasis. A haphazard study of a structure, an unintentionally partial coverage of a topic, an impressionistic commentary, a sporadic explicitness, an inconsistent use of terms or procedures, a failure to take account of previous work on a subject: these are not features we expect to see in a scientific approach – though it is a matter of regret that they can sometimes be found in work going under the heading of linguistics. In principle, however, linguists would try to avoid these failings and adopt a systematic approach in their investigation into language. The need for system in our dealings is perhaps obvious enough; after all, this principle is by no means the prerogative of scientific method. F. N. Kerlinger, in his book *Foundations of Behavioral Research*, talks about the scientific approach as 'a special systematized form of all reflective thinking and inquiry'. It is the extent to which our 'system' has to be developed and made explicit which is the distinctive feature of scientific systematicness. In the case of language, the structures being examined are so complex, and involve so many variables, that it would be impossible to reach any general conclusions about them unless they were studied in a highly organized way. But how does this organization manifest itself?

One of the most obvious ways is in the manner in which linguists have tried to establish standard procedures to be followed in analysing a language. This was a dominant characteristic of much early work in linguistics. It was felt that there is so much complexity immediately encountered when we are presented with a language to investigate that it was essential to simplify immediately, to select certain aspects of the language as the things to study first. In looking at this approach, we must remember that any selection is of course necessarily artificial. There is no obvious priority in the stream of speech – no set of features which analysts must address themselves to first if the job is to be done properly. I am reminded of the old question about the best way to describe an elephant: does one begin with the trunk, or the tail, with its size, or its weight . . .? Different linguists may choose to begin their analysis with different aspects of the data, and relate subsequent aspects of this data to their starting-points in a multitude of different ways. For example, one group of linguists may find it more satisfactory (what this means we shall be going into below) to begin an investigation by studying the pronunciation system (the 'phonetics and phonology') of a language first, establishing what the vowels and consonants are, and working out the way in which these units combine into syllables and other stretches of speech. After doing this, they may move on to the study of the structure of words ('morphology'), and, after this, to the study of the way words pattern in sequences to form sentences ('syntax'). Later still, they may attempt to study the various meanings which these words and word-sequences convey (the 'semantics'). This would be one way of imposing some organization on the material and working through it. It is, as it happens, a method which was very popular in linguistics until recently. But, as we shall see in Chapter 4, there is nothing natural about this approach; and a different group of linguists might well use almost the reverse procedure. This other approach might begin with the study of the various relationships of meaning which exist between words or word-sequences; after this it might establish which syntactic or morphological patterns express these meanings; and only after that might it move on to a study of the way in which these patterns would be pronounced. Nor is this the only alternative. And similarly, once one has arrived at an analysis of some data, there are many alternatives as to how the features of this analysis may best be presented.

The point to be made here and now is not which procedure is the most valid, or gets the best results, nor should we concentrate on understanding our procedures at the expense of the more important, theoretical goals (these questions will concern us later), but rather that any procedural factors which we are aware of should be made as explicit *as possible* in doing research into language. The emphasis is important. It is never possible to make our procedures absolutely explicit: there are too many unknown factors which lead us to make the decisions we do – factors arising out of our own personalities and situations; and as we shall see below (p. 121), this indeterminacy has been a major reason for the current diminution of emphasis on research procedures. But without *some* attempt at a clearly defined procedure of analysis, any research is liable to degenerate into chaos, and it is highly unlikely that any of the general explanations being sought by the investigator would ever be achieved. It is, I suppose, possible to 'pick up' a fair knowledge of a language's structure and, ultimately, about the structure of language in general, by working in a sporadic, impressionistic way; but apart from the purely practical reasons for not doing so (for example, the waste of time involved – such as by covering the same ground more than once without realizing it), there are all-important theoretical reasons (such as failing to notice relationships of importance between features of language).

This last point leads us on to the second main aspect of systematicness in linguistics. The need to study phenomena using a procedure which is as methodical and standardized as possible is perhaps obvious enough; but there is a presupposition here. It is one thing to decide to investigate or outline the structure of (let us say) the noun phrase before we go on to the verb phrase in a language; but this requires the prior recognition that there *are* such things as noun phrases and verb phrases that can be studied. In other words, when approaching the analysis of a piece of language, linguists have some ideas about what they should be looking for, what they will find there – they have in mind a more or less precise working hypothesis, or descriptive framework, within which they hope to be able to fit their observations about the language's patterning. This framework, of course, is itself a systematic construction; it is a preliminary version of the final description which they one day hope to produce, a first approximation which they know to be inexplicit and incomplete in some respects, but which nonetheless provides enough of a conceptual apparatus to make some progress. Some of the variables and relationships within this framework will be fairly precisely defined, the product of their own and others' previous experience of language; others will be extremely vague – no more than guesses. And, in a way, the point of the whole exercise is to substitute precision for vagueness on all counts. Ways of doing this I shall discuss below.

A point that can be emphasized immediately is that linguists will improve their understanding of phenomena only if they use their descriptive framework consistently within any stage of their investigation. The importance of consistency is paramount – not only for clear thinking in general, but specifically because of the pressures imposed on linguists by the need to make comparisons between samples of language. Linguists are typically comparative animals. By this I mean that their regular task is to compare two bits of language, to determine whether they display the same structural principles, to decide whether the analysis they have given to bit A also applies to bit B, and so on. We have already seen something of this concern in our discussion of explicitness – and consistency is the offspring of explicitness. The bits of language to be compared may of course be any size – single sounds, words, sentences, or even whole discourses or texts. Now, when faced with any comparative exercise, it is obviously crucial to be systematic, and this means having both a reasonably explicit descriptive framework and a standard procedure, as suggested above – for otherwise no comparison can be made. If one bit of language has been analysed in terms of method and framework A, whereas the other has been analysed using method and framework B, comparison becomes difficult, and sometimes impossible. It is like using two different measuring systems simultaneously. Faced with two tables, if we are told that one table is 36 ins. long, and the other is 48 cm. long, it is not immediately apparent (to most of us, at any rate) which is the longer – even in these metric days. In order to decide this, it is necessary to turn one measure into the other, that is, to adopt a common conceptual apparatus and analytic procedure. With language, things are far more complex, as there are a very large number of points of comparison, all defined by reference to sets of criteria. But the principle is the same: only by using the same approach can a systematic comparison of two bits of language be easily effected.

We must remember too, in this connection, that it is not simply a question of keeping single terms constant in meaning in making our analysis, but of keeping the relationships between whole sets of terms constant also, and bearing in mind the effect of introducing a new term, or redefining an old one, on the definitions of the other terms used hitherto. The terms which we use to describe a language are to a very great extent interdependent: one term defines the meaning of another, and is in turn defined by it. Alter the meaning of one term and by implication you have altered the meaning of some other, and perhaps, as in a chain reaction, the meaning of a very large number of terms indeed. To see this, an analogy may help. If given a set of objects of different sizes, and asked to classify them into 'big' and 'small', we can do so, even though we may not feel too happy about where to draw the dividing line. Now, given the same set of objects, and asked to classify them into 'big', 'medium-size' and 'small', we can also do so – but note what happens. Some of the smaller items classified under 'big' *and* some of the larger items classified under 'small' are put together to form the new category. The result is not one new category, but three new categories, as 'big' and 'small' have both been redefined in the process. This kind of thing happens all the time in language. A very simple example of this would be when beginning the analysis of a language. For instance, we may have isolated a few noun-like words, and we are trying to make the concept of 'noun' precise, so we are looking for criteria. We notice that these words sometimes end in the syllable *-ik*, sometimes in the syllable *-om*. By comparing a number of examples of the way in which these forms are used, and by asking the right kind of questions, we conclude that *-ik* is a 'singular' form of the word, used when only one instance of the object in question is being referred to, and that *-om* is a 'plural' form, used when more than one object is being referred to. Then a little later we find that these same words can be used with the ending *-ap*, with the meaning 'two (objects) being referred to' – what grammars would call a 'dual' number for the noun. The point is that the discovery of this new category forces us to redefine one of those we have been working with: plural no longer means 'more than one', but 'more than two'. This process of redefinition is continually occurring in the early stages of analysing a language, and is implicit in any change we make from the use of one descriptive framework to another while analysing two samples of the same language. The problems arise, of course, when we are dealing with more complex meaning contrasts – contrasts which are not as easily definable as 'one', 'two', and 'more than two', and which affect more of the grammar than simply nouns. To keep tabs on all the variables is quite complicated, and it is accordingly not surprising that a linguist may see similarities or differences between two accounts of a phenomenon which may vanish when observed from a slightly different angle.

We can see how such problems arise in more complex matters by the study of style, which is a comparative subject *par excellence* (cf. p. 26, ff.). Here the typical tasks are to see how a person's style develops or changes (for example, in two poems, novels, speeches . . .), or to see if there are similarities between the styles of a number of people which would allow them to be grouped together ('scientific language', 'journalese', and so on). In order to do this, it is essential to isolate and describe the salient features of each style – to pick out from the samples of language certain features which we can say with some definiteness do identify the use of language as such-and-such – Shakespearian, scientific, typical of that kind of newspaper, etc. If we are examining five samples of language in this way, it is clearly going to be essential to use the same descriptive framework in each case, and it will be more convenient and clear if the same analytic procedure is used at all points (e.g. dealing with any morphological features of stylistic distinctiveness before syntactic). Unfortunately, this does not always happen, and, worse, people do not always realize it. Unless our criteria are absolutely explicit, it is all too easy to allow a different range of phenomena under a given heading in sample A than in sample B. For example, if we are trying to make sense of a phrase I came across recently, a critic who said that 'A's style was very concrete, far more so than B's', it is important to see what this impression of concreteness is based on. One measure of this, which has been suggested in other connections, might be the ratio of nouns to verbs in the author's usage: if there were a significant preponderance of nouns over verbs in A's proportions, then the style might indeed be labelled 'concrete'. This is the sort of analysis which is very often attempted. The problem is that an investigator might analyse A using one definition of noun, while another (or even the same person) might analyse B using a different definition. To make use of our earlier example, the first might allow in 'proper names' (and other similar marginal cases); the second might not (cf. p. 80). Then it would certainly be true to say that A had a higher ratio of nouns to verbs than B, and that A had therefore a more concrete style – but only because the definition of noun allows more in the first case than in the second. Such variation between basic terms in an investigation is, I suspect, rather more common than is generally supposed. It is something which ought to be studiously avoided.

Systematicness refers to other principles too, apart from the use of specific procedures and a consistent descriptive framework. It refers to the need for strict testing of our hypotheses, beliefs, guesses, insights, and the like, about language, or some aspect of language. The rigorous testing of hypotheses is central to what I mean by a scientific approach in linguistics. The operative word in this statement is 'rigorous', but first a word of explanation about 'hypotheses'. A hypothesis is a statement which suggests or predicts a relationship between two or more variables. If X happens, it says, in effect, that Y will happen also. Some elementary hypotheses in language study might be: 'vowels become nasalized when followed by a nasal consonant'; 'pronouns always go before verbs'. These may be hypotheses for a specific language or group of languages, or for language in general. More complex hypotheses are: 'sound-changes are regular', 'bilingual people are less intelligent than monolingual ones', 'animal communication has nothing in common with human language'. A hypothesis is in principle a very specific statement: it states a relationship which can be demonstrated, or shown to be false, to a greater or lesser degree, in one or more experiments. Moreover, a hypothesis, if it is well-formed, should assert only one relationship at a time. The entities being related may be quite complex in themselves (and may be based on a number of other hypotheses), as in the concepts of 'bilingual people' and 'intelligence' above, but there is still only one major correlation being postulated in each case. (We may, however, test more than one hypothesis at a time, using certain statistical techniques.)

Hypotheses are made to be tested; that is their purpose. They formulate a problem or an insight in such a way that it becomes possible to obtain some evidence for or against a point at issue. This is very important as far as understanding the traditional picture of science is concerned. For what is the nature of the evidence that we allow in to validate or falsify our hypotheses? This will be the central question underlying our discussion of objectivity below. From the point of view of understanding the role of hypotheses in relation to systematicness, I must rephrase what I said at the beginning of this paragraph: hypotheses are made to be tested – rigorously. The opposite of 'rigorous' here is 'careless', 'impressionistic', 'casual', and the like. Putting it positively, by a rigorous test, I mean that within a particular frame of reference the research is explicit, disciplined, thorough, and (as far as techniques allow) comprehensive. The conditions in which the experiment takes place are made clear, so that others can replicate it if necessary and verify its results. In a word, rigour inspires confidence. Now there is very little of language which can be tested in the same way as material objects (research into the physical properties of sounds is an obvious exception), as mentalistically-inclined linguists have been quick to point out (see below, pp. 103, ff.), but the need for rigour is central no matter what kind of test we frame. One way of ensuring that a test is rigorous is to *control* as many variables in a particular experimental situation as possible – their presence in the situation has to be accounted for, the effect of any one variable on the other variables in the situation has to be known. Out of a multiplicity of possible explanations for a relationship, all explanations bar one are shown to be impossible. We can only test a hypothesis if other variables not part of the hypothesis are held steady in some way (that is, we eliminate the possibility of their having any causal role in affecting the relationship we are testing); and the ways in which we can do this are part and parcel of what I mean by systematic. A simple example of controlling a variable would be to show that in a particular construction, consisting of three words, let us say X, Y, Z, the first word is the reason for the form the third takes, and not the second. In the sentence *John is a bigger man than Jim*, the construction *bigger man than* illustrates the X Y Z situation. *Than* (and the structure which follows it) is dependent on there being an adjective in the comparative in the preceding construction, in this case, *bigger*. This may be obvious. If it is not (and presumably there was a time in language study when it was not), we could show this by hypothesizing a relationship between the two most likely variables (e.g. '*than*-structures are dependent on the occurrence of a comparative adjective in the preceding noun phrase') and testing it. What other possible explanations have to be eliminated? For the sake of illustration, here are two trivial ones (trivial, because we know from general experience of language study that languages do not work like this normally): perhaps the *than*-structure can only be used if the noun that precedes it is three sounds (or letters) long? This can be eliminated by finding examples which show length to be a quite independent variable, e.g. *a bigger elephant than* . . . . Well, then, perhaps the *than*-structure can be used only if the verb is in the present tense? Again, an explanation which is easy to eliminate. The necessity of having the comparative adjective is shown by seeing what happens if it is omitted: *John is a man than Jim* is not a possible sentence. But this is not the end of the story; the example is not quite as straightforward as it appears. For in our examples, the use of the *than*-structure seems to be dependent on more than just the adjective in the comparative form: the use of the indefinite article seems to be important too, for it is not possible to have *John is the bigger man than Jim*. The role of the article system in relation to comparison in English needs to be gone into a little, it seems. But this would take us beyond the purpose of this example.

Rigorous testing is an ideal. The trouble with language is that the variables to be controlled are sometimes not at all obvious. One reason for this is that, because we have been brought up in a traditional conceptual framework, we are often blinded to the existence of relevant variables. We look to see the relevance of the features which we know to be important in Latin grammar, say, and not beyond. One very clear, but complex example of this is in connection with the tense system of a language. If we stick to a traditional conception of tense, then the hypothesis 'tense in language signals time' is likely to be accepted without question. It would follow from this that the present tense of a verb signals present time (that is, the activity is taking place at the time of speaking, as in *John is going*), the past tense signals past time (as in *John went home*), and so on, for the whole range of tenses we may want to set up. But the hypothesis can be shown to be false, if we rigorously examine the posited relationship and ask the (related) questions: Is there a one-to-one relation between tense and time? Do the tenses have any other jobs to do in language apart from signalling time relationships? and, Are there any other ways of signalling time relationships in language (i.e. other variables) apart from using the tense system? Let us answer these questions one at a time. Just taking the two tenses given above, we can find examples which illustrate the need for alternative explanations. *Sir X dies*, says a newspaper headline. This does not mean that Sir X is dying while the headline is being read. It means he has just died. Or again, I might call to see someone and say upon entering the room, *John says you want to talk to me* – that is, it was said some time before. But in both cases, the present tense is used. Present tense can signal past time as well as present time, in some contexts, it seems.

That tenses have other jobs to do in language apart from telling the time is obvious from a consideration of the following example: *I was wondering whether you could look at this*. Here, the wondering was not taking place some time before, in the past: you are still wondering, while you speak, and you will be wondering for a little while yet, until you get an answer. The past tense form *was wondering* means far more than any time relationship can convey. It expresses *tentativeness* of meaning. It is a much humbler, or politer way of introducing the question than to say *Could you look at this?* To use the present tense would make the request far more businesslike – and in addition provides a hint of ambiguity: *I am wondering whether you could look at this* could also mean 'I am not certain whether it is appropriate for you to do so at this moment' or even 'I am doubtful of your capabilities in this matter' – these interpretations being highly unlikely when the past tense is used. The 'tentative' meaning of the past tense is quite common in English.

In answer to the third question, whether there are any other ways of signalling time relationships than the use of the tense system, we may simply refer to the adverbs of the language. The 'adverb of time' is a familiar category from traditional grammar, but its importance for the expression of time relationships in English (and in many other languages too) is generally underestimated. The reason for its importance is that when it occurs in a sentence, its meaning very often outranks the meaning of the tense form which occurs along with it. We can illustrate this from the sentence *I'm going to the cinema*, as said by someone while leaving the room. Here the present tense refers to present time, a simultaneous activity. But if the same person said while leaving the room, *I'm going to the cinema tomorrow*, the meaning would be quite different. The activity being referred to by the sentence would no longer be the one taking place at the time of speaking. Or again, if the sentence had been *I'm going to the cinema far too often these days*, the implication would be the one sometimes referred to as 'habitual' action. Now here are three sentences uttered on identical occasions referring to three different times of action, but with the same (present) tense form in each. It is clear that something else must be causing the difference, and this is of course the use of the adverb of future time (in the second example) and the adverb phrase of frequency (in the third). Such cases could easily be multiplied.

To take the concept of 'time' and to investigate systematically all the features of a language which are part of its expression is by no means an easy task, as the concept in question is so profound. English is the language on which most linguistic work has been done, but even here, work on the verb system and related features of time expression is by no means complete. And there are many other areas of language in a similarly uninvestigated state. It is perfectly reasonable to maintain as an article of faith that a complete analysis of a whole language is possible; but no such analysis is anywhere near conclusion at the present time (though restricted areas of language have been studied fairly completely). The point I want to emphasize, however, is that how near we can get to this ideal depends entirely on the extent to which our approach is systematic, in the sense of this chapter. Without systematicness, the goal will never be achieved.

Systematicness is such an all-embracing concept that it is not possible to cover all its implications in a chapter such as this. We shall have cause to refer to further of these implications later on. Meanwhile, we must look at what is involved in the third characteristic of a scientific approach, which I have labelled above as *objectivity*. I have left this characteristic until last – even though in many people's minds it is precisely what they intuitively associate with a science – because its status sometimes generates controversy in linguistics. I think every linguist would grant explicitness and systematicness a fairly fundamental role in any linguistic approach, though their ways of defining and evaluating them may differ somewhat. But the status of empirical evidence has been called into question by a sufficiently large number of influential people to make it necessary to approach this topic with particular care. And whether one considers this questioning of empirical method a scientific blasphemy or not, the fact remains that the questioners have developed an extremely thorough frame of reference for their views which, like it or not, has contributed more to our knowledge of human language than anything before. It is ironic, in a way, that linguists should have been made aware of their responsibilities as scientists by a theoretical school which does not regard a major feature of traditional science as primary. But I shall discuss this view further shortly. It makes little sense until it is seen in the context of the usual scientific approach, as practised by chemists, sociologists, biologists, and others. Here, objectivity is a cardinal feature of scientificness. The questions they ask, the conclusions they reach, and the evidence they cite must be capable of being publicly observed and tested. The usual word which attempts to summarize this point is 'empirical'. An empirical test is one in which the examination of phenomena takes place under controlled, experimental conditions, the results being available to direct observation and judgement, so that if the experiment were replicated, the same results and the same popular judgements would be obtained. Putting this another way, the results are 'verifiable'.

In all this, certain connotations of the term 'objective' are important. The word implies all sorts of good things. It implies open-mindedness in matters of analysis, a critical approach where we are in principle suspicious of any hypothesis until some experimental evidence is brought to bear on the point. It means taking care to avoid our own preconceptions which might selectively support a hypothesis – such as by making the effort to think out a problem from a fresh angle, or by getting colleagues to read through our research drafts for criticism. It also means making use as far as possible of standardized procedures – procedures which would be accepted by most or all linguists as being valid, not needing separate justification each time they are used. This last point needs illustrating, as 'standard' can mean two things here. Firstly, it can refer to techniques whose general validity is recognized – or at least, where this validity is determined on grounds other than those established by linguistics. Examples would be the use of statistical or other mathematical reasoning (set-theoretical techniques, for instance) or the use of formal logic. Secondly, it can refer to techniques which have been widely used in linguistics, whose value is recognized and (more important) whose limitations are fairly well under-

Linguistic *Science*

stood. An example would be the use of the so-called 'minimal pair' test in phonology. This is a method which most linguists use when they come across a language for the first time and they want to find out its sound-system. Of all the sounds that it is possible to produce, some are going to be used in a language for purposes of communication and others are not. In speaking English, for example, it would not matter if I put a broad nasal twang on every vowel I uttered, because it does not make any difference to the meaning of what I am saying – it would just sound (to British ears, at any rate) as if I were an American, or had a cold. But if in speaking English I put an /a/ vowel in place of each /e/ vowel, or a /b/ instead of a /p/ it would make a considerable difference. I would frequently be misunderstood. 'I like pets' would sound like 'I like bats', and so on. The minimal pair test, briefly, is a technique which establishes which sounds in a language 'make a difference', and which do not. It works like this. You take a word – on its own, to begin with – and you alter one of its sounds: if you get a different word thereby – that is, if a speaker of the language tells you the words no longer are the same – then you have a 'minimal pair', and the two sounds which alternate to produce the two words are considered important sounds in language. They are part of the sound-system, and would be called 'phonemes' by most linguists. Examples would be /pet/ and /bet/, or /bet/ and /set/, or /set/ and /sat/, and so on. Sooner or later you would come to the end of the possible substitutions you could make and you would assume that your inventory of the important sounds was complete. It is more complicated in practice than this, of course, as we shall see in Chapter 4; and certain assumptions the test makes can be criticized (for example, it assumes certain norms of perceptual ability in the person who judges whether the two words are the same or different). But on the whole it works, as a technique for establishing the sound-system of a language, and some linguists have made names for themselves by being able to operate this technique with great skill and speed – rumours of linguists who can establish the phoneme system of a brand-new language in an hour or so are well-founded. The minimal pair test is a standard technique. Other examples of standard techniques these days would be the use of transformation equivalences to show the relationships between structures, and of acceptability testing to determine the linguistic status of a particular utterance. These techniques are referred to often in this book, so I shall not go into them here: an instance of the former is on pp. 207–8, of the latter on p. 65.

Another way of looking at objectivity in science is to see it in relation to its antonym, subjectivity. In its extreme form, a subjective approach is one where the investigator's analysis and data derive wholly from his 'feel' or 'belief' or 'intuition' about things, no reference being made to empirical evidence. At its worst, subjectivity produces a vague and biased impressionism – unfortunately a feature of much of the traditional approach to language study referred to in Chapter 2. At its best, it can add an invaluable qualitative dimension to study, and provide a source of useful hypotheses (cf. p. 107). But even at its best, subjective investigation would be classified as strictly unscientific by the criteria of standard scientific method. Speculation may be sophisticated and stimulating, but it is non-science. There are many such speculations to do with language that cannot be given any objective test: such matters are not necessarily uninteresting or trivial – quite the contrary, very often – but they are not considered scientific questions. Propositions which cannot be tested – 'metaphysical explanations', as Russell and others once called them – are easily found in connection with the discussions into the ancestry of language, for example. We may firmly believe that God 'invented' language, but without some verifiable evidence, the issue remains outside the realm of science. It is, if you like, pre-scientific. And, as we have seen, pre-scientific hypotheses can attract a great deal of attention without achieving any positive results.

So far in our discussion of scientificness, the evidence which has been required to substantiate linguistic hypotheses has been, implicitly or explicitly, empirical in character. This, I have said, is the standard scientific approach. If data, methods and results cannot be publicly observed and measured using standard techniques, then the scientist, it would be argued, has some justification for not accepting them – or at the very least for keeping an open mind about them. In the case of linguistics, the data that we would refer hypotheses to would be, in these terms, the actual usage of people – the spoken or written manifestations of language. In an empirical approach, the aim would be to determine the patterns in the data – patterns of sound, grammar, vocabulary, meaning, or anything else. On the basis of a few samples, we should set up hypotheses about the structure of the data, and then refer these hypotheses to further data to check the analysis. This collection of spoken and/or written usage which is used to verify our hypotheses about structure is usually called a 'corpus' (plural 'corpora'). A 'corpus-based' approach is one which restricts itself to the analysis of a limited sample of language in this way. In the 'middle ages' of linguistics (the forties and fifties) this approach was especially widespread. A particularly influential example of its use was the book *The Structure of English*, by Charles Carpenter Fries, which appeared in 1952. The approach was called by many names, 'structural' linguistics being perhaps the most common (though there is far more to structuralism in language study than the use of a corpus, as we shall see in Chapter 4). This approach is by no means of historical interest only, however. There are a number of large-scale surveys of usage using corpora taking place at the moment (though they do not actually restrict themselves to corpora): the approach has considerable positive value in its detailed focusing on points of uncertainty and dispute in language, such as in plotting the effects of stylistic variation or language change on norms of usage. But a corpus-based approach has its limitations too, and a knowledge of these, it has been argued, is fundamental for assessing the conceptual basis of the discipline, in particular its basis as a science.

The approach developed in the late fifties known as 'generative grammar', associated primarily with the name of Noam Chomsky, was pivotal in stimulating a sharp reaction against the empirical approach of the previous decades, which had been so prejudiced against postulating any kind of 'mental' constructs. Chomsky argues that linguistics is concerned with far more than the range of patterns to be found in any corpus – and in this I do not think any linguist would disagree with him. To begin with, he says, a corpus, in the nature of things, can never illustrate a whole language, but will only reflect a partial and selective picture. Moreover, he says, 'a record of natural speech will show numerous false starts, deviations from rules, changes of plan in mid-course, and so on' (*Aspects of the Theory of Syntax*, p. 4). These mistakes and non-fluencies are due to many factors, such as poor memory, and being distracted while we are speaking; but the important point is that we have the ability to recognize them for what they are and discount them. We do not take them into account when we are listening to what someone is saying. But this suggests – the argument continues – that we have learned a way of distinguishing mistakes from correct utterance, for discriminating between sentences. We can therefore postulate that people have mastered a system of rules which allows us to sort out language in this way – and this system of rules, it should be noted, is something that is not contained within the corpus, but lies outside it, presumably in the mind of the speakers of the language.

The existence of this system of rules can also be postulated by an argument from creativity in language use. It is nowadays almost a truism (since Chomsky's repeated emphasis on the point) to say that each of us has the ability to produce and understand a vast number of new sentences – sentences which we have never encountered before (or, at least, which we cannot remember encountering). A sentence like *Fifteen bright green garden-chairs were scattered all over my next-door neighbour's pussy-cats* is almost certainly going to be a new sentence for everyone reading this book; but it is easily understood. In a way, the central task for linguistic theory is to answer the question 'How then did we reach our understanding of it?' Presumably we have mastered ('internalized' is a word often used here) a technique for breaking each new sentence up into bits which are more familiar (e.g. numeral + adjective + noun, as in *three green bottles*), and we reach a synthesis of any new sentence by reference to these bits. The magnitude of our ability is indicated by the fact that there is an infinite number of sentences in any language which we can arrive at by manipulating bits (words, phrases, etc.) of this kind. Language, it has been said, makes infinite use of finite means. And once again, this argues for the existence of a system of rules present in anyone who has learned a language which is the means whereby they interpret and produce new and old, acceptable and unacceptable sentences, and much else besides.

But surely (the argument continues), the study of this system of rules is ultimately more important than the study of the actual sentences themselves? For this system is a blueprint which specifies all the possibilities in a language, whereas any collection of sentences (as in a corpus), no matter how large, presents only a partial picture of what can be done. Chomsky thus makes a fundamental distinction between a person's knowledge of their language – the system of rules they have mastered – and their actual use of the language in real-life situations. He calls the first 'competence', the second 'performance'. Linguistics, he says, has as its most important task the study of competence. He makes this point succinctly in *Aspects of the Theory of Syntax* (apart from a lengthy footnote on mentalism, which I am omitting here):

The problem for the linguist, as well as for the child learning the language, is to determine from the data of performance the underlying system of rules that has been mastered by the speaker-hearer and that he puts to use in actual performance. Hence, in the technical sense, linguistic theory is mentalistic, since it is concerned with discovering a mental reality underlying actual behaviour. Observed use of language or hypothesized dispositions to respond, habits, and so on, may provide evidence as to the nature of this mental reality, but surely cannot constitute the actual subject matter of linguistics, if this is to be a serious discipline. (p. 4)

The implications in this shift of focus are far-reaching. Competence, as the quotation makes very clear, is an *underlying mental system*; it underlies actual behaviour, and is thus not available to direct empirical study. If it is not directly observable, then (carrying the argument a stage further) the main way in which we can find out about it is by introspection, by asking ourselves how we react to (or interpret, or analyse) a given sentence. The native speaker of the language and the linguist (who may of course be two personae in the one individual) are therefore credited with a linguistic intuition, which allows them to analyse language according to requirements (e.g. detecting ambiguities, ignoring mistakes, understanding new sentences, and so on). And the conclusion follows from this: if the aim of linguistics is the description of competence, and if the only direct access to this is our intuition about language, then intuitions become part of the evidence for the nature of this competence. Putting this another way, if competence is the 'actual subject matter of linguistics' (cf. the above quotation), then our intuitions must be part of the data on which a theory of competence is based.

Intuitions as data; part of the object, as well as the tool of investigation. Such a statement, on the face of it, would get no truck from scholars in other sciences. It is not likely that physicists, or sociologists (apart from those influenced by the present approach), would be willing to allow their own intuitions about their data to rank as data. They would know that such a move would inevitably arouse criticisms of subjectivity, and that it would be difficult to defend themselves against the charge that their results were preconceived. They would also know how misleading and irrelevant it can be to allow intuitions a place as data. Physiologists, for example, would not allow their internal, kinaesthetic sense of what happens inside their arms when they move their hands to serve as data alongside their anatomical, radiographic and other investigations: the two 'modes of knowing' would be considered independent, and only the latter would be considered as 'doing physiology'. (Questions of whether such boundary-lines are right or wrong are not relevant at this point: I am simply trying to characterize the scientific situation as it has come to develop.) For Chomsky, this 'anti-mentalist' attitude is considered far too restrictive, as far as language is concerned. Linguistics *is* mentalistic in character, he argues (in his later work); and to compare the reactions of the physicist or sociologist is irrelevant. Linguistics is part of the study of the mind, and can legitimately be called a branch of cognitive psychology. And as a mentalistic discipline, there is nothing wrong with the idea of intuitions being used as data.

I am not consciously trying to arrange a confrontation at this point between mentalists and anti-mentalists in linguistics, or to suggest that there is any clear-cut opposition between generative and non-generative linguists, as has sometimes been done – and I would warn newcomers to linguistics to avoid seeing the situation in this way. To begin with, there is no necessary identity between 'being a generative grammarian' and 'being a mentalist'. It is quite possible to establish an underlying system of rules and concepts without this leading us into mentalism. There are, after all, a number of basic phenomena in the physical sciences which are not directly observable, but which do not have an intuitive basis either, and which would be accepted as proper subject-matter for empirical research, e.g. the concept of the atom. The identification of generative grammar with mentalism is a relatively recent development, and one which a number of generative grammarians avoid. Secondly, one should not underestimate the amount of contact which exists between mentalist generative grammar and other approaches. In particular, it is important to realize that this kind of generative theory by no means excludes empirical evidence from its domains: on the contrary, Chomsky frequently stresses the need for hypotheses about language to be empirically testable, and criticizes those which are not. Nor would the mentalists deny the relevance of empirical data, in the sense that in working out their system of rules for competence, and finding that their rules were not producing the sentences to be found in any corpus, they would conclude that something was wrong somewhere, and presumably go back to re-examine their consciences. A point of contact with empirical data, an 'objective correlative' (to apply T. S. Eliot's literary critical term in a context where it was never intended), has to be made sooner or later. From the other 'side', no anti-mentalists would in fact restrict themselves to the patterns they found in a corpus, as if they were the linguistic equivalents of jig-saw puzzle enthusiasts. A corpus-based linguist is not necessarily a *corpus-restricted* one – and I have never in fact met any 'corporate' scholars who believe that their rules do not in some way transcend their data – that is, account for the patterns in their corpus and a lot more besides. They may not be very clear as to how this transcendence is effected, or how it is best explained; and they may have taken quite for granted a number of theoretical assumptions which derive from outside their corpus; but they would agree completely with the stated aim of linguistics to establish an abstract system of rules to explain linguistic phenomena. (Where they would differ from mentalistic linguists is over the question of whether these abstract formulations need be given any psychological reality.) They would also be aware of the inevitability of making use of their own intuitions in selecting and sorting their linguistic evidence; though they would try to minimize their reliance on these intuitions, and would stop short of investigating their nature as an end in itself.

The difference between the two linguistic approaches is not so much a question of their use of empirical data, as of what *other* kinds of data can also be legitimately introduced; and it is the claims which seem to be being made here which strike the outsider as being tantamount to a radical redefinition of the term 'science'. I say 'seem' to be being made, because the available literature on the subject is not always clear as to exactly what position is being argued, and certain crucial terms are used in a highly ambiguous way (hardly a good advert for linguistics). The sense in which the word 'intuition' is used is probably the main cause of trouble. On the one hand, there seems to be a suggestion that the proper sense of 'intuitions' in generative theory is not at odds with empirical methods, in that what is being referred to is no more than the observed reaction of informants to their language's acceptability, meaningfulness, structure, and so on. On the other hand, there is the suggestion that a great deal more than this is involved, and that the native speaker's own intuitions about structure are in their own right part of the subject-matter of linguistic analysis. This second position certainly seems far from an orthodox empirical viewpoint. The opposition may of course be a false one. Perhaps it is just a question of individual linguists' practices being unsatisfactory – for example, in failing to use systematic, empirical techniques in testing the generality of a native speaker's intuitions, in presenting too selective a picture of intuitively observed data, in mixing up their own intuitions as linguists with those as native speakers, and so on. (I shall develop this point below.) But whether real or imaginary, stereotyped or not, many scholars do believe that there is an opposition in principle between the mentalistic view of linguistic analysis and the so-called 'empirical' one; and they would interpret the quotation from Chomsky above, along with other remarks of this kind, accordingly. Indeed, the way in which Chomsky himself reiterates and uses the opposition between rationalist and empiricist positions in some of his publications strongly suggests that he too believes in an opposition in principle.

The claim that mentalistic information should be granted a comparable status to empirical evidence is the crux of the matter, and the reason why many people think that this development has disturbing implications for any definition of linguistics as a 'science'. For, it would be argued, if anyone wished to make use of the definition of linguistics as the 'science of language', and at the same time to affirm their faith in the saving powers of mentalistic generative theory, it would become necessary for them to re-define, in effect, what they meant by science, in order to incorporate the emphasis on the intuition which the standard view of science avoids. They would have to say, for instance, that linguistics is 'not the sort of science' in which empirical evidence is the sole kind of evidence, that it is not a science 'in the usual sense', and so on. Whether one should use the term 'science' at all in this way is a matter of dispute. It would certainly be unfair to deny any claim to scientificness on the part of 'mentalistic linguistics', since it pays far more attention to the needs of explicitness and systematicness than many another school of linguistic thought does, and has devoted far more space to problems of formalization than anyone else. Moreover, it is probably true that intuition has a more important role to play in language study than in any other field of inquiry. If we emphasize the uniqueness of language as being perhaps the defining feature of the species ('homo loquens', cf. pp. 247, ff.), then it should not be surprising that its adequate understanding might force us to advocate principles which would be considered, by all other standards, unorthodox. The nature of the evidence which should be allowed into linguistic discussion is still a source of some controversy, and the issues are by no means fully thrashed out yet – hence it may be premature to expect the dispute over the term 'science' to be resolvable. But at least the existence of the problem has now been recognized, and the subject will be all the better for that.

The difficulties may, of course, be only temporary (from the viewpoint of the future history of science, at any rate), but the new student of linguistics has to be aware of them, for two main reasons. A new definition of science established by a field of inquiry purely for itself will inevitably incur the disapproval of other scientific disciplines, particularly of the philosophers of science: it will, indeed, be considered arrogant. But more important than this, a philosophical divergence of the kind involved in the mentalist approach is going to make it extremely difficult, if not impossible, for linguistic information to be ultimately integrated within the general framework of scientific knowledge. In principle, at least, knowledge from one science can be correlated with knowledge from another, because the same premisses of investigation are shared. If linguistics develops a mentalistic basis for its development, it might be argued, it will simply detach itself from the mainstream of scientific investigation, and come to be considered a scholarly eccentricity – at least until such time as other sciences become self-avowedly mentalistic (at which point the eccentric would be seen to have been really a prophet all the time). Meanwhile, until a mentalistic intellectual climate develops a concept of 'empirical-plus' science, there seems no choice but to refer to the more extreme trends in mentalistic linguistics as 'not strictly scientific' (or some such circumlocution); at least this way there is a chance of retaining intelligibility and consistency as far as presenting linguistics in an introductory way is concerned, and avoiding the perpetuation of false dichotomies.

The claimed opposition between empiricism and rationalism in language is indeed already being attacked by the devising of sophisticated empirical techniques for the description and classification of intuitive responses to language. Psycholinguistic research into 'acceptability' has taken place which could well develop into a 'bridge' between the two positions. But in talking about empirical research into intuitions, we must be very clear as to what is meant, if we want to avoid some of the ambiguity referred to above. To begin with, we have to distinguish clearly between the intuition of native speakers (those who are 'linguistically naïve', as it is often put) and the intuition of the linguist, i.e. the analyst. The two 'intuitions' work in different ways. The native speakers' can only be safely used to provide information about what they feel is in the language – about what is a normal usage or meaning, or what is deviant; it cannot be safely asked to provide opinions as to how this data should be analysed (the dangers inherent in such a request were outlined at the end of Chapter 2). Reliable intuitions on the latter point are the product of training and professional experience – and in this respect, of course, the linguist is no different from, say, a physicist. The difference between linguist and physicist, though, is that the linguist may be a native speaker as well: the two kinds of intuition can reside in the one person, as mentioned above, and it is here that the dangers associated with subjectivity lie. On the other hand, if linguists can keep their own intuitions apart from those of the native speakers', then it may well be possible to obtain an empirically-orientated account of what it means to make use of one's intuition. The use of someone else's intuition has in fact long been accepted as a standard technique in linguistics (especially that branch known as 'anthropological linguistics', on which see Chapter 5), where, in analysing a foreign language, we take native speakers of it ('informants'), and by asking them questions we would elicit statements from them about their language – about the meanings of words or structures, and so on. It should be clear that the minimal pair test mentioned on p. 99 has a very important intuitive basis, as it is the informant who decides whether a particular pair of words means the 'same' thing or not. In a research situation where both the analyst and the language being studied are English, for example, the use of informants (other than the analyst) is still useful, as it has the effect of distancing the linguist from the data. Moreover, it suggests a method whereby techniques of observation and experiment become possible. If the questions put are carefully controlled and the reactions obtained carefully described, classified and quantified, then there is a strong likelihood of obtaining an objectively verifiable account of some aspects of their intuitions. For example, we might obtain some insight into someone's linguistic competence if we presented them with a number of structures and asked (in so many words) which of them were acceptable English. If we can devise a way of asking the questions which does not precondition the answers, and if the other, non-linguistic variables in this situation can be controlled, then the replies should stand as direct evidence of the workings of the intuition in relation to these structures. It should be possible to replicate the experiment, try it on other people under different conditions, and thus gradually build up a picture of underlying competence in terms which would satisfy the behavioural scientist. Investigations into linguistic acceptability are already in progress.

The main effect of Chomsky's approach to linguistic analysis has been to bring linguists face to face with issues which for the most part had not been tackled, or even recognized in some cases, previously. In particular, it focused considerable attention on the aims of the subject, which had been hazy, to say the least, hitherto. What *are* the aims of linguistics which have emerged from this discussion? Out of a number of possible contenders, there is one aim which is generally considered primary, and it is an aim which linguistics shares with all science: the construction of theories. Contrary to what many people believe, the basic aim of science is not to collect facts about the world. Nor is it the improvement of mankind. In Chapter 1 I gave plenty of emphasis to these pragmatic aspects of linguistics; but while the practical value of a subject is always an inherently attractive introduction to it, it is not and cannot be the whole story. The basic aim of science is to establish theories. What, then, is a theory – a linguistic theory, in particular?

Clarification of this concept requires that we first rid our minds of some of the popular senses and bad connotations that the term 'theory' has acquired. Many people tend to be scared of the word 'theory' – especially if they have had an arts training. The story goes of the lecturer who said 'And now, ladies and gentlemen, let us turn to matters of theory.' He looked down at his notes for an instant, and when he looked up again, his audience had gone. Apocryphal, perhaps. But for many, the term 'theory' connotes a level of complexity and abstract reasoning and a divorce from reality that they would far rather do without. This is both a pity and a misconception. A theory, if it is a good theory, is never divorced from reality: on the contrary, as we shall see, much of the point of theory-construction is in order to *explain* reality – or data, or whatever one likes to call it. In our case, the 'reality' we want to understand and explain is language. We want to find out 'how language works', as it is usually and metaphorically put. Only a theory can do this for us.

To begin with, when we talk about a theory, there are two everyday senses that the phrase is not intended to imply. In the first sense, 'theory' means no more than 'conjecture'. *This book is based on the theory that* . . . Here the term can mean anything from 'firm belief' to 'vague feeling'. *You're theorizing* provides a similar meaning – and we should note that the implication of this sentence is wholly critical. Secondly, *in theory, three things should happen* means 'if everything goes according to plan, then . . .' We are referring to an ideal, hopeful, but fictitious set of circumstances. Needless to say, neither of these senses is implied by the term in the phrase 'linguistic theory'. An adequate definition of a theory is quite complicated, naturally, but it seems feasible to break the notion down into various interdependent ideas. (This approach to a definition is not original: compare, for example, that of Kerlinger's, in his book referred to above, p. 86, or the views of such philosophers of science as Ernest Nagel.) Essentially, we may say that a theory is an *explanation* of phenomena, or data. We are presented with some aspect of reality which we wish to 'make sense of', 'establish some organization in', or the like. In our case, the immediate data to be explained are the spoken and written sentences of an individual language-user; or, if we extend this to include the generative position, the set of intuitions about language which constitute that language-user's competence. One point should be made clear straight away: a theory is not simply a summary of the data (a view implicit in the fallacious idea of science as a collection of facts, referred to above), nor is it an explanation of a particular selection of data only (as in a corpus). A theory set up solely to account for patterns found in a particular sample of data would be a theory in a very restricted sense, one which would not be very helpful as far as our reaching any understanding of language as a whole was concerned. The whole point of a theory is that it purports to be a *general* explanation: the explanation that the theory proposes will handle all the data which were first investigated, but it will handle other data besides, and indeed any other data that would be produced within the same frame of reference. A common phrase, as we have seen, is to talk of a theory 'transcending' the data which it originally took into account. Putting this another way, a theory makes claims about the pattern, or system, which underlies the data and *predicts* that this system will equally well explain future samples of data. The extent to which its prediction turns out to be true is one measure of the theory's validity.

How, then, does a theory explain data? We have already seen a little of how this is done – by establishing relations between the variables in the data through the systematic use of hypotheses. If the criteria of explicitness and systematicness are followed, then we end up with a general frame of reference which presents an organized view of the data. We can show that there is regularity there: the potentially infinite variation in language data can be explained with reference to a finite set of structural principles, and a finite number of categories. (Or, if we wish to put this more in the idiom of generative theory, we will define an ordered set of rules that will assign an analysis to all possible grammatical sentences in a language, which will unambiguously specify their syntactic structure, pronunciation and meaning.) A theory, then, posits a systematic set of principles and categories which will account for all conceivable data. In passing, it should be noted that there are many ways in which we can see a system in something – particularly in a thing as multi-faceted as language. From one angle, language's 'system' may seem quite different than from another. It is thus easy to see how different linguistic theories have developed and will develop, each postulating a different set of principles and categories to account for language data. What these theories are, and how their various merits and demerits may be analysed, will occupy us more in Chapter 4. Right now, we should simply note that one possible definition of linguistic theory could be 'the study of linguistic theories'. The existence of this theoretical multiplicity is an extremely healthy sign.

For many linguists, this general idea of a theory is at once too ambitious and too abstract an idea to be directly applicable to data, and they prefer to work with something more concrete, namely, a *model*. Another way of answering the question put in the last paragraph, 'How does a theory explain data?' would be: 'by providing illuminating models'. This term has many meanings, in linguistics and elsewhere, but its central meaning is clear: a model is a detailed and systematic analogy constructed in order to help visualize some aspect of the structure or function of language that is not directly observable, and whose significance might otherwise be missed. In other words, it is intermediate between the very general concept of 'theory' and the highly specific concept of 'hypothesis'. Linguistics makes use of many models in this way – mathematical models, using statistical or algebraic concepts and formulae; physical models, which enable us to produce a 'working analogue' of the phenomena (as in much work in phonetics and computation); and so on. The value of a model lies in the clarity and concreteness of the relationships it proposes. In the light of a particular model, we obtain some insight into language that we had not obtained hitherto. If a model ceases to provide fresh insights – or if it fails to provide any insights at all – it will be discarded and a new model sought. From this, we can see that models are temporary things – it is sometimes said that science progresses through the search for new models to suggest new insights. Models are also selective things – only certain aspects of language are highlighted, and others may be totally ignored. Our choice of a model to guide our research must then be a careful one, and we must use it critically. If we choose a model which seems to illuminate certain features of language, we must remember it may be blinding us to the existence of other features, and we must beware that we do not assume that all parts of the model are equally relevant to language – for often they are not. The analogy may be misleading in some respects, and we have to watch out for this. The traditional model of language in terms of 'parts' of speech, we have already seen (pp. 73–4) was misleading in a number of important respects, though it contains an essential insight (the idea of a 'class' of items) which should not be ignored. Or, to take a more recent view, it is illuminating to see language in terms of a model which distinguishes various 'levels', or 'layers', of structure – phonetics, phonology, morphology, syntax and so on. But it is misleading if we take this model too literally, and assume that these levels work independently of each other, for they do not. Syntactic information enters into the definition of morphological constructs, phonological information controls our analysis of phonetic data (see pp. 172–4), and so on. Other linguistic models are referred to throughout Chapter 4. It is easy to see why people prefer to talk about models rather than theories. The way in which a model focuses the attention on a particular aspect of language and suggests in its analogy a coherent and testable account of it clearly makes it a very attractive notion. But the notion of model does not make the notion of theory redundant: the value of a model lies very much in its specific applicability to the clarification of a particular area of language – in other words, it lacks the comprehensiveness and generality which a theory claims to provide. There can be many models derived from a consideration of the properties of any one theory. Putting it this way shows how the two concepts are in fact complementary.

So far I have suggested a purpose of theories and a means whereby they achieve this purpose. I have not, however, discussed the form a theory takes; this is a fascinating but intricate subject which it is not possible to go into in a book of this kind. To talk about the formal properties of a theory would involve us in such things as the nature of primitives, axioms, postulates and theorems, how these concepts are interrelated, and the kinds of deduction one can make using them. (A primitive term is one not derived from or reducible to something else, a term which the theory need not bother to explain. An axiom is a statement about one or more primitives; it is a necessary proposition within the framework of the theory, not open to dispute. A postulate is a proposition advanced with the claim that it be taken for granted, i.e. considered axiomatic; within a theory it requires no proof of its validity, and usually encapsulates some essential presupposition or premiss. A theorem is a proposition deduced from a set of axioms; it thus admits of rational proof, and is frequently expressed using special notation.) Much valuable work has gone on over the past few years into how the set of abstract relationships which obtain between the features of a theory might best be given a formulation in mathematical and/or logical terms. What I should like to emphasize is that theoretical argument at this level, in terms of the definition, evaluation and testing of the properties of different theories is of a quite different order from that discussed hitherto in this chapter. The conception of a theory as a purely intellectual, deductive system is something which can be developed quite independently of the conception of a theory which accounts for patterns in data. To bring language data into the subject-matter of the present paragraph is not essential, and would, for some scholars, be an irrelevance. Having said this, however, it is important to realize that linguistic theories, on the whole, do not consider problems of formalization to be their main concern – applicability to data, in some sense, is usually primary.

Three further points of clarification and three of caution should now be added to this discussion of theory. Apart from a brief mention of different schools of thought, I have talked about linguistic theory so far as if it were a single notion, the purpose of it being to establish a set of categories and principles which would explain the salient characteristics of human language *as a whole*. We may, however, adopt a more restricted set of theoretical aims. We may wish to develop a theory which will explain the structure of a particular language, or some aspect of a given language, in which case the idea of 'linguistic theory' would have to be restricted to 'English (or French, etc.) linguistic theory', 'theory of English (French, etc.) grammar', 'theory of the article in English', and so on. Or, from another point of view, we might concentrate on trying to explain the basis of the transmission of speech in soundwaves ('acoustic theory'), or the basis of pronunciation systems in various languages ('phonological theory'). 'Syntactic theory', 'morphological theory', and 'semantic theory' ('theory of meaning') provide other examples of this breakdown. It should be noted, however, that any breakdowns of this kind presuppose the existence of some more general linguistic theory to provide the basis for making these discriminations in the first place. On what grounds dare we distinguish between syntax and morphology, between acoustic and phonological, and so on? There *are* grounds, and one task of a linguistic theory is to make the reasons for these distinctions clear (see Chapter 4). Ultimately, also, it is to be hoped that the various analyses made of the different areas of language can be integrated in some single linguistic framework. 'An integrated theory of linguistic description' is the claim made by the title of one linguistics monograph. An eminently desirable goal, it is true, but at the moment still nowhere past the stage of wishful thinking.

A second clarificatory point arises from this, namely, that the present-day emphasis on theory subsumes many of the other, and more limited, aims of linguistics which have been suggested over the years. In particular it subsumes the idea that the aim of linguistics is to provide descriptions of languages (for teaching purposes, for fun, or whatever). As we have seen, a description of a particular language, or group of languages, will always take place within a more general theoretical perspective – a framework of linguistic and other assumptions which transcend the specific language of investigation. We have already seen something of the nature of these assumptions in our earlier discussions of explicitness; and clearly many of the distinctions mentioned in the preceding paragraph are of this general nature. It would be misleading and naïve to begin our description of English with the words, 'For this language, I am going to make a distinction between pronunciation, grammar, and meaning' – for what language would we ever study which would not require some such distinctions to be made? They are concepts relevant to general linguistic theory, not to the study of English only. Ideally, linguists engaged in a description of English would specify only those aspects of structure which are idiosyncratic to English. Concepts applicable to (or, more strongly, required for) the analysis of *all* languages they would take for granted as having been specified by some all-embracing general theory of language. These latter, 'universal' concepts, are entities which we shall return to in Chapter 4.

Another aim of linguistics, far more ambitious than any we have had cause to mention hitherto, also arises out of our discussion of theory, and that is the need for evaluation. As I briefly mentioned a few pages ago, there are now many competing linguistic theories and (by implication) descriptions of language. It is an important aim of linguistics to provide a means whereby alternative accounts of language can be compared and evaluated. Is there a way of deciding which theory is 'best'? What measures of evaluation are there? What does one mean by 'best', anyway? Is there any such thing as a linguistic philosopher's stone? The nature of such a sophisticated notion as an evaluation procedure is naturally very little understood at present. It is, after all, only recently that far more elementary matters to do with the nature of theory as such have been approached in an adequate way. But at least the existence of the task of evaluation has been recognized, and until a procedure is formalized, our awareness that sooner or later we shall have to come to terms with this problem can indeed provide assistance in the solution of more immediate analytic tasks. For example, in the analysis of a very restricted area of language, such as the vowel system of English, the facts are so well known that it is possible to produce a number of alternative descriptions of the data, operating with the same or with different theoretical assumptions, quite quickly. We are thus faced with the task of deciding which of the various available descriptions is the best. Some measures are fairly obvious. If one description provides rules which will account for all the available data, this description is likely to be better ('more powerful') than one which generates only three-quarters of the forms in the data. Some linguists refer to this as the 'comprehensiveness' or 'exhaustiveness' criterion. Or again, if one description explains all the data in a more economical way – economy here being defined in terms of the number of symbols or rules needed to do the explaining – then this is likely to be the better description. This is one thing that some linguists mean when they talk about the 'simplicity' criterion. There are others, involving such notions as ease of applicability to a particular purpose (e.g. automatic translation, speech synthesis, language teaching), or elegance (an evaluative property which might warm the heart of the more artistic student of the subject). But such measures have hardly received any formalization, and there are others which are even more hypothetical. Notice, though, the phrase 'is likely to be' in the two evaluation measures cited above. It is not the case that a simpler solution to a descriptive problem is always going to be the better one: sometimes a simple solution to one part of a language is possible, but only at the expense of a vastly more complex account of some other part. And because the chain-effects of decisions of this kind can become extremely complicated, there seems little likelihood at present of the idea of a 'best' description becoming anything more than a useful fiction. An absolute measure of assessment in language description (a 'decision procedure', as it is sometimes called) is, as Chomsky was the first to point out, a pipe-dream of an over-reaching linguist. The only measures of assessment which seem capable of being turned into something concrete are relative ones ('My grammar is better than yours in the following respects . . .'), and it is to these that the phrase 'evaluation procedure' is properly applicable.

My first cautionary point follows from this. It is foolish to accept a theory uncritically before at least the more important of its claims have had a chance to be properly investigated. No linguistic theory has been worked out in anything like its full form at the present time. What we have, for the most part, is outline and programmatic, with a minimum of illustration of how the theory would be applied in actual analysis. It seems to me quite premature to make the kind of extravagant claims for a theoretical position such as are often made these days – saying, for instance, that such-and-such a theory explains 'the facts' of something 'correctly'. There are two misconceptions in this little phrase alone, as the inverted commas indicate, and as our discussion above should have made clear. (But since it is fashionable at the moment to talk about the views of someone else who agrees with you as being correct, perhaps I am reading too much into that!) Of course, we have got to adopt some consistent theoretical approach in our investigations into language; I am not advocating throwing all theoretical responsibility to the winds. Moreover, there have to be some people who can lead as theoretical innovators. But what I am arguing is that, particularly when *beginning* to study linguistics, we should withhold our full assent (if I may borrow a theological metaphor) until such time as all the claims of any theoretical innovations have been explored and a fair proportion of the hypotheses arising out of them tested. True science, it has been said, is humble and self-critical; and a readiness to look out for weaknesses in the approach we favour can be beneficial. It can save embarrassment as well: there is at least one textbook which was written to present generative theory in a way in which it might be used by schoolteachers – but by the time it appeared, the version of generative theory it used had been thoroughly out-dated by the appearance of radically different approaches by some leading generative theorists. The speed at which linguistic theory has developed in recent years has been exceptionally rapid. In quieter times, it is less likely that application would run so quickly ahead of theory. But in principle the danger is always present.

More worrying than this is the point that if a theory is accepted prematurely, it can very easily lead someone to force interpretations on to data which in retrospect seem no more than distortions, or to overlook features of the data that the theory says are not important, but which later prove to have been significant. The dangers are sometimes not immediately apparent, but they accumulate gradually, until someone realizes that what has been constructed is not a well-founded theoretical framework, but a flimsy fabric of fictions, partial truths, red-herrings and pseudo-problems (that is, problems which are totally a product of the theory we use, and which would not have been considered as problematical at all, if some alternative theoretical approach had been followed). An example of a pseudo-problem would be if a theory led us to assert that in order to establish the phonemes of a language (this is in itself a pseudo-problem, to some linguists, see p. 179), we had to determine changes in the meaning of words by reference to the 'observed behaviour' of the native speaker: such an assertion is often made, but it is in fact impossible to determine phoneme differences in this way (presented with any minimal pair, a native speaker may not react behaviourally at all), nor is it necessary to make any such requirement. An example of more basic fabric-weaving is provided by the way in which certain of the wider implications of the rationalist position of Chomsky *et al.* are developed – or so it has been argued. Some say that to postulate an innate predisposition for language in the mind of the child (see further, Chapter 5) is just such a piece of fabric, an unnecessary hypothesis forced upon one by the previous postulation of the concept of competence. If the idea of language competence had not been proposed to begin with, and defined in mentalistic terms, it is argued, there would have been no need to rephrase the question 'How do we acquire language?' as 'How do we acquire competence?' and no need, accordingly, to have to phrase a mentalistic answer to this question by postulating innateness. This criticism would be seriously weakened if there were any evidence from a theoretical standpoint *other* than generative theory to suggest the existence of such innateness. It is possible that psychological tests of various kinds may do this, but even if they do, it is going to be a difficult job reconciling the notions of adult and child competence. The danger, of course, is that of imposing too much grammatical structure on the mind of the child: it is very easy to get into the habit of talking about certain structures as being innately present, the only reason for wanting to do so being that such structures have an important role to play in the analysis of adult grammar.

Another example of a red-herring is in connection with linguistic notation. It is absolutely crucial to keep problems of theory and description apart from notational problems. A specially devised notation, for symbolically representing the linguistic variables we are studying and their relationships, is of inestimable benefit to consistent and productive inquiry in linguistics, as it is in logic, or mathematics, or music. To develop a notation for handling a problem is half the battle. It allows a more immediate and precise perception of a broader group of structural patterns than would be possible if the research were continuing 'in long-hand'. In linguistics, as I remarked at the beginning of this chapter, special notations are very much in evidence, particularly in the field of phonetics and syntax. They are sometimes extremely complex – though no more so than the structures they are attempting to summarize – and part of learning to do linguistics is learning to master the technicalities of a particular notational system. These days a considerable amount of linguistic exemplification, as well as basic reasoning, is carried on in symbolic terms – and the theoretical development of the subject has benefited much as a result. The danger, of course, is obvious: that the notation comes to be treated as if it had a reality of its own – as if the symbols *were* the language, instead of merely an attempt to reflect it abstractly. Sometimes a choice of notation does convey important theoretical implications, as we have seen already (p. 83 above); but very often it does not. Sometimes it hides a theoretically important point – a relationship between two sounds or structures may be quite obscured because someone uses totally different symbols to refer to them; or, conversely, a choice of similar symbols may suggest a closer relationship between two sounds or structures than perhaps exists. And it is extremely easy, if we are not careful, to find ourselves arguing about an issue which is purely an artefact of our notation, and which has no theoretical or descriptive validity at all. A notation, it should be clear, makes a good servant, but a bad master.

It is also important in discussing questions of linguistic theory to avoid confusing matters of theory with matters of procedure. A clear distinction between the two is essential, as I suggested earlier (p. 88), but it has often not been made, and the two have sometimes got very mixed up, theoretical problems usually being ignored at the expense of procedural ones. This was quite understandable, in a way, bearing in mind the emphasis of early, anthropological linguistics on procedural matters ('field methods') in their studies of American Indian languages (see p. 141). At that time, linguistics was seen as a 'technique for reducing languages to writing', and the central problems were viewed as methodological ones: *how* are the best results to be obtained? The modern reaction to this approach is to place far less emphasis on methods of arriving at an analysis, and more on the characteristics of the analysis itself. It is pointed out that there is no one method of arriving at a given result: all kinds of factors can enter in, some controllable, some not – such as testing informants, observing behaviour, using our own intuition, borrowing from earlier descriptions, having sudden flashes of insight, and so on, in various combinations. Consequently, it is argued, procedures of analysis are less important than matters involving theoretical or descriptive considerations, and should not be concentrated on at the expense of the latter. What counts is the result, and it is the analysis of this which should be the main aim of modern linguistics. The minimal pair technique referred to on p. 99 is one possible procedure for arriving at the units of pronunciation of a language, but there are other ways of analysing pronunciation which do not require reference to this, and it is the units themselves which are the main point of interest. Or, to take a different example, the justification of the term 'noun' in a grammar is the extent to which this term can be shown to be necessary to produce rules that will account for all the sentences in the language. It is needed, in other words, in order to define the patterns which exist in the language: without it, we should not be able to explain all these patterns. But how we might arrive at an explicit notion of noun-ness – establishing criteria, examining usage, considering their 'naming' function, and so on – is a different (though still important) question, and one which is independent of the use we propose to make of the concept in the grammar as a whole. An analogy with numbers suggests itself: we need the number ten, let us say, in order to perform various kinds of calculations; it has a definite role to play in developing a numerical conceptual apparatus. But how we arrive at the concept of 10 in the first place (e.g. by increasing 1 by 1 nine times) is strictly irrelevant. Distinctions of this kind, between theory and procedure, have received particular emphasis in the writings of generative theorists.

One further cautionary comment might be added to all this. In talking about 'theories' 'accounting for' 'data', it is all too easy to slip into a way of thinking in which we see these two concepts as being totally independent, and this would be highly misleading. It is naïve to think of data as a kind of virgin territory, out of which bits are selected to build theories around. As mentioned earlier (p. 89), the very process of selection of data for study implies a theoretical stance of some kind – assuming, that is, that any selection was principled and not random. Of course, this theoretical position may not have been worked out to any great extent, but it is there nonetheless. Our theoretical background will affect the way in which we handle our data. And the opposite also applies: the continual process of analysis of data will suggest modifications to be made in our theory. The interplay is inevitable. It may be necessary to talk about 'theory' and 'data' for purposes of economical discussion; but we should remember that these concepts are two sides of a wafer-thin coin.

Linguists, like everyone else, have to use language to express themselves; and, like everyone else, they have to be very careful that they do not fall into the trap of taking their metaphors too literally. A good example of these dangers is when we talk (as I have above) of the main aim of science being the construction of theories. By this I do not mean to imply that we can begin a theoretical investigation with no theoretical views at all. The idea that scientists approach a topic with a mind completely free of preconceptions, a *tabula rasa* in relation to their research, is as wide of the mark as it is naïve. This was a point made at length in John Dewey's *How We Think*. He distinguishes various stages in scientific reasoning. The first stage is the development of intellectual uncertainty – a vague unrest or curiosity on the part of a group of researchers that a problem exists. The second stage is to express this problem – to give it a tentative statement, an intellectual expression of what had earlier been no more than an emotional attitude towards it. Third, they think around the problem, trying to form a hypothesis. Fourth, they deduce the consequences of this hypothesis in the light of their previous experience and in the context of whatever theoretical principles are known already (as a result of which they may decide that the problem is one which cannot be solved at present because of technical difficulties; or one which will lead nowhere, and which should consequently be abandoned; or they may see that the hypothesis is part of a different problem which should be approached first; and so on). Fifth, they test the implications of the hypotheses set up previously. Finally, they obtain results which allow them to evaluate their hypothesis and modify the terms of their theory. Now, this is a helpful breakdown of events; but Dewey stresses that the stages are interdependent, that the boundaries between them are not clear, and that the importance we may attach to any one stage is a variable. But as a breakdown of events that are relevant to scientific investigation, his account is helpful, particularly as regards the isolation of stages one and four, whose importance in research is frequently underestimated – stage one, in particular. In the early stages of inquiry, it is often the case that researchers have a very unclear idea of the problem which they are investigating. We can see this in journal articles which conclude by saying, in effect, 'Well, I haven't actually proved very much in this paper, but at least I now have a much clearer picture as to what the relevant problems are – I now know what questions have to be asked.' This preliminary research – if such it can be called – is extremely important, especially in a subject like linguistics, where there has been so much confused thinking in the past. But it is essential that this sorting-out of hypotheses be done carefully, for otherwise there is a real danger of doing a great deal of work on a topic which is really trivial or irrelevant. Also, we should not underestimate the importance of the early 'thinking around' the problem. As I have said, to think that we can begin to construct a theory with no theoretical preconceptions at all is naïve. We always begin an investigation with *some* vague, half-formulated ideas and assumptions – some derived from intuition, or common-sense, or misunderstanding, or, of course, earlier theory. The general processes of education have provided all of us with preconceptions about most things – and language is no exception. Indeed, as Chapter 2 suggested, language study has more preconceptions about it than many other subjects – ideas about language in general, or about the foreign language we may be studying, or about our own language. Sometimes, even, we intuitively know the theoretical answer to a research question, before the research actually begins – or at least we have a fairly good idea as to how things will work out. But for scientists, un-formulated, vague ideas and theories are not good enough, nor are brilliant, intuitive explanations of events. They must subject their own preconceptions and feelings, as well as others', to critical examination: otherwise they will be unable to defend themselves against charges of subjectivity, question-begging and un-intelligibility. They must, literally, prove their point to the sceptical outside world, and it is in their procedures for getting at this proof that their central task lies. That is why they need the scientific approach characterized in this chapter – not because they have to prove the point to themselves (though this may happen), but in order to prove it to others. And the more their methods are explicit, systematic and objective, the more they will be likely to make a genuine contribution to scientific knowledge of their subject.

Looking back on this chapter, and reflecting on the current

research in progress in linguistics, it must be admitted that the high ideals of scientific inquiry are by no means always lived up to by linguists. Examples of slanted studies, hidden assumptions, unintentionally partial accounts, and so on, abound – if one can burrow one's way through the polemic which sometimes surrounds them. Still, I fall back upon some such truism as 'Bad drivers do not invalidate the Highway Code.' There are sufficient examples of excellent linguistic analyses around to make me feel that it is only a matter of time before linguistics gets through its petulant adolescence and applies the rigorous standards which its practitioners have been advocating. But let us move on now to the study of more specific topics.

Interlude: An Example

My characterization of a scientific approach to language study has been fairly abstract and general; necessarily so. In order to put flesh on these ideas, and to suggest something of the sometimes unexpectedly hidden complexity of language's structure, I propose now to illustrate one possible approach to an analysis of a particular area of language, trying to see it in a way which would agree with the ideals of the above discussion. I think this would also be useful as a preliminary to the more academic discussions of Chapter 4. I have chosen English as my language of illustration; as this will be the language most familiar to most readers, the nature of the problem to be solved, and my suggestions for its solution, will be more immediately appreciated. I have also tried to select a topic – adjective order – which will clearly add weight to the dictum 'Never take things for granted in language'. Most native speakers of English, I am sure, are unaware that there is any particular problem here. Perhaps this is not surprising. Long sequences of adjectives are uncommon in everyday speech, and the question of adjective order is one which receives little mention in traditional grammars. It is in fact only recently, in connection with foreign language teaching, that the issue has been raised at all.

A few preliminary observations are necessary. I have chosen a topic 'right from the middle of the grammar', so to speak. I shall have to assume a knowledge of certain concepts as a background for my discussion – concepts such as 'sentence', 'word', 'definite article', and 'noun'. In a more complete description of English structure than there is space for here, these concepts would naturally have to be identified and interrelated, and explained using similar procedures to those outlined below and in the relevant sections of Chapter 4. The fact that this has not been done here should not, however, cause a problem, as they are sufficiently familiar concepts not to warrant any explanatory digressions, and any problems which have to be faced concerning their definition exist quite independently of the issue being investigated here. I shall assume, then, that we already know (i.e., previous grammatical analysis has already established) the following concepts (indicated by inverted commas) which I need in order to start my inquiry. The 'sentence' *The chairs are by the window* commences with a 'phrase' *The chairs*, which 'consists of' two 'words', an 'article', *the*, and a 'noun', *chairs*. Between the article and the noun it is possible to insert a number of words of various grammatical types (*the big chairs, the very big chairs, the garden chairs, the vicar's chairs, the three chairs*, etc.), one type of which is generally referred to as 'adjectives' (*big, small, happy, interesting, red, marvellous*, etc.). I also assume that various criteria have been established in order to determine the membership of this class of adjectives (cf. pp. 79–81), and that marginal cases have been dealt with in some way. In other words, I am going to talk as if I have available a dictionary in which all the adjectives in English are listed, and I have a sentence-frame into which I can insert these adjectives if I wish (*The big chairs are by the window*, etc.). I can now begin the problem. What happens when more than one adjective is inserted? Do they have to go in a certain order?

The first problem, as Chapter 3 suggested (p. 123), is to be aware that there is a problem. After all, for the most part in English there *is* no problem of this kind. If we want to insert two adjectives into this slot, then there seems to be no particular reason why either one should come first. It is possible to say both *The cheap, comfortable chairs are by the window* and *The comfortable, cheap chairs are by the window*. It is entirely a question of personal choice. In neither case are we producing a sentence which sounds 'odd', 'unaccept-able', 'incorrect', or the like. Most sequences of adjectives seem to display this flexibility. The adjectives may not always be contiguous, of course: sometimes they are linked by *and* (the last two in a sequence, in particular, e.g. *the fascinating, cheap and comfortable chairs . . .*). And sometimes one adjective is stressed to imply a particular contrast (e.g. *The* CHEAP *comfortable chairs are by the window, not the expensive ones*). But in either case the flexibility of the order is maintained: we could say *the cheap, fascinating and comfortable chairs* . . ., or any other permutation, if we wanted to. On the basis of this, and hundreds of other examples displaying a similar flexibility, then, we might be forgiven for thinking that there was no problem to be solved here at all.

And yet there is a problem. We can imagine it arising, as scientific problems often do, in a quite casual way. Perhaps a foreign learner of English would say *The red large chair is near the window*, and the teacher would correct him, and tell him that *The large red chair* . . . is the necessary order. But why is this so? The answer is by no means self-evident; and a research task clearly presents itself. The first thing to be done is to ascertain how general a problem this is: how many sentences can we think up which display order restrictions of this kind? Perhaps the problem is a trivial one. Perhaps **the red large chair* is the only example of its kind in the language – an idiomatic archaism which has to be learned as a unit, which does not reflect a general tendency in the language (like the unique plural of *child, children*)? But it is not, as the following examples show. Each of these phrases has one order for its adjectives which seems (to me, in the first instance) to be the natural, correct order; alternatives seem artificial, forced, wrong (though, as we shall see, they may occasionally occur under certain very specific circumstances).

steep rocky hill	*a long black wooden stick*
nice smooth floor	*a high red brick wall*
kind old man	*smart brown leather shoes*
big black sheep	*small round pink face*
pretty purple silk dress	

Other evidence that the restrictions involved are fairly widespread might be found by a search through the literature on English syntax. There linguists would find that the problem has not gone completely unnoticed, but that the explanations given are not very helpful ones. Those traditional grammars that recognize the existence of the problem usually 'explain' the order by saying that the most general adjectives come first, the most specific last – in other words, the most obvious or important attributes of the object (referred to by the noun) are placed before the less obvious. Sometimes this works, as an explanation, but usually it does not. In the phrase *small round pink face*, for example, which is the most important feature of *face*? Is it its smallness, its rotundity, its pinkness? The answer, I suppose, is that it all depends: different attributes strike different people in different ways. But there is no choice over the order: even if we feel that it is the pinkness of the face that is its central attribute, the order stays the same – **pink small round face* is not acceptable. Or, to take another example, *big black sheep* is the fixed order, but the obviousness of the qualities cited depends very much on the situation as it presents itself in the real world: in a field full of large white sheep, the blackness will stand out; in a field full of small black sheep, the bigness will stand out. In other words, the above 'explanation' fails to explain the grammatical facts at all, and in view of its dependence on all sorts of extraneous factors in the real world (such as the size of the sheep, the angle at which we view the face, and the like), it can hardly be said to have any consistent basis. An alternative explanation must be found; but at least, having read through this material, linguists will now feel more confident that their research task is non-trivial. It is always reassuring to discover that someone has thought of a project before you (as long as the earlier project failed to achieve its aims).

The next step is to try to determine the extent of the restrictions more precisely. In order to do this, linguists must accumulate more data illustrating the point at issue, and must obtain a wider range of judgements about the acceptability or otherwise of the sentence patterns. Regarding the need for data, there are two sources they can use. First, there is themselves – their own intuition. It is usually possible for experienced linguists to think up a few more examples of the phenomenon they are investigating. But soon, particularly if the construction is a rare one (as in this case it is, for, as I have suggested, adjective sequences are not all that common), they will be forced to look elsewhere for data. This is the main difference between linguists and the armchair grammarians of Chapter 2: when linguists' intuitions cease to supply fresh examples – or even before this – they go outside themselves, obtaining the reaction of their colleagues to the problem, and, most important of all, systematically working through as wide a range of samples of spoken and written language as they have the time and energy to muster. This is the first aspect of the empirical side of their work. As we have seen (p. 103, ff.), it is a policy which many linguists do not feel the need to follow: they prefer to spend more time with their own intuitions, and less (or none) working through actual samples of usage. To this extent, their work is less empirically based; and to the extent that empirical evidence is central to a science, it is less scientific. But I have already discussed this point.

However, most linguists, I think, would not feel confident about the ability of their intuitions to supply a whole range of illustrations relevant to the present problem, and would examine other materials also. The kind of thing involved here would be to see whether the order restrictions were stylistically governed in some way. Do they only occur in speech, or in writing, or both? Do they occur in both formal and informal styles of speaking and writing? Do they occur in certain occupationally restricted uses of language only, such as journalese, scientific English, or legal English? And so on. This process can take a long time if we have to find this information for ourselves, and these days there are collections of data being made available on computer tape for general use, to avoid these practical difficulties. But in principle, someone at some stage has to work their way systematically through as representative a range of usage as they can find, if their statements are to approximate at all closely to 'the language as a whole'. And it is important to remember at this point that this means transcribing the spoken language to take into account any phonetic property that might be relevant to deducing a general explanation. For example, it is possible, though general experience of languages says that this is unlikely, that the particular sound or letter an adjective begins with may affect its order. Rather more likely, the length of the adjective, measured in terms of the number and position of the stressed and unstressed syllables, may affect its place in a sequence. (Why *this* is so would require reference to other questions, to do with the nature of rhythm and euphony, or the kind of subject-matter involved; but this would distract us too much from the present argument.) Most important of all in this connection, the intonational movement over the noun phrase as a whole must be indicated, and it requires a few paragraphs to see why this is so.

Intonation is the most important means we have of organizing our speech into units of communication. In some respects, its function is similar to the use of punctuation in writing, but it is far more complex than punctuation. In writing, the two following sentences have different meanings:

> *Would you like whisky, or gin, or tea?*
> *Would you like whisky, or gin, or tea . . .?*

The use of the dots indicates that the list of drinks could be extended, whereas in the first sentence there are three, and only three possibilities to choose from. In speech the difference is made by intonation: in the first sentence, the last word is given a falling pitch-movement, and produces an impression of finality. We can indicate this with a downwards accent-mark over the word, as follows:

> |*would you like whisky or gin or tèa*|

(The vertical lines indicate pauses at the beginning and end of the sentence. There is no need to mark the beginning of the sentence with a capital letter, as these do not exist in speech.) The second sentence ends with a rising movement on *tea*, giving the impression of non-finality; this could be indicated with a rising accent-mark over the word, as in

> |*would you like whisky or gin or téa*|

This is not of course the complete transcription of the sentence. The other words have to have some pitch-movement too. (We cannot say anything without giving our utterance *some* pitch.) But the remainder of the two sentences can be said in an identical way, without this affecting the difference in meaning signalled by the different ending, and so I shall not go into this further here.

Now, if we look at our speech data for noun phrases containing adjective sequences, we find that there can be considerable variation in their intonations, but that a number of basic patterns are present.

(How to establish basic patterns in intonation is an important question, but again one which is a side-issue from the viewpoint of the present discussion.) To begin with, a noun phrase may not have any separate intonation pattern at all: it may simply form part of a larger pattern, as *the big chairs* in *the big chairs are by the window*, where *window* is the word that receives the main emphasis. But if someone now asks *What's by the window?*, and I say *the big chàirs*, I now have to give it a pattern of its own. (Not to do so would make my answer sound incomplete, or cut off: compare the effect of the dash in the following written dialogue.

> 'Do you mean to say you know who did it?' the inspector asked.
> 'Of course,' replied Smith. 'The clue was in the furniture. The big chairs —'
> The inspector stared aghast as a bullet-hole appeared in Smith's forehead.)

The normal pattern is to put the main pitch-movement on the noun in the noun phrase, as in *what a marvellous dày, what a kind old màn*. To put it on the adjective immediately implies that the speaker attaches special importance to the adjective emphasized in this way. For example, *what a kìnd old man* implies that kindness is his most striking attribute; *what a màrvellous day* implies that the speaker really does feel the day is marvellous; and so on.

And now we come to a relevant fact for the problem of adjective order. If there is more than one adjective, then this placing of the point of most emphasis can sometimes disturb the expected, normal order. For example, in the sentence *get the long black stick in the corner*, the order *long black* is normal. But if there are a number of long sticks in the corner, all different colours, including one black, and it is the black one I want, then I can single it out in one of two ways. I can say either *get the long blàck stick*, or *the blàck long stick (yes, that's right, it's the blàck long stick I want)*. In other words, singling out a particular attribute usually means putting extra intonational emphasis on it (there are other ways of doing it, using syntactic means, but this is a separate issue); and when an adjective has an emphatic intonation, it can come first in a sequence, whatever its normal position elsewhere. It is important to remember that the singled-out adjective itself must carry the main intonational movement: it would sound very odd to say *it's the black long stìck* or *it's the black lòng stick*; though we can never rule out the possibility of such patterns turning up sometime or other. Normally, however, the rule is clear: if one adjective is being given special emphasis, whatever restrictions on order operate elsewhere do not apply. So we have to eliminate cases of special emphasis from our problem.

But there is a second case of intonation outranking the syntactic restrictions on order, and this is in the case of a 'listing' sequence. Imagine that we have written a shopping list, and we are reading aloud the items to someone to see if we have forgotten anything, as in

I need some whisky, bread, bananas, bandages and tea.

The intonation of this sentence is quite stereotyped in English: each item in the list (except the last, if the list is completed, as we saw above) is given a separate intonational emphasis, and the pitch movement is a rising one, as in

|i need some whísky|bréad|banánas|bándages|and tèa|

(There will usually be a slight pause between each item, which the vertical line indicates.) This sequence of rising tones is conveniently referred to as a 'listing' intonation pattern. Now the relevance of this is that adjectives can be uttered in a listing pattern too, and when they are, any restrictions on their order vanish. If we are describing the characteristics of a face, for example, and we are thinking them up as we go along – perhaps hesitantly – then the following are all perfectly acceptable:

|well she has a róund|pínk|smáll|delíghtful face|
|well she has a pínk|smáll|róund|delíghtful face|
etc.

The restrictions on the order of *small round pink face* no longer apply; and the same goes for any other adjective sequences. In other words, our problem has to be defined still more narrowly, in order to exclude this kind of possibility. Whatever rules we shall establish in order to explain adjective order, we shall have to state that they do not apply under certain circumstances, of which the two intonationally-induced situations discussed here are perhaps the most important. There are other circumstances that have to be defined in a similar manner; but my discussion is not intended to be comprehensive, so I shall not refer to them here.

So far I have been illustrating the need to accumulate a fairly large amount of data as part of the investigation. I suppose any of the above conclusions could have been arrived at through a process of introspection, but not many people – linguists included – have that kind of general conscious awareness of intonational nuance which would result in their being able to state the above conclusions reasonably quickly, and, more important, with confidence. The use of a corpus of data rapidly provides a source of examples which linguists can then apply their intuition, as native speakers, to the analysis of. As Chapter 3 suggested, no corpus is ever going to tell the whole story; but in the early stages of investigating this kind of problem, any supplement to our intuition is beneficial. This is no more than an application of the old idea that two heads are better than one.

I mentioned on p. 129 that there is a second requirement which must be met before we can determine the nature of the data to be explained, and I have assumed in the discussion so far that this was being done. At the same time as they search out examples of adjective order to analyse, from a wide range of sources, linguists must be ascertaining as objectively as possible just how acceptable or otherwise particular sequences of adjectives are. Up to now I have been taking the acceptability or otherwise of a sequence as given, on the basis of my own intuition; but of course this needs to be confirmed. Perhaps, due to my particular regional background, or personality, I am accepting some sequences which others would reject, or vice versa. More likely, as a professional linguist, anxious to avoid the bogey of prescriptivism, perhaps I am adopting *too* open-minded an approach to my data, and allowing in too much as an acceptable sequence. How can I avoid these difficulties?

Techniques of testing the acceptability or otherwise of language patterns are nowadays quite sophisticated, and this is not the place to illustrate their principles and methods in detail. But I can give an idea of the kind of problem present by instancing some of the range of factors which need to be controlled in any investigation. First, a number of informants need to be selected. Exactly how many will vary, depending on my feelings as to how much variability I am likely to find in the results, and depending also, of course, on practical considerations of time and people available. They all have to be native speakers of the language, they have to be as unpre-conceived as possible about linguistics ('linguistically naïve', as it is usually put), and they should come from as nearly homogeneous a background as possible (regional and educational variables being the most important). These characteristics of the informant sample would have to be made quite explicit, in case further research on a different sample produced a significantly different set of results. Secondly, the way in which I ask the questions has to be very carefully controlled. (In many cultures, of course, getting to the stage of asking questions systematically is the end of a very long process of getting to know the people and learning to follow their customs of greeting, and so on. W. J. Samarin's book, *Field Linguistics* (1967), illustrates these difficulties very well. In work on English, however, this is not normally a problem.) I cannot come straight out and ask informants about adjectives, for instance: this would be treating them as linguists, which they are not; and in any case they are liable to have a host of misconceptions about such terms, and about my purpose in questioning them, deriving from half-remembered schooldays. Nor can I ask them directly about a certain sentence containing an example of my problem, as this would be to draw their attention to the phenomenon under investigation, and this in turn would be likely to prejudice the results. I have to 'hide' the problem in some way – for example, by putting a phrase with an adjective-sequence problem into a larger context – and ask them to react to the acceptability of the utterance as a whole. I have to ensure as far as possible that my instructions to the informants are unambiguous, and that they have understood what I expect them to do. I should also check that they have *some* intuitive sensitivity about language deviance by giving them some very clear-cut sentences to react to (an informant who cannot tell that there is something wrong with *the garden nice chairs* is not going to do very well with *the pink small face!*) And if the test sentences are of spoken English, I must ensure that they are accurately and consistently produced from the intonational point of view, and free from any distracting features, such as hesitation. Extra controls can be added by inserting the same (or a very similar) test sentence more than once into a question session. Other effects well known in experimental design (such as those due to fatigue) also have to be borne in mind when constructing a test. To avoid fortuitous linguistic patterns influencing the results, the relationship between any specific adjective sequence being tested and other features of the sentence should be varied (e.g. the adjectives should be presented in noun phrases as subject and as complement, they should be followed by a selection of different nouns). Any grading in the complexity of the sentences being presented should be made clear (e.g. presenting sequences of two adjectives before three). And so on. (This is *not* intended to be a complete check-list of relevant factors.)

Compared with all the preliminaries which a researcher has to go through, the analysis of the results (that is, the informants' reactions) is easy. (Note the time it has taken before I have got round to talking about results at all.) What kind of results are likely to emerge from an approach such as this? I can report on only one small experiment carried out along these lines, but this I think will be sufficient to illustrate the kind of hypotheses which might be established about this area of sentence structure. The statistical analysis of informants' preferences (which I will not go into here) showed that they did react along definite, non-random lines, and that there was a consistent tendency for adjectives to be preferred in a specific order in the vast majority of cases *where certain characteristics were present*. These characteristics – as the sensitive reader may already have guessed – concerned the types of meaning into which the adjectives could be classified. For instance, on the basis of obtaining favourable reactions for *small pink face, high red building, short brown boot*, and the like, and unfavourable reactions to the alternative order, it would be reasonable to suppose that the basis of the ordering was to do with the obvious semantic parallelism between the phrases – namely that in this case an adjective of 'size' preceded an adjective of 'colour'. (The labels used for semantic classes are quite arbitrary, incidentally 'Dimension' vs 'hue' might do equally well.) Similarly, it was possible to hypothesize, on the basis of this experiment, that adjectives of 'age' preceded adjectives of 'colour' also (*an old red hat*, *a new black dress*, etc.), that adjectives of 'size' preceded adjectives of 'age' (e.g. *a tall new chimney*), and that any or all of these classes would precede an adjective of 'nationality' if one were used (e.g. *a tall English convict*), or an adjective of 'material' (e.g. *an old wooden chest*). Putting these preferences together, we find possible sentences illustrated by *those large new red English wooden chairs*, which might now be hypothesized as representing the statistically normal order of adjectives in the noun phrase (assuming normal intonation, as we noted above). Most other adjectives – that is, those not assignable to the above classes – seem not to have any order-restrictions, and could be used randomly in between the determiner (*those*) and the first adjective (*large*) in the above example.

The statistics underlying this analysis were fairly conclusive: most pairs or triples of adjectives tested in this way showed one hundred per cent preference for a particular order; for some (e.g. the 'size'–'age' combination), the tendency was still dominant, but not total. One analytical problem presented itself in the case of a few adjectives whose semantic classification was uncertain (e.g. are *fair-haired* and *flaxen* adjectives of colour or material? Is *colourful*, in *He was a colourful figure*, an adjective of colour?); but these were very much a minority. The most important issue arose in connection with two or three 'exceptions'. I put the word 'exception' in inverted commas here, because to say that a particular utterance's structure is exceptional is not to say very much. It is a helpful statement only if we can provide some reason for its exceptional status. Can we see *why* the structure does not conform to type? In order to do this, we have to see whether the exception itself can be classified, or related to some other structure in the language which might be influencing it. In other words, we have to expect to look much further into language than the originally very restricted aims of the research anticipated. One kind of possible counter-example which would cause this sort of 'theoretical extension' we have already discussed, namely, that due to intonation. But there are others, and all have to be systematically followed up in a scientific approach. I shall illustrate just one, with the phrase *a fair-haired young man*, for which this was the definite preferred order. This is however Colour (or Material) before Age, a reversal of the expected order. Why? One possible explanation is that there is a structural relationship of some kind between *young* and *man* which is 'stronger' than that between *fair-haired* and *man* – so strong that there is a tendency for the words *young* and *man* to be used together, at the expense of any 'normal' order. Evidence of this might be provided by the use of the phrase *young man* as a unit elsewhere in the language (as in *Come here, young man*). *Young man*, it might be argued, is sometimes used almost as an idiomatic unit, and the existence of this unity elsewhere in the language might be sufficient to influence the departure from expected order which is illustrated here. It is certainly a possible explanation, though at the moment it is an extremely vague one. Moreover, it has introduced a new concept into the story, the idea of 'structural relationships of various strengths'. But such a major theoretical construct needs to be formalized and justified. It would hardly promote the cause of precision and economy in grammatical analysis if such a vast notion were introduced into the grammar merely to handle the case of *the fair-haired young man*! This would be like killing a fly with a hand-grenade. What we have to do is to ascertain that such a construct can be independently motivated – in other words, that it is needed elsewhere in the grammar in order to explain other structural patterns unrelated to the adjective order case. If it can be, then it can be made use of here. If not, then it would have to be discarded, and an alternative explanation hypothesized. (In this case, the answer is yes.) The idea that words have different degrees of predictability of co-occurrence with other words is basic to such familiar concepts as idioms, similes and clichés; and in some theories of language the concept of mutual restrictiveness on specific word-combinations is considered an issue of importance. (The *collocations* of Halliday's linguistic theory (see p. 210), and the *selectional* restrictions of generative grammar are cases of theoretical notions set up to handle co-occurrences of this type.)

To continue this illustration would go beyond my purpose, which was solely to indicate some of the more complex considerations which might arise even in a very restricted and apparently straight-forward piece of study. I am not of course suggesting that all the above principles and procedures are universally adhered to among linguists; as the theoretical discussions in the next chapter indicate, there would be numerous points of dispute over my presuppositions and priorities. And I have omitted to deal with some questions which are in many respects more important – at least from the viewpoint of general linguistic theory: questions of how order re-strictions of this kind should be incorporated and formalized in a general theory, questions of how other ordering problems in English relate to this one, questions of what implications this example has for the debate on the boundary between syntax and semantics (see p. 231), and so on. All I have tried to do is illustrate something of the state of mind typical of many linguists, to show the mixture of intuition, careful observation, training in methods of analysis, and application of consistent and clear theoretical reasoning which are the hallmarks of a scientifically responsible approach to language study. As such, it has been a very selective picture. In my next chapter, I shall try to balance this selectivity by reviewing the fundamental ideas in the background and present state of linguistics in a more systematic and general way.

4. Major Themes in Linguistics

It should be clear by now that linguistics is a healthily controversial subject. But not everything in linguistics is controversial. On the contrary, after fifty years or more of full-time study as a science, a considerable amount of agreed theory and practice has accumulated. Eavesdropping on a conversation between linguists these days, it would not take long to identify a fairly large number of terms and issues about whose definition and value the participants would be largely in agreement. There would be a tacit acknowledgement that these ideas could be taken for granted for the purposes of discussion. Most of them turn out to have had a formative role in the development of the subject in this century; and along with some information about the scholars who first expounded them, and the 'schools' of thought which developed with them, there is clearly a case for a separate, if lengthy chapter on these 'fundamentalist' notions. And this is it.

Origins

The subject we now call linguistics began to take its present form at the beginning of this century. The interesting thing is that it seems to have developed in an almost independent way in two places at once – Europe and America. But the two approaches were radically different, each being very much the product of its own history, and each taking advantage of the kind of linguistic material which it found immediately available. The Europeans had a continuous tradition of philosophical thought, as we have seen (in Chapter 2), which stemmed from Classical times; and an immediate background of historical study of language which came from nineteenth-century 'comparative philology' (of which more below). Most of the data about language concerned the development of Classical and, to a lesser extent, modern European tongues. Based entirely on written records, their discussion of language had usually been from the viewpoint of textual interpretation – for example, in biblical studies, literary criticism, or history. Work on living languages had been considered secondary, and limited to the activities of a few who attempted to plot the differences between regional dialects, and to construct 'dialect atlases'. A few 'occasional' studies of new languages had been made by missionaries and colonial officials in various parts of the world, as was suggested in Chapter 2; but these had been narrowly pedagogical for the most part, and were usually made within a Latinate analytical framework.

The tradition which the early European linguists grew up with and reacted to was very different from that available to American scholars, who had had relatively little direct contact with the European situation. American research began by turning to the sources most readily available, the American Indian languages, and the orientation was completely different. There was no written record in the case of these languages, and there were no earlier descriptions – hence it was impossible to develop a purely historical interest or to use writing as the basis of linguistic analysis. These languages were also *so* different from European languages that it was obvious that Classical procedures and terminology were going to be of little value; and in any case, many of the scholars involved had developed a strong distrust of the distortions which they were aware Latinate descriptions could impose. There was also a reaction against the use of meaning as the basis of an analysis of a language – again a contrast with the way in which considerations of meaning, logic, and so on had been used for the definition of grammatical categories in the European philosophical orientation (cf. p. 54). The first task of the linguist, it was felt, was to describe the physical forms that the language had: saying what those forms meant was a logically later activity. The emphasis was therefore on a meticulous description of the individuality of each language's structure, based on the only available source – the living speech activity of the users. This dynamic role given to language was largely due to the initiative of the anthropologists of the time, who stimulated this kind of approach from the very beginning as part of their drive to accumulate information about the dying Indian tribes. Franz Boas, one of the pioneers, emphasized the need for the linguist to 'go into the field', to get an accurate, detailed description of the human behaviour involved – before it was too late, and all the informants were dead! In 1911, the first volume of the *Handbook of American Indian Languages*, which he founded, was published. Ten years later, another anthropologically orientated book, subsequently extremely influential, appeared – *Language*, by Edward Sapir. These two books, and the students of their authors, were a formative influence on the development of linguistics in America, as we shall see in due course.

There was thus a simultaneous development in language studies on both sides of the Atlantic, with neither side in the early days knowing much about what the other was doing. However, it is usual to try to date the beginning of a science by referring to the publication date of some pioneering work; and those who have tried to do this for linguistics generally give the honours to a European. Despite the tendency these days to see the origins of linguistics in the work of almost every scholar since Plato, it is generally accepted in more sober mood that the work of the Swiss scholar Ferdinand de Saussure holds pride of place as the first real essay into linguistic theory as we understand it now. To call him the 'founder' of the subject, as is sometimes done, is perhaps a bit extreme, in view of the American work taking place at the same time. Moreover, there were other strands to the early history of linguistics which contributed to its foundation – for example, the general reaction (reflected in Chapter 2) against the principles and practices of traditional grammars, which had developed in the late nineteenth century in the context of a fresh pedagogical interest in language teaching, and associated with such names as Henry Sweet (satirized by Shaw as Henry Higgins in *Pygmalion*), Harold Palmer, and the Danish linguist Otto Jespersen. But there is no doubt that Saussure's pioneer thinking on theoretical issues had a fundamental and lasting effect on language study – and a very specific one too, in view of the fact that his was a dominant formative influence on at least three schools of linguistics later (those of Geneva, Prague, and Copenhagen). A number of his theoretical distinctions are striking anticipations of current issues – his distinction between *langue* and *parole*, for instance, which I shall shortly discuss (p. 159, ff.) appears with very little difference in the competence/performance distinction of generative grammar.

But it is not possible to understand what Saussure did without seeing him in his own time, and especially against the intellectual linguistic background of the nineteenth century, against which so much of his work is a reaction. Let us, then, begin near the beginning, with an excursus into the nature of nineteenth-century 'comparative philology'.

Comparative Philology

The easiest way to identify comparative philology is by saying that it is what most people coming across linguistics for the first time expect the subject to be about – the history of language and languages, and the study of the origins and development of words and their meanings ('etymology'). In fact, as we have seen in the first part of this book, this would be a highly misleading interpretation, for the history of language comprises but a small component of the discipline as a whole. It is, moreover, a component which many people have come to disparage, in view of the melodramatic approach to much historical study in earlier centuries (in connection with the origins of language), and the pedagogical tendency to confuse matters of history with matters of current relevance in language structure (cf. p. 63). The psychological gap between linguistics and philology has indeed been very great – and it still is, in some parts of the world, particularly on the continent of Europe. Linguists would get very emotional if they were referred to as philologists by mistake; and many philologists would look rather pityingly at the new upstart discipline which they would feel lacked the decades of painstaking textual analysis on which their approach was based. These days, however, there are many signs that the old opposition between the two fields is coming to an end. From the point of view of linguistics, at any rate, it is beginning to be realized that any opposition was due more to the use of different procedures in the analysis of data than to any radical difference of opinion as to the intrinsic interest of historical vs non-historical data. Nowadays, the problems which historical linguistics raises and the facts which its methods bring to light are seen as highly relevant to the development of linguistic theory as a whole. It has been recognized that a linguistic theory will be of very limited value unless it can provide an account of the mechanisms underlying language change – either as seen in the individual (as when a child learns a language, this being sometimes referred to as 'linguistic ontogeny'), or in the community as a whole (as when a language changes from one distinct form into another, e.g. Latin becoming French – 'linguistic phylogeny'). And with an increasing number of linguists becoming interested in historical matters and using modern techniques for their analysis, it is likely that an integrated approach to historical phenomena within linguistics will not be long in being formalized. There is, however, considerably less ecumenical spirit in many schools of traditional philology, and any attempt to identify philology with linguistics would still be premature. Even with the same subject-matter, and the use of similar techniques, it will be a long time before the pejorative connotations the two labels have acquired are eliminated. Accordingly, it is still prudent even these days to keep the terms 'historical linguist' and 'philologist' distinct, the former referring to someone trained in linguistics who is applying this knowledge to the study of the older states of language, the latter to a follower of the older, nineteenth-century traditions of study.

The contribution of the nineteenth century towards the development of a scientific approach to language cannot be underestimated, even though the preoccupation throughout this period was almost totally historical. Earlier study of language history, as we have seen, was largely haphazard and vague. There was little objective, systematic analysis of the similarities and differences between language forms, or of the chronological changes in a language. If similarities were noted, it was often to dismiss them as coincidental; differences were dismissed as unimportant, or reinterpreted to suit the presuppositions of a particular (e.g. original language) theory. If the changing nature of language was considered at all, it was as part of a natural process of corruption, measured against the changeless status of Latin. Above all, no one, with the possible exception of some early Jewish scholars, had noticed anything systematic about either resemblances or differences. The first to point out objectively the fact of a systematic language similarity was a French Jesuit missionary named Coeurdoux, who showed in 1767, with many examples, that Latin and Sanskrit had definite grammatical and lexical correspondences; but his suggestion was not published until much later, and by that time, Sir William Jones had said the same thing more emphatically, and included Greek and Celtic in his observations. He had had an opportunity of studying Sanskrit in detail while Chief Justice in Bengal, and in a speech to the Asiatic Society in February 1786, largely to do with matters other than language, he made a statement which was to inspire the basic principle of comparative linguistics:

The Sanskrit language, whatever be its antiquity, is of a wonderful structure; more perfect than the Greek, more copious than the Latin, and more exquisitely refined than either, yet bearing to both of them a stronger affinity, both in the roots of verbs and in the forms of grammar, than could possibly have been produced by accident; so strong, indeed, that no philologer could examine them all three, *without believing them to have sprung from some common source, which, perhaps, no longer exists.* (My italics.)

Even though this was unsupported in detail, Jones's impressions were in print, and thus circulated widely. Within the following thirty years, the effects of the stimulus became apparent, and the reverberations of the theory took over a century to settle.

The first systematic attempt to study the implications of Jones's statement in detail was made by a Dane, Rasmus Rask, in an essay written in 1814, called *An Investigation into the Origin of the Old Norse or Icelandic Language.* It was followed shortly afterwards by Franz Bopp's first major work, *Concerning the Conjugation System of the Sanskrit Language in Comparison with those of the Greek, Latin, Persian and Germanic Languages.* This was published in 1816, three years before a third scholar, Jacob Grimm, enlarged and further systematized Rask's statement in his *German* (i.e. Germanic) *Grammar.* By 1833, the techniques and data amassed by these three, supplemented by much extra information from contemporaries, led to the production of Bopp's comprehensive handbook, which was extremely popular and went through three editions: the *Comparative Grammar of Sanskrit, Zend, Greek, Latin, Lithuanian, Gothic and German* took nineteen years to prepare, and by its third edition incorporated Old Slavic, Celtic and Albanian.

The study began in an empirical way within its own field. However, it was not long before the comparative philologists shifted their focus of attention. From the comparative data which was being described, they began to deduce the features of a language which they assumed must have been in existence before the earliest records, which would account for the similarities in the forms of say, Sanskrit, Greek and Latin. The hypothesis that the languages were related produced the further hypothesis that they had a common source. At first it was thought that Latin and Greek had descended from Sanskrit (which had always held a patriarchal position in the eyes of European scholars); but further research indicated that all three languages were 'cognate' – that is, had a common ancestor, which, in this case, had not survived in any recorded form. Work thus began on determining this old language's characteristics.

Modern Romance languages, of course, showed a similar pattern. The similarities existing between certain words and forms in Italian, Spanish and French, for example, indicated clearly that they came from the same parent language. The fact that the three words for 'father' had so much in common (Italian, *padre*, Spanish, *padre*, French, *père*) would be just one case in point among thousands. But one could then go further, and suggest that the word, as it stood in the original parent tongue, must have had a *p* in it, because this is a common factor in the three modern languages; similarly the presence of an *r* might be deduced; and if sufficient comparative work was done, the reason for the vowel discrepancy might become clear, and the parent language vowel determined. In such a way, one could arrive at an ancestor form *pater – which in this case exists*, in Latin. By studying a large number of such cases, dealing with more complex grammatical constructions as well as with letters, the totality of the Latin we know could be deduced, as it were, backwards.

This reasoning, then, was applied to Latin, Greek and Sanskrit, which showed a very similar set of correspondences. Here the forms for 'father' were: Latin, *pater*, Greek, πατήρ (*patēr*), Sanskrit, *pitar*. The conclusion reached suggested that the parent language from which the three had derived would have had a word for 'father' of the form *pətér*. The asterisk in front of this form, or any other in comparative philology, indicates that it is a reconstruction along these lines which is not attested in written records. (It is a different use of the asterisk from that usual in contemporary, synchronic linguistics, where it refers to an unacceptable usage, as on p. 80 above.) In other words, a reconstruction is a kind of hypothesis based on the consideration of a multiplicity of examples taken from as many cognate languages as would seem to be relevant. (The theoretical status of these reconstructed forms has been a source of recent debate in historical linguistics.) Thus, in deducing the older word for 'brother' one might well wish to consider as part of the evidence Latin, *frāter*, Greek, φράτηρ (*phrātēr*), Sanskrit, *bhrātār*, Old Church Slavonic, *bratrŭ*, Gothic, *broðar*, Old Irish, *brāthir*, Old English *brōðor*, and so on, from which one could arrive at a form *bhrāter*. (Most large dictionaries provide 'etymological' information of this kind.)

A further eye-catching example of relationship is the present-tense indicative conjunction of the verb 'to be' in Latin, Sanskrit and Greek (the forms of the latter two languages have been transliterated for ease of comparison):

sum	ásmi	eimí	PIE	*ésmi
es	ási	éssi		*ési
est	ásti	esti		*ésti

The regularity of sets of phonetic correspondences existing in such listings was soon established beyond reasonable doubt, and provided the stimulus that led scholars to suggest lines of phonetic relationship between the languages. Thus, for example, the presence of an *a* vowel in the verb paradigm given above for Sanskrit corresponds systematically with an *e* vowel in the other two. The weight of evidence is therefore for an *e* vowel in the parent language (called Indo-European), the *a* having developed from this **e* by some process of phonetic development. If this was so (and scholars assumed it was), the process could be described as 'Indo-European **e* became Sanskrit *a* and Latin and Greek *e*'; or in a more simple shorthand: 'IE */e/⟩Skt/a/, L. Gk. /e/.' Such formulas were worked out in great detail and became known as 'sound-laws'. This was originally a metaphorical use of the word 'law', because the formulas were only representing what were thought of as very strong tendencies for the sounds to behave in such ways; they were not originally considered as exceptionless laws at all – an attitude to be sharply reversed later by the neogrammarian school of comparative philologists, discussed below.

The original parent language, then, was gradually reconstructed word by word, as far as the evidence of the written remains allowed, and is now called Proto-Indo-European (or PIE for short). It was assumed that it was being spoken before 3000 B.C. The languages which developed from it were thus called the Indo-European 'family' (according to the then popular model of linguistic description), and the relationship of one member language to another was described in kinship terms: Sanskrit, Greek and Latin were 'sister-languages'. Such a procedure accounted satisfactorily for the inter-relationships of most European languages (Basque being an odd exception) by postulating various sub-families or groups of languages within the main family that had some kind of common structural core. From the practical point of view, PIE was given more attention by scholars, partly because there was more written material available in the daughter-languages, and partly because the users of the languages within the Indo-European complex were politically and economically more important. This is, of course, by no means to say that a language of Indo-European stock is somehow intrinsically 'better' than any other: a culture may be more powerful than another, but this does not affect the status of the languages used which are, linguistically speaking, of equal standing (cf. p. 70).

Thus, the major language 'families' of the world were suggested, and those of Europe given more detailed treatment: the Germanic

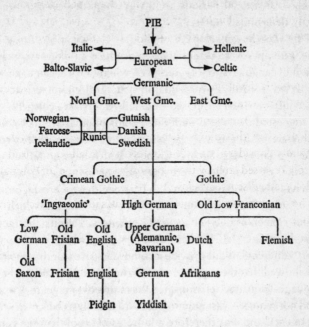

THE GERMANIC FAMILY OF LANGUAGES

family, the Romance, the Balto-Slavic, the Celtic, the Hellenic, and so on. The figure above shows one way, using the family tree model, of relating the languages of the Germanic group, of which English is a member. We should remember, of course, that arbitrarily to date and label language states with different names, as is usual in comparative work, is a distorting process. Language is *continually* in a state of flux; it is always changing. Latin did not suddenly become French overnight, nor Old English Middle English; and it is impossible to pin down the exact moment when any two dialects diverged to the point of unintelligibility, at which point we say they are separate languages (though there has been one movement in recent years which has tried to do just this – the technique variously called 'lexicostatistics' or 'glottochronology'). The names given to the different language states postulated in the comparative method are averages, approximations only, as are the dates. Transitional periods are always present between two arbitrarily determined states.

This was the *genealogical* method of classification. At the same time, attempts were being made to produce an alternative classification of languages, the *typological*, wherein each language would be placed according to its major structural characteristics. This procedure was first proposed in detail by A. von Schlegel in 1818. He suggested that there were three kinds of language that could be characterized in this way: at one extreme there were *analytic* (or *isolating*) languages, such as Chinese, which have no inflections; at the other extreme there were *synthetic* (or *inflectional*) languages, such as Greek or Sanskrit; and in between there were *agglutinative* (or *affixing*) languages, such as Turkish or Korean, which string verbal elements together in long sequences. Despite the fact that most languages fell between these points, Schlegel's theory had many adherents. It did provide a comprehensive standpoint at least, and showed that there were general structural tendencies in the ways languages indicated relationships. Its main advantage, too, was that it did not require a vast quantity of textual analysis before making its statements, and was therefore a more useful tool than the genealogical model for classifying languages which had no written records. The two techniques are not incompatible, of course; but for many reasons the genealogical approach remained more popular, and despite support by Sapir and other linguists, no broad classification has yet been produced on typological principles that is satisfactory.

It is important to be aware that the comparative method was largely empirical, and (under German stimulation) thorough; it was based on textual evidence, information about speech being deduced from an examination of writing; again, it was primarily concerned with comparison of individual sounds (rather than words, or meanings); and it tried to show the systematicness behind the linguistic variation which it noted – an aim which was not always successful, in view of the fact that insufficient attention was paid to the structural character of the language states being compared before comparative decisions were made. But such an ordering of priorities (non-historical description preceding historical comparison) was not seen as important until Saussure. Meanwhile, as the century progressed, techniques were clarified, principles were more precisely stated, and a scientific atmosphere became more normal.

The remainder of the century saw the accumulation of a great deal of information on the history of languages, and, in particular, on the details of Proto-Indo-European. Sanskrit was of the utmost relevance in such work, and was hailed as such by many linguists; Max Müller, for example, in 1868, said, 'A comparative philologist without a knowledge of Sanskrit is like an astronomer without a knowledge of mathematics.' An important reflex of this detailed study, however, was an increasing theoretical linguistic interest which took the newly discovered facts about language into consideration. Scholars began to meditate on the underlying principles which the facts of sound-change and related developments suggested. In particular, there was the growth of an evolutionary attitude to language, stimulated by Darwin's work. If plants and animals have a birth, development and death, then why not language too? Early on, W. von Humboldt had emphasized the fact of linguistic flux, in an attempt to explain the phenomenon in terms of the changing mental power of the users of language; and certain aspects of his thinking have been commended by Chomsky as striking anticipations of important features of current linguistic theory. August Schleicher first tried to develop the theory systematically, making Hegelian philosophy take account of the Darwinian theory of natural selection; to him, the typological classification of languages as isolating, agglutinative and inflectional was an example of a Hegelian triad of thesis-antithesis-synthesis. Synthesis being the climax of development, the standard of excellence in language was thus tied to the amount of inflection it possessed: Latin, Greek, and Sanskrit were indubitably best on this count, Chinese least of all, and all languages since Proto-Indo-European were in the stages of a slow decay, as the comparative method showed quite clearly that this parent language (*Ursprache*) was probably more inflected than any of the attested languages.

A fundamental objection to this approach, emphasized by many scholars, is that language has little in common with an organism, such as a plant. It has no separate physical existence, therefore it has no separate life or death. Language change resides primarily in the users of the language, and only indirectly, via these speakers, can language be seen as an abstracted whole. Language is but one aspect of an organism's behaviour, an activity which is continually changing; it is no more than a set of useful conventions. There is a further, more specific objection, that if languages like French and English are biologically distinct, on different 'branches' of the family tree, then once they have split up, how could the one influence the other in any direct way? Yet this has often been the case, as is shown by the number of words borrowed from French in recent centuries by the English. But despite these objections, such theories had a great influence on the development of linguistics during this part of the nineteenth century. The emphasis till then had been on philology in its more widely accepted sense, i.e. language study as an end to understanding a nation's culture (in particular, its literature). But with the stimulus of natural science, linguistics came to be studied as a more autonomous discipline, with the suggested status of a physical science. It began to be studied for its own sake. Otto Jespersen, in his book *Language: Its Nature, Development and Origin*, published in 1922, calls this the 'emancipation' of the subject. It was supported at the linguistic level by further developments among contemporary scholars.

The work of Jacob Grimm and others had already produced a more 'mechanical' outlook on linguistic data, with more and more sound-'laws' being formulated. But there was still a large amount of material that could not be accounted for, and sound-changes which seemed to be exceptions to the otherwise readily perceivable patterns of development. But when Karl Verner proved in 1875 that one set of unsatisfactorily explained sound-changes could be shown to fit a regular pattern by formulating a new phonetic principle hitherto ignored, a new attitude in linguistic scholarship became apparent; it was supported in other publications appearing at the same time (by Saussure, for example) that showed the relationship between Sanskrit and Indo-European more clearly. Certain scholars thus began to assume that *all* exceptions were explicable in the same way, that is, that they only remained exceptions because insufficient study had been made of the material to determine the underlying principles of development which could be formulated as laws. Sound-changes were not haphazard, it seemed: a comprehensive, objective examination of the data, paying careful attention to the mutual influence exerted by sounds, could produce a satisfactory explanation of a regularity behind all sound-changes. 'Sound-laws have no exceptions' became a canon of the new attitude, held by men who were called by their older contemporaries, a trifle sarcastically, 'neogrammarians' (*Junggrammatiker*). Of major importance in their doctrine was the concept of analogy (cf. p. 70), as this was seen as the linguistic force which tended to normalize differences in language.

This approach thus focused attention on the physical side of language; but its methodological rigidity naturally evoked some heated criticism. It was too mechanistic an approach, it was said, which left the human being out. Language had two sides, not one: there was form, but there was also function (or usage), and this social (or pragmatic) province provided an indispensable perspective for language study. But this criticism the neogrammarians largely ignored.

The criticisms were largely valid; the social basis of language had yet to be thoroughly expounded. However, the result of the movement was to inject a greater scientific precision and awareness into linguistics, and this supported the tendency to see the subject as a kind of natural science. The perspective was still evolutionary – all explanations continued to be historical in the following years – but there was a more rational, empirical approach to language, especially in its contemporary, living forms, which was first developed in theoretical detail in the work of Saussure. The old, fanciful, vague theorizing was gone; reliable major work, synthesizing and codifying the results of widespread scholarship, was becoming available. The comparative method had been proved to be of great use in historical linguistics, and a number of important points had been raised and clarified.

For example, such philological procedures firmly dissolved all the old theories that one of the spoken languages of the world was the oldest. Moreover, it caused further confusion in the anthropological camp among those who maintained that whichever language it was that Adam and Eve spoke in Eden, it was sure to have been a simple language; for the comparative method indicated that the further back one went in reconstruction, the more complex the inflections of language appeared to be. Indo-European was much more inflected than either Greek or Sanskrit; and there was no evidence that Indo-European was anywhere near the starting-point of mankind's language. There was a geographic coincidence between the linguistic judgement and the historical, in so far as both sets of evidence pointed to a place of origin for civilization to the north of the Indian sub-continent, but it was all very hypothetical, and how long a variety of Indo-European was being spoken in that place was indeterminable.

While we can be optimistic about the gains linguistics has had from comparative philology, it is not to be thought that philology provides all the answers, even within its own field. In the Indo-European family, for example, for a variety of reasons, Basque, Sumerian and Etruscan have no obvious place. And the relationship of Indo-European to any other of the world's great language families (for example, the North American Indian languages, or the Malayo-Polynesian family) is impossible to ascertain in the present stage of study, though attempts, some misguided, have been made. Nor is philology likely to make much progress in this field: with primitive cultures there are rarely any written records and hence no basis for historical reconstruction. It is highly probable that many languages of non-Indo-European families have already disappeared, leaving no trace, and there are many hundreds of tongues that remain unanalysed to date.

There are also some important limitations to the comparative method as such, which should make us wary of relying too uncritically upon it. It concerns itself overmuch with dead languages, and with letters, rather than sounds. Secondly, it is preoccupied with the superficial similarities existing between languages, as opposed to the underlying differences. For example, the method does not allow for independent changes arising within a language once it has left its parent, which might not affect the parent at all; and an attempt to read such new features into the structure of the parent language (as the method is bound to do) can only produce distortion. Thirdly, and more important, there is the charge that the theory embodies a fundamental inconsistency in comparative procedure. The method characterizes a language as, say, Indo-European, by pointing to certain linguistic changes that have occurred in the course of its subsequent history; but in doing this it ignores other changes that have also occurred, which may be equally characteristic. Nor is there any criterion or principle furnished by which we can explain which type of change is relevant for deducing a parent language, and which is not, and this is dissatisfying. English may be Germanic in one sense, but it is Romance in another, especially when we consider it from the point of view of vocabulary. Fourthly, the method assumes that as soon as two languages split off from a parent, they no longer influence each other formally – which is by no means necessarily true – witness the influence of English on a variety of languages. Fifthly, the method fails to consider a variability in the degree of precision attainable at various periods of reconstruction: the further back we go in history, the more time and space we allow in between language states, and thus the more unknown influencing factors. It is not possible to talk of Indo-European with the same degree of certainty as of Old English, but the sound-laws are poker-faced, and equate all ages in their formulas. And finally, there is the assumption that Proto-Indo-European was a single language which can be deduced from all the forms evidenced in daughter languages. It is rather more likely (in view of certain contradictory pieces of evidence in the reconstructions, and in view of what we know about the nature of language) that the parent language involved *many* dialects, not just one which has been miraculously preserved in extant languages. But to determine the dialectology of Proto-Indo-European would be a task to wither even the most ardent German philologist's spirit.

The twentieth century, as we know, brought a reaction to purely historical studies, and today the most valuable and alive aspect of comparative linguistics is the subject of *dialectology* (or *linguistic geography*), which studies variation in speech forms of a language, and thus deals in the state of contemporary languages emphasizing speech to the almost total exclusion of writing. It is at this point, then, that we can take up the trail of modern linguistics, beginning with the work of Ferdinand de Saussure, whose contribution to our subject remains outstanding.

Saussure

We are fortunate in having any of Saussure's theoretical ideas to read at all. The chief book we have under his name was, in a way, unpremeditated. The *Course in General Linguistics* (*Cours de Linguistique Générale*) was published in 1916, three years after his death. It is a collection and expansion of notes taken by Saussure's students during various lecture courses that he gave. Understandably, it is rather fragmentary in character, and in many places there are hints only of the theoretical position which subsequent exegesis has concluded Saussure must have held. There is also very little in the way of detailed illustration of his views. But its influence has been unparalleled in European linguistics since, and it had a major formative role to play in the shaping of linguistic thought in Europe over the thirty or so years which followed its publication. In particular, it moved the subject away from the nineteenth-century emphases in language study. In Saussure, we can see a clear reaction against many of the ideas raised in my preceding section: again and again he emphasizes the importance of seeing language as a living phenomenon (as against the historical view), of studying speech (as opposed to written texts), of analysing the underlying system of a language in order to demonstrate an integrated structure (in place of isolated phonetic tendencies and occasional grammatical comparisons), and of placing language firmly in its social milieu (as opposed to seeing it solely as a set of physical features). The tradition of study which has grown up around Saussure has been to extract various theoretical dichotomies from his work and to concentrate on the clarification of these. I shall follow this tradition, and look briefly at the more important of them.

In opposition to the totally historical view of language of the previous hundred years, Saussure emphasized the importance of seeing language from two distinct and largely exclusive points of view, which he called *synchronic* and *diachronic*. The distinction was one which comparative philologists had often confused, but for Saussure – and, subsequently for linguistics – it was essential. Synchronic linguistics sees language as a living whole, existing as a 'state' at a particular point in time (an *état de langue*, as Saussure put it). We can imagine this state as the accumulation of all the linguistic activities that a language community (or some section of it) engages in during a specific period, e.g. the language of the present-day working-class in Manchester. In order to study this, linguists will collect samples within the stated period, describing them regardless of any historical considerations which might have influenced the state of the language up to that time. Once linguists have isolated a focus-point for synchronic description, the time factor becomes irrelevant – whatever changes may be taking place in their material while they are collecting it, they consider trivial. To consider *historical* material is to enter the domain of diachronic linguistics. This deals with the evolution of a language through time, as a continually changing medium – a never-ending succession of language states. Thus we may wish to study the change from Old English to Middle English, or the way in which Shakespeare's style changes from youth to maturity: both would be examples of diachronic study. Saussure drew the inter-relationship of the two dimensions in this way:

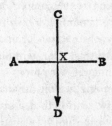

Here AB is the synchronic 'axis of simultaneities', CD is the diachronic 'axis of successions'. AB is a language state at an arbitrarily chosen point in time on the line CD (at X); CD is the historical path the language has travelled, and the route which it is going to continue travelling.

We might think this a fairly obvious distinction, if it had not been the case that some quite eminent nineteenth-century scholars had failed to draw it. And it needs to be drawn. We have already seen some of the confusion which can arise if the two dimensions are not treated independently, each with its own aims (p. 63). Neither excludes the other completely, of course: there must always be a point of intersection (in the terms of the above diagram). But being aware of the distinction allows us to focus attention more unswervingly on language from a given, consistent angle. Moreover, giving due emphasis to the synchronic (which had been the neglected dimension before Saussure) helps to clarify the important point that a diachronic investigation always presupposes, to some extent, a synchronic study. It is impossible to consider the way a language has changed from one state to another without first knowing something about the two states to be compared. This need not be a pair of *complete* synchronic descriptions, of course – to complain that it should be would be a distortion of what linguists actually do in practice (cf. p. 119 on pseudo-problems) – but some non-historical analysis is essential as a preliminary. Saussure rounds off his discussion with various analogies, of which his analogy with chess is perhaps the most famous. If we walk into a room while a chess game is being played it is possible to assess the state of the game by simply studying the position of the pieces on the board (as long as we know the rules): we do not normally need to know the previous moves from the beginning of the game. And likewise, the state of the board at every move is implicit in any pattern of play we may wish to study. The synchronic/diachronic distinction, Saussure claims, is very much like this. And, without wanting to push the analogy too far, we can agree with him.

More recently, and especially after the work of Roman Jakobson (cf. p. 254) the focus of attention in discussions of synchrony and diachrony has settled on the point of intersection, as clearly the potentiality for change in a language system is a factor which has to be carefully considered in attempting any characterization of language competence. But originally, it should be remembered, the aim was to distinguish between the two points of view, with the primary purpose being to impress upon scholars who had hitherto ignored it the primacy of the synchronic dimension. As a result, the living language received more attention than it ever had before, and speech, in particular, came into the ascendant. This leads us on to a second Saussurean dichotomy: the distinction between *langue* and *parole*. The problem which he was here trying to solve arises out of the intolerable ambiguities which surround the basic term of our discussion, *language*. (Look the word up in any major dictionary, and you will see how many senses it has developed.) Saussure made a distinction between three main senses of language, and then concentrated on two of them. He envisaged *langage* (human speech as a whole) to be composed of two aspects, which he called *langue* (the language system) and *parole* (the act of speaking). Briefly, the division is as follows. *Langage* is that faculty of human speech present in all normal human beings due to heredity, but which requires the correct environmental stimuli for proper development (*contra Psammetichus et al.*, and see p. 264). It is our facility to talk to each other. It happens to make use of apparatus in the chest and head for the production of sound – apparatus, it is normally pointed out, which was not primarily for this purpose, each of our 'vocal organs' having other, biologically more primary functions than speech (lungs for breathing, nose for smelling, etc.). *Langage*, then, is a universal behaviour trait – more of interest to the anthropologist or biologist than the linguist, who commences his study with *langues* and *paroles*.

Langue was considered by Saussure to be the totality (the 'collective fact', as he put it) of a language, deducible from an examination of the memories of all the language users. It was a storehouse: 'the sum of word-images stored in the minds of individuals'. The idea is very similar in principle to the notion of competence as defined by Chomsky (see p. 103), though it differs in its cumulative emphasis. It is certainly a mentalistic concept of a language system: Saussure argues strongly that the characteristics of *langue* are really present in the brain, and not simply abstractions. *Langue* is also something which the individual speaker can make use of but cannot affect by himself: it is a corporate, social phenomenon. Thus, when we say 'The verb *to be* has the following forms in standard English – *I am* . . .', we are making a descriptive statement about the *langue* of English – something which is valid for all speakers of this dialect at the present time. Putting it loosely, *langue* = grammar + vocabulary + pronunciation system of a community.

Ultimately, *langue* has to be related to the actual usage of individuals, for it has no reality apart from its validity as a reflector of the system underlying acceptable usage, which a community manifests in its everyday speech. And this leads to the correlative Saussurean concept of *parole*, the actual, concrete act of speaking on the part of an individual; the controlled (or at least, controllable) psycho-physical activity which is what we hear. It is a personal, dynamic, social activity, which exists at a particular time and place and in a particular situation, as opposed to *langue*, which exists apart from any particular manifestation in speech. *Parole* is, of course, the only object available for direct observation by linguists: it is identical with the Chomskyan notion of performance. The *langue* of a community, it would seem, can be arrived at only by a consideration of a large number of *paroles*. As such, *parole* is not of primary importance to linguists. They want to make statements which apply, not just to the speech of individuals, but to the language as a whole. To study the speech of a single person may tell us much in cases of psychiatry, aphasia, or stylistic analysis, but these studies are all dependent on some more general and abstract concept of a language system, which it is the ultimate purpose of the linguist to establish.

Making a conceptual distinction of this kind is certainly an aid to clear thinking on the subject, and linguistics as a whole has benefited. The two concepts have also been modified, over the years, as different schools of thought have taken them up and built further conceptual structures on their basis. Other concepts relevant to the discriminations being made have been related to them or developed out of them. In particular, we should note two terms. The first is the use of the term *dialect*, referring to the language system of a smaller community than that referred to by *langue*; the second is *idiolect*, referring to that part of the *langue* of a community which exists within individuals at any stage of their linguistic development. My idiolect is *my* total command or knowledge of my language. It is an important addition to our terminology, as it

helps to clarify the difference underlying the following three questions, which is sometimes missed: 'Is there a word *psychosis* in
English?', 'Do you know what *psychosis* means?', and 'May I hear
you pronounce that word again?' Reformulating these questions,
the first asks 'Is the word *psychosis* part of the English *langue*?';
the second asks 'Is it part of your idiolect?'; and the third is intended
to elicit a feature of *parole*. At the moment, many questions about
langue tend to be rephrased as questions about idiolect by linguists.
'Is such-and-such possible in English?', someone might ask (about
a particular structure, or pronunciation, or meaning). 'I don't
know', might go the reply. 'It's not in my idiolect, anyway.'

Saussure's third main theoretical contribution was to clarify the
concept of a language *system* – and many linguists feel that it was
this facet of his thought which had the most profound influence on
subsequent scholarship. To understand his position here, we must
first look briefly at his view of meaning. The nineteenth century,
we must remember, had spent very little time discussing the nature
of this concept; but before that it had been a hardy annual. Discussion of the possible naturalistic basis of meaning – positing a natural
relationship between 'words' and 'things' – had taken place since
Plato (cf. p. 50). Saussure accepted that there must be two sides to
meaning, but emphasized that the relationship between them was
arbitrary. His labels for the two sides were *signifié* (that is, 'the
thing signified') and *signifiant* (that is, 'the thing which signifies').
Other pairs of terms could be used to make the same kind of
distinction: 'concept' vs 'acoustic image' is one possibility which
Saussure himself suggested; 'content' vs 'expression' is another,
later suggestion – though this terminology rather implies that
meaning exists on one side of the opposition only, whereas Saussure
was insistent that meaning was a *relationship* between two equally
participating characteristics (the objects, ideas, etc. on the one
hand, and the language used to refer to them on the other). This
insistence subsequent scholars have been largely in agreement with.
Saussure calls this relationship of signified to signifier a linguistic
sign. The sign, for him, is the basic unit of communication; a unit
within the *langue* of the community. Being a relationship, and part
of *langue*, it is thus a mental construct – but we must remember

that Saussure viewed such constructs as nonetheless real (he refers to the sign as a 'concrete entity', at one point). *Langue*, in this way, can be viewed as a 'system of signs'.

Saussure's view of a language as a system of mutually defining entities is a conception which most linguists have some sympathy with – though few have actually continued to use his term 'sign'. It is a view which underlay Saussure's earlier work in comparative philology too, especially in his investigation of the Indo-European vowel system, where he postulated various abstract elements on the grounds of their function in a system (not, as his contemporaries would have done, on the grounds of their phonetic form). It is fundamental to his (and subsequently many others') account of *structure* in language. Any sentence, for Saussure, is a sequence of signs, each sign contributing something to the meaning of the whole, and each contrasting with all other signs in the language. This sequence can be seen as a *syntagmatic relationship* – that is, a linear relationship between the signs which are present in the sentence. For example, in the sentence *He can go tomorrow*, we have a syntagmatic relationship, consisting of four signs in a particular order. We would refer to this particular configuration of signs, defined in a more abstract way (e.g. Pronoun + Auxiliary Verb + Main Verb + Temporal Adverb) as a *structure*. Now in addition to the syntagmatic relationships that we can see in a language, there are also *paradigmatic* ones (Saussure's term was 'associative', but the mentalistic overtones of this were too much for subsequent researchers who wanted to make use of the basic idea). A paradigmatic relationship is a particular kind of relationship between a sign in a sentence and a sign *not* present in the sentence, but part of the rest of the language. For example, in the above sentence, there is a clear relationship between the first sign *he* and the other signs *she*, *you*, *I*, etc. This set of signs form a little system in themselves ('the personal pronoun sub-system'), one of which can be used at this point in the structure, and only one (we cannot have * *You he can go tomorrow*, for instance). Putting this another (and more recent) way, we have a 'choice' as to which sign we can use at any place in the structure (cf. p. 211). It is worth noting, in passing, how in a system of this kind the meaning, or 'value', of each sign in the system is derivable by reference to the other signs which are co-members of it. The pronoun system is a particularly clear example: we can gloss the meaning of *he* by saying 'third person, male, singular'; but we could also 'gloss' it by a process of elimination, as in 'X can go tomorrow, and X is not I, you, she, it, we or they'. For Saussure, this view of meaning arising out of the relationships *between* signs in a system, and not out of the signs as such, was basic; it was neatly summarized in his (admittedly rather extreme) formulation: 'In language there are only differences.' The principle was novel and influential; it will emerge repeatedly below (e.g. pp. 178–9).

We thus have another dichotomy, of syntagmatic vs paradigmatic, as illustrated in the following diagram:

He	can	go	tomorrow	syntagmatic relationships
she	may	come	soon	
I	will	ask	next	
you	could	sleep	now	
•	•	•	•	
•	•	•	•	
•	•	•	•	

(paradigmatic relationships)

But as any one sign within a sentence has both a syntagmatic and a paradigmatic role (the functions of *he*, for instance, being partly a matter of its relationships with the other personal pronouns, and partly its relationships with the other words which follow it), it is perhaps wise to avoid talk of dichotomies at this point, with all their implications of mutual exclusiveness. *Both* kinds of relationship are necessary to carry out the complete analysis of any sentence.

We have here, then, the basis of a concept of language as a vast network of structures and systems; and it was the Saussurean emphasis on syntagmatic relationships in structure which was taken as the keynote of a number of theories of language thereafter, and which underlies many other linguistic approaches to language today, though terminology sometimes differs considerably from that found in Saussure. The Linguistic Circle centred on Geneva produced a considerable amount of work, particularly on the more 'social' aspects of Saussure's thinking. Other 'schools', based on the linguistic circles of Copenhagen and Prague in particular, went in different directions, but owed much to Saussure's original ideas (see p. 254). British linguistics was also much influenced by Saussurean notions, although less directly. And it is largely on account of Saussure that the idea of *structuralism* achieved the status which was to make it the major linguistic theme of the next thirty years. I shall have more to say about this shortly.

An ideal way to relate the history of linguistics would be stereophonic – the development of Saussurean (and other) themes in Europe recapitulated in one ear, and the simultaneous development of methods of linguistic analysis in America in the other. To concentrate on one area without reference to the important points of contact between them would be over-simple; on the other hand, there are so many of these points of contact that to give them adequate attention would produce a chaotic picture. I have tried to get some kind of balance in what follows by covering each theme from both historical and present-day points of view in the same section of my discussions. Such a 'panchronic' approach (as it might be called) has the benefit of integrating the significant moves in the history of the subject with the areas still felt to be of significance today. Certain issues will inevitably be omitted as a result; but omissions cannot be avoided in an introductory book, and need hardly be apologized for if the major thematic material does not suffer, as I hope it will not. Using this technique, then, and taking the period from 1900 to 1985 as our focus of attention, I think it is possible to discern some seven 'ages' in modern linguistics – areas of concentration which were developed at a particular time during this period and which would be singled out for separate attention in any contemporary course on the subject.

1 Phonetics

Phonetic research, as we saw in Chapter 2, has long been of interest to a variety of people: since the Renaissance we have seen the inquiry of elocutionists, language teachers, spelling reformers, shorthand inventors, auxiliary language enthusiasts, and missionaries, to name but a few. At the beginning of the nineteenth century, it was given a real boost with the discovery of the work of the Indian phoneticians (cf. p. 44); by the end of the century, the developments in physiology and acoustics, and the accompanying progress in instrumentation (as reflected in Alexander Bell's system of Visible Speech), had stimulated a considerable amount of experimental research into all branches of phonetics. Also in the late nineteenth century, various attempts were made (for example, by Henry Sweet) to produce a phonetic alphabet; and the International Phonetic Alphabet, which is still the system in general use, came to be formulated in 1889.

In other words, at the beginning of the present century, much of the attention was taken up with the devising of appropriate techniques for the transcription of speech. This emphasis was also to be found, independently motivated, in America, where as we have seen (p. 141), the focus of interest was to make a detailed description of the dying Amerindian tribes – particularly of their languages. It is a perfectly understandable emphasis, both then and now. A phonetic transcription is no more than an attempt to make a permanent and unambiguous record of what goes on in our speech. The point which has to be emphasized is that to get such a record, we have to devise a fresh technique: our usual alphabets, which we use for everyday writing, are insufficient to do this task precisely. After all, there are only 26 basic letters in our English alphabet, but there are over forty basic sounds (or 'phonemes', see below, p. 174). We all know how English tries to get round this problem: it uses the same letter or letters for different sounds, as in the many ways in which the *ough* combination can be pronounced; and it gives the same sound all sorts of different spellings – the same vowel /i/ appears in *sit, women, village, busy* and *enough*, for example. This method is both uneconomical (two or more letters for one sound), and, more important, highly ambiguous: we cannot predict all the time from seeing a group of letters how a word will be pronounced. English is particularly difficult in this respect, as we can see from the groups of words like *bough, bow* (of a ship, or of a head) and *bow* (the weapon or the knot), where the second sounds like the first, but looks like the third. Many other languages show a much better correspondence between sounds and letters, such as Finnish or Spanish, and some, of course, like Irish Gaelic, have a much worse relationship. But the general point should be clear: if we want to talk about speech sounds accurately and unambiguously, we need to use a notation devised for this purpose – and over the years this has usually been in the form of a special alphabet. It should go without saying that this is especially necessary if the language being studied has never been written down before (*i.e.* the people are not literate) – and the majority of the world's languages are like this.

Another reason for devising a special transcription is that we sometimes want to show differences between two people's pronunciation of the same word or phrase – when we are comparing dialects of a language, for example. If we want to write down how a Cockney speaker says the word *no*, as opposed to a Welshman, then it is no use taking the standard written form of the word, as all literate speakers of English spell it identically, regardless of how they pronounce it. We have to devise new, different 'spellings' to show the phonetic differences: thus we can indicate that the tongue moves from low in the front of the mouth to high in the back for the Cockney pronunciation by transcribing the word as [nau], and we can show that the tongue stays in one place, quite high up in the back of the mouth, for the Welsh pronunciation, by transcribing it as [noː] (the colon indicating that the vowel is relatively long in duration). Other differences could be shown in the same way. People are sometimes scared of phonetics because of the alien appearance of its transcriptions; but if they remember why it is necessary to go to such lengths, and realize what benefits can be obtained through using a phonetic transcription, then the strangeness should seem trivial, and the initial difficulty they are bound to have in mastering it should not be a deterrent.

One further point should be made about phonetic notation – and indeed I have had cause to make it already, in an earlier chapter – namely, that the notation must not be confused with the phonetic description which it is attempting to reflect. The aim of phonetics is not to provide a notation: it is to analyse speech into its basic units, which may *thereafter* be transcribed in some way. The phonetic description, and its underlying analysis, is primary; a

notation secondary (though, as we have seen, nonetheless important). These priorities were not, however, clearly seen in linguistics
until the mid thirties. A great deal of the early work in language
analysis was taken up with arguing the pros and cons of a particular
notation – what were the merits of using symbol X over symbol Y
for the notation of a given sound? What criteria should be borne in
mind when using symbols? It took some years before criteria for
the underlying phonetic analysis were discussed in anything like
the same degree of detail. But despite the confusion, the development and use of phonetic transcription was of major importance in
the early history of linguistics, as it provided a consistent means of
getting large quantities of data from unfamiliar languages widely
circulated, and it was this data which was to have a fundamental
role in the arguments about the phonetic structure of language
which were developing at the time.

The basis of phonetics is, however, completely independent of
any transcriptional considerations. As suggested above, phonetics is
the science of human speech-sounds; it studies the defining characteristics of *all* human vocal noise, and concentrates its attention
on those sounds which occur in the world's languages. It looks at
speech from three distinct but interdependent viewpoints: it studies
the vocal organs, through the use of which we articulate the sounds
of speech; it studies sound waves, which is the physical way in
which sounds are transmitted through the air from one person to
another; and it studies the way in which human beings perceive
sounds through the medium of the ear. These three 'modes of
knowing' are usually labelled *articulatory*, *acoustic* and *auditory*
respectively. As part of their training in these areas, phoneticians
have to learn to recognize the different sounds which occur in the
parole of any language, and to produce them for themselves – they
have to train their ears to notice fine distinctions in sound, and
they have to be able to control their vocal organs in a conscious,
direct way. In order to do this, they have to know a fair amount
about the anatomy and physiology of the chest, throat and head.
Moreover, in order to find out about the physical characteristics of
a sound, using such machines as the oscillograph or spectrograph, a phonetician has to be a bit of a physicist as well. It is not

surprising, then, in view of these highly specialized techniques of study, that some linguists consider phonetics to be a quite separate area of investigation, and talk about the 'linguistic sciences' – by which they mean phonetics *and* linguistics, the former dealing with the general properties of human soundmaking, the latter with those properties which are of importance in the system of a particular language. This view is very much a minority one, however, and I shall not adopt it in this book. For reasons which will become clear below, phonetic analysis has to be incorporated within linguistic analysis in general if a satisfactory linguistic theory is to be developed.

In the early, anthropological period of linguistics, such a problem did not even arise. It was assumed that the first task of the linguist was to 'reduce the language to writing', and this was done, using the articulation of sounds as the main technique of description. To get the feel of an articulatory description, and to see something of the kind of terminology involved, we can look at some of the sounds we can make, using the front of the mouth in particular. First of all, we can articulate sounds using both lips: such sounds are described as *bilabial*. If we observe languages carefully, we can find three types of bilabial consonant, differing in the manner in which they are pronounced. First, we may press the lips tightly together, allowing air from the lungs to build up behind them, and then release the air suddenly, to produce an explosive effect: examples of these sounds, known as *plosives*, would be the [p] sound as in English *pit* and the [b] sound of *bit*. We should in passing note the important difference between these two sounds: the first is pronounced with the lips quite tense, with a puff of air (*aspiration*) upon release of the lips, and with the vocal cords not vibrating; the second is pronounced with the lips more relaxed, with no aspiration, and with the vocal cords vibrating. Differences of this kind are usually summed up using a single pair of labels, *voiceless* and *voiced*: [p] is a voiceless bilabial plosive, [b] is a voiced bilabial plosive. The square brackets used in phonetics help to show that we are talking about sounds and not about the letters of the everyday alphabet. In this particular case, we use the same symbols for [p] and [b] as are used in normal English orthography; but, as we shall see, this does not always happen.

The second kind of articulation using both lips takes place by pressing the lips firmly together, as for plosive sounds, but allowing the air to come out through the nose in a continuous stream: this produces a *nasal* sound, which may be both voiceless [ɱ] (as in the Welsh word *mhen*, 'my head') or voiced [m] (as in English *mat*). Third, we can put the lips very closely together, but not pressed tight, and produce a continuous hissing noise: such sounds are referred to as *fricatives* (because of the friction which we can hear during their articulation). Bilabial fricatives would be written down with the symbols [ɸ] and [β] for voiceless and voiced sounds respectively, in the most widely used system of phonetic notation that we have (that of the International Phonetic Association): we can find examples of the former in Japanese or German, of the latter in Spanish. They are not quite the same as the *f* and *v* of English, described below.

Plosives, nasals and fricatives may of course occur in other parts of the mouth, along with further types of articulation which I shall not be illustrating here. For example, if we look at the range of sounds which is pronounced when the bottom lip is placed against the top teeth (*labio-dental* sounds), we find more fricatives ([f] and [v] as in English *fat* and *vat*, for example) and nasals (such as [ɱ], which may be heard to occur in a word like English *comfort*, where because the [m] precedes an [f] sound, its place of articulation is slightly changed). And if we listen to the sounds we can make with the tongue against the teeth (*dental* sounds), we find plosives [t̪] and [d̪], such as occur in French. (These are slightly different from the [t] and [d] of English, which are generally pronounced with the tip of the tongue against the gum behind the top teeth, and not against the teeth themselves.) We would also find fricatives [θ] and [ð], as in English *thin* and *this* respectively. All these sounds are quite easy to distinguish, largely because we can feel the movements of the vocal organs very clearly, and indeed see much of what is going on if we care to look in a mirror. The further back in the mouth we go, however, the more difficult it becomes to sense changes in our articulation, and the more we need training in order to be able to understand what is going on. It may come as a surprise to learn that the initial consonants in English *keep* and *car* are articulated in quite different positions, the tongue touching the roof of the mouth further forward in the first [k] sound than in the second. And there are many other sounds equally difficult to distinguish.

II Phonology

In the early period of American anthropological linguistics, there was a very marked emphasis on the use of phonetic methods to obtain some kind of relatively objective transcription of speech data. It was regularly maintained (and still is, by some) that this phonetic description of the data was a necessary first step to any kind of analysis of a language. The reasoning behind this view went something like this. If we are presented with speech in an unfamiliar language, we do not know in advance which bits of the speech are the important bits (that is, the bits which 'carry the message') and which are not. To take a bizarre, but clear example, if, in speaking English, I happened to cough or sniff slightly in the middle of a sentence, no one would take any notice, as far as following my meaning was concerned. There is no pair of words distinguished in meaning by the presence of a cough-sound in the one and its absence in the other (cf. the minimal pair technique, p. 99). The glottal affricate sound which might have been the basis of my cough, or the voiceless nasal sound which would have been my sniff, would be disregarded because, as native speakers of English, we know that these sounds are incidental and not part of the pronunciation system of the language. But who is to say that sounds such as these should always and everywhere be like this? Perhaps there are languages where glottal or nasal sounds of this order *are* important factors in the communication of meaning. There are, in fact, many languages (e.g. Burmese, Arabic) where vocal effects which might appear to the English speaker to be no more than a catch in the throat, or a husky voice, or a nasal twang, are just as important for the construction and differentiation of words as the sounds [p], [b], [s], and so on, are in English. And the conclusion follows: as we never know in advance which sounds a language is going to use as part of its pronunciation system, we therefore need to make a note of *everything* that we hear when we first come into contact with a language – a complete record of all the vocal effects, no matter how bizarre to our ears, which our informants present us with. This was held to be an ideal approach in the early decades. The next step was to sort out which sounds were important for causing differences in meaning and which were not, and to establish rules to account for the variations in sound involved. And it is the theory and procedures of doing just this which have developed into that branch of linguistics known as phonology.

But first let us look more closely at the kinds of linguistically unimportant differences which turn up in speech: they are far more sophisticated and complex than the sniff example suggests. There is, to begin with, an infinitude of insignificant, minute differences between any one person's speech on any two occasions. Visual displays of speech (using such machines as the sound spectrograph) have shown that it is next to impossible to pronounce a sentence – or even a sound – in exactly the same way twice running; and even when the ear is the judge, it is not really possible to avoid introducing audible differences into two renderings of the 'same' bit of language. This should not be too implausible an idea to accept if we remember just how many variables we have to keep constant in order to achieve any total identity: to pronounce a [t] sound exactly the same way, we should have to keep the tongue in an identical position behind the teeth, move it at the same speed and in the same direction away from the teeth-ridge, keep the pressure of air from the lungs and the muscular pressure of the tongue absolutely stable, and so on. The slightest change in any of these factors would cause a difference in the quality of the sound, which techniques of acoustic analysis could clearly display, and which in many cases would be quite audible. And each of us, of course, introduces a multitude of such differences into our speech with every utterance – and it does not seem to matter. On top of this, we have to consider the extreme unlikelihood of any two people having precisely the same dimensions for their vocal organs, and, as a consequence, the unlikelihood of two absolutely identical articulations. Different people have their own voice qualities – tones of voice by which we recognize them for who they are – 'That sounds like X's voice,' we say. Here, then, is a second factor which contributes to the infinite phonetic variation of speech. The surprising thing, considering all this variation, is that we learn to communicate at all. But we do. Despite all the intimations of chaos, people who have learned a language find themselves able to identify and discriminate sounds systematically in the vocal noise occurring around them. Somehow a *t* sound remains a *t* sound, no matter who pronounces it, or where, or when. We recognize it as a *t*, and not as a *p* or a *k* or a cough; and we automatically discount any idiosyncratic articulation of it which may be audibly present. Phonology is really no more than the study of the way in which language allows us to carry out this vastly complex task with unselfconscious ease.

We can put this another way by saying that language is not merely randomly articulated human noise, which would be something like the beginnings of baby-babbling. It is patterned noise – sound with organization. Out of the total range of audibly distinct sounds a human being can produce (a very large number indeed), only a limited number are used in any one language. We refer to the kinds of sound which occur in a given language, and the patterns of relationship into which they fall as the *sound-system* of that language; and the study of the properties of sound-systems is technically what we mean by phonology. Phonology is, then, different from phonetics, in that phonology deals with sounds and contrasts between sounds only within the context of some language (maximally, in any language), whereas phonetics studies sounds without any specific reference to their function in a language's sound-system – it is sometimes called 'general' phonetics, accordingly. For example, a statement beginning 'a plosive is a sound made in the following way . . .' is a phonetic statement; one such as 'there are six short vowels in English . . .' is a phonological one. This at least is the distinction traditionally made between phonetics and phonology in linguistics, and the basis of the original conception of the phoneme, as developed in the 1920s. A rather different conception of the relationship between phonetics and phonology and of the phonological system of a language exists in generative grammar, and I shall refer to this in due course.

We can illustrate the traditional distinction between phonetic and phonological features of language very clearly by looking at some of the sounds which occur in English from both points of view. We can take two sounds which are phonetically quite distinct, but which phonologically can be shown to be but two versions of a single basic entity. (Phonological entities are transcribed within slant lines, as opposed to square brackets, and this shows that what is being referred to is functioning as part of a specific linguistic system.) The /l/ sounds in the words *leap* and *peel* are pronounced very differently in many dialects of English. The first, sometimes called a 'clear' [l] is articulated with one part of the tongue (at the tip) touching the gum behind the top teeth, another part of the tongue being raised simultaneously to near the front portion of the roof of the mouth. If we say *leap* very slowly, spending a long time on the [l], this articulation can be clearly felt. We can get an even clearer picture of where the tongue is by very sharply breathing in through the mouth while keeping the tongue steady in this position: the cold air will rush past the part of the tongue involved in the production of the sound and give a very clear sensation of where it is in the mouth. The second kind of /l/, sometimes called a 'dark' [ł], and distinguished by a slightly different symbol in transcription, is in a very different place, however: the tip of the tongue stays behind the front teeth for the sound, but the part which is raised towards the roof of the mouth is now much further back – a good inch away. From the phonetic point of view, therefore, there are two quite distinct sounds for /l/ in English; and once we have learned to listen for the difference, we can distinguish one from the other quite readily.

If we now consider these sounds from the phonological view-point, we reach a different conclusion, the two sounds being seen as fundamentally the same, since they have a single job to do. The reason is that the language organizes these sounds so that they have exactly the same function in helping to communicate and distinguish between words and meanings, despite their differences in pronunciation. The /l/ sounds, to begin with, do not occur haphazardly: there is no question of our using clear [l] one moment, and dark [ł] the next, depending on how we happen to feel at the time. We are restricted in our use of the sounds; and if we look carefully at the way in which they are distributed in the words of the language, we find that the restrictions form a nicely complementary pattern: we use clear [l] before a vowel, and dark [ɫ] at the end of a word after a vowel, or before a consonant. This is a very important discovery, because it accounts for the central phonological fact about this pair of sounds, namely, that we cannot make use of the contrast between them to help build up words which are different in meaning – as we can with, say, [p] and [t]. If we substitute a [p] sound for the [t] sound in the word *cut*, we get a different word – which shows that [p] and [t] are sounds which have an important role to play in distinguishing meanings in English. But substitute a clear [l] for a dark [ɫ] in any English word, and we do not get a different meaning: we get the same word with a slightly odd accent. In this way we can show that the two kinds of /l/ are really one, from the point of view of the job they do in identifying meanings. The large phonetic difference is not matched by a corresponding phonological one. There is one phonological unit (or *phoneme*) only, which appears in two different forms, its sound depending on whereabouts in a word it happens to be. Technically, in this approach, we would talk about the phoneme /l/ having two *allophones* [l] and (ɫ). 'Allo-' simply means 'variant of, in a particular position'.

This example also illustrates the statement that phonology is concerned with the study of the sound-system of a particular language, and that the conclusions we reach about the phonology of one language should never be generalized into the study of another. Just because in English the /l/ situation is as above, we must not run away with the impression that these sounds function the same way in other languages, for we would soon be shown wrong. In Russian, for example, a similar, though not identical phonetic difference to that between [l] and [ɫ] *does* carry with it a phonological difference: there are pairs of words, different in meaning, where the main phonetic difference is in the *l*-sounds used, for example, the words for *hatch* (of a ship) and *onion* are люᵛ and лук respectively, the first beginning with a clear [l], the secᴏ d with a dark one.

There are many other examples of differences at the ᴏnetic

level of analysis which are unimportant at the phonological level (for 'level', see p. 113). The /t/ sounds in words like *take*, *stake*, and *outpost*, for example, are all different, phonetically, because of the nature of the phonetic environment in which they occur, but phonologically they are all 'the same' (strictly speaking, allophones of the same phoneme). The [t] of *take* is clearly aspirated, where the [t] of *stake* is not (plosive sounds preceded by [s] are never aspirated in English); and in *outpost* there is no explosion for the plosive at all, due to the presence of the following [p] sound, which 'covers' it.

A full statement of all such variations of sound in a language, so as to determine which variations cause differences in meaning and which do not, is a very complex matter; but it is crucial to be able to do it, for otherwise we would not be able to explain native speakers' ability to impose order on the welter of phonetic details they hear around them, and, of course, use. This complexity is more than just the phonetic problem of being able to hear and transcribe the sounds accurately: there are theoretical problems also. We can see something of this if we look briefly at the way in which alternative views of the phoneme have been formulated over the years, and at a recent movement in linguistics which has tried to do away with the notion of the phoneme altogether.

To begin with, of course, there was no phonemic tradition available for scholars to use at all, though a number of people had begun to think about the matter. The term 'phoneme' had been used in the nineteenth century, but it referred to a unit of sound (that is, a phonetic unit – what we would usually these days call a 'phone'), and not to an abstract notion involving contrastivity. The germ of the phoneme idea was present in the work of the Polish scholar J. Baudouin de Courtenay towards the end of that century, but it remained undeveloped for some years. It was also implicit in the *parole–langue* distinction of Saussure, but again the importance of the concept was not brought out. In early American work in the 1920s, too, there was undoubtedly a tacit recognition of the distinction between 'important' and 'unimportant' sound-units in language; but the absence of any overtly formulated analytic principles led to a great deal of confusion. In reading this early literature, we

Linguistics

are often not sure, when someone talked of a 'sound' in a language, whether a phoneme was being referred to or not. The idea of phonemic contrasts in speech is certainly present in the early work of Edward Sapir, for example; and in a paper he wrote in 1925 called *Sound Patterns in Language*, the distinction is very definitely there, though not given any precise formulation.

The idea of the phoneme was not formulated with any precision until the thirties, and when its explanatory potential was realized, it sparked off a host of divergent interpretations and exegeses. The first, large-scale, explicit, theoretical treatment of the phoneme concept is to be found in the work of the linguists centred on Prague in the late twenties. The *Principles of Phonology (Grund-züge der Phonologie)* of the Russian linguist N. Trubetskoy was the principal exposition in this area, and its influence on subsequent phonological theorizing was vast. The 'Prague School' (see p. 254) argued the need for a separate account of phonology, distinct from the methods associated with phonetics – in other words, applying the Saussurean distinction of *langue* and *parole* to the concept of sound. The phoneme, for them, was an abstract, functional concept – the smallest distinctive unit operating within the network of structural relationships which constituted the sound-system of a language. The operative word in this rather imposing definition, though, is 'distinctive'. The phoneme was a concept which kept words apart, making phonological *oppositions*. To give a specific example, it was the *difference* between *pit* and *bit*, and not the characteristics of the *p* or the *b* seen in isolation.

Now this interpretation was rather different from others that were being suggested at that time. Some scholars conceived of the phoneme as being no more than a convenient way of eliminating some of the problems caused by phonetic details in transcription: the way was open to the development of a less detailed, 'broad' transcription (as it was called). More influential than this were views of the phoneme in altogether more concrete, physicalist terms than the very abstract approach of the Prague School. The phoneme, to some, was a *class* of sounds. The /l/ phoneme, for example, would be said to 'consist of' its various allophones, [l], [ł], and so on. To others, the phoneme was not so much a class of sounds, as a class of *features* of sound. To take the same example, the /l/ phoneme would 'consist of' such features as laterality of articulation (the air is expelled round the sides of the tongue), alveolarity (the front of the tongue is against the alveolar ridge), and so on. Leonard Bloomfield's definition of the phoneme runs: a 'minimal unit of distinctive sound-feature', and he talks about phonemes being 'lumps' or 'bundles' of features of sound. Now whether we define these features as articulatory, or acoustic, or some combination (room for further dispute here), it should be clear by the use of the phrase 'consist of' that the phoneme idea is very much more physical in these approaches than in that of the Prague School. The phoneme must in some way share some of the physical properties of the allophones or features which are its members.

This, broadly speaking, characterizes two radically different accounts of the phoneme: is the minimal unit of the sound-system best viewed as an abstract notion of 'opposition' or a concrete notion of 'class' of sound? Both positions were developed at length in the thirties, and many intermediate positions grew out of them. A useful collection of articles which covers much of the debate at this time is to be found in *Readings in Linguistics* Volume I, edited by Martin Joos, and published in 1958. I cannot outline all the issues involved here, but one line of subsequent development it is essential to trace, for it leads directly into a major controversy in phonological theory at the present time. This development arose out of the work of the Prague School, and in particular in the work of one of its members, Roman Jakobson, who was later to leave Europe and continue his research in America. The Prague group's phoneme, as I have said, was a very abstract notion. It made contact with reality, with the physical world of phonetic data, by their postulating the concept of *realization*. A phoneme, it would be said, was realized as various sound-features. (The abstract *langue* was manifested in *parole*, as Saussure would have said.) Each phoneme was defined in terms of a set of 'distinctive features', features which stood in clear opposition to other features in the data. Thus, there would be no point (it would be argued) in talking about a /p/ phoneme as voiceless, aspirated and tense, as these 'features' only make sense when we consider what they are opposed to (namely, the /b/ phoneme, which is voiced, unaspirated and lax). The difference between the two lies in the *opposition* of voicing, aspiration, tension, and so on. Exactly how much aspiration, or voicing, defined in absolute terms, there may be in various articulations of the /p/ and /b/ is not important, as long as they are kept distinct somehow: it is the relative values which are the main ones, and these values can simply be characterized as a set of oppositions. We end up, then, with a set of distinctive features which underlie all the phonological contrasts (i.e. phonemes) in a language.

The next stage in the development came in the fifties. Before this, the distinctive features were defined purely in articulatory terms (i.e. in terms of the way in which the vocal organs worked during utterance). With the development of better devices for acoustic analysis, it became possible to formulate the characteristics more comprehensively and accurately using acoustic data. It was then postulated that a very small number of distinctive features (twelve pairs of contrasts, in fact) would be enough to analyse all the phonological oppositions in any language. In *any* language. In other words, this hypothesis was claiming that in the final analysis the pronunciation systems of every language were built up out of different combinations and modifications of the same basic 'alphabet' of phonetic bits. The problem to be faced was how to specify the rules which governed the way in which these bits were to be put together, and if possible, to determine any 'universal' phonetic laws which would be applicable to the sound-systems of all languages. The search for phonological universals had begun, and with it, the question of how to devise a notation to adequately handle the complexity involved. With the advent of generative grammar in the late fifties, such issues, and many others arising out of them, began to be faced squarely. But there came with this a side-effect which was originally unexpected, and which is quite ironic under the circumstances – namely, the conclusion that the concept of the phoneme is not really needed for the analysis of sound-systems, the concept of distinctive features being equally able to cope with the job. It is argued that to set up a separate level of analysis for phonemes is unnecessary. In a particular word, e.g. *cats*, the phonemic approach would say three things about the final

-s: first, it is [-s] and not [-z], because the preceding word ends in a voiceless consonant (cf. p. 57); secondly, the [-s] is an allophone of the phoneme /s/; thirdly, the phonetic details of its pronunciation are voiceless, fricative, etc. – i.e. its distinctive features. The generative grammar approach asks, Why is it necessary to make the second statement? Could we not explain the same facts by going straight from the first point to the third (technically, from the 'morphophonemic' level of representation to the phonetic level)? Nothing is added, it is claimed, by inserting an extra level of analysis in between; or at least, the onus is on the phonemicists to show that any such level *is* needed. This was an interesting attack on the need for a separate concept of the phoneme, and it carried with it a whole new conception of the relationship between phonetics and phonology. Counter-arguments were not slow in forthcoming – for example, that an analysis in terms of distinctive features was too complex, or that it presupposed phoneme-like units anyway. But the implications of these arguments are still being worked through. At the present time little general agreement has been reached about the formal properties of phonological theory.

Whether we agree with the arguments of the generative grammarians over phonology or not, one thing has emerged with striking clarity from all the discussion, namely, the impossibility of keeping the two levels of phonetics and phonology strictly apart when beginning the analysis of a sound-system, as was recommended in the early days of linguistics. Whatever theoretical framework analysts work within, they do not 'do the phonetics' first, and 'do the phonology' later, as the above breakdown into two sections might suggest is possible. On the contrary, they do both tasks more or less simultaneously. There is a continuous switching of viewpoint from one mode of examining the data to another. A set of phonetic details may suggest a particular phonological hypothesis, which in turn suggests a reassessment of the relative importance attached to one phonetic feature, as opposed to some other, and the process continues. Any rigid separation of phonetics from phonology seems quite unrealistic (cf. my point above about the linguistic 'sciences', p. 168). We cannot keep phonological considerations out of our phonetic analysis. If we are linguists, then assumptions about the nature of sound-systems in general will be brought to bear on our task right from the very beginning. If we are linguistically naïve, then we will read our own language's sound-system into the foreign language's – for instance, in the Russian example, we will not notice the difference between the two kinds of *l*, because they are not different in English (and this of course is one main reason why we have difficulty in learning them). A phonological analysis is very much a single process, but involving considerations of both phonetic detail and abstract relationship. The important point to remember is that in any theoretical exposition of phonology, we must make it quite clear how we are distributing our emphasis over such issues.

I have spent so much space on the phoneme concept because of its unequalled status as a concept for organizing people's thinking in the first half of this century. Whether it is retained in future linguistic theory or not, the fact remains that not only was it an important explanatory concept in its own right, as a way of organizing phonetic data, it was also a source of hypotheses, many extremely valuable, about other aspects of language structure. We can see this in the way in which the fundamental idea of 'a unit functionally contrasting with another unit', which is the basis of the phoneme concept, was applied in other areas of language, most of which had nothing to do with pronunciation at all. People looked for phoneme-like phenomena elsewhere; and when they thought they had found some, they were labelled similarly. A whole host of technical terms was introduced in the thirties and forties, all based on the idea of the '-eme', and it is still possible to find linguists coining new terms using it, so major has been its influence. The 'emic' approach to linguistic analysis, as it is sometimes called, is not however a single, integrated theory. It is rather a label which characterizes the attitudes of scholars who approach language from a similar point of view, trying to establish basic functional units which will classify and interrelate the variety of structural patterns which face them. In its early days at least, the analogy was very much with the phoneme, and the emphasis was on the way in which the phoneme's emphasis on function helped to explain the mass of phonetic details which might accumulate in analysing a language. The 'emic' approach was thus opposed to an 'etic' approach – that is, one in which the physical patterns of some aspect of a language were described with no explicit reference to their function. More recently, this opposition has become somewhat blurred, in the work of various scholars, but the two terms 'emic' and 'etic' are still current, referring to two, largely idealized states of mind.

An early extension of the term was in developing an area of phonology which had been largely ignored in the earliest discussions of the phoneme. The discussion of phonology above, it may have been noted, was totally concerned with the 'segmental' aspects of the sound-system of a language – that is, with the description of its vowels, consonants, and combinations of these to form syllables, words and so on. It thus omits the description of the 'suprasegmental' aspect of the sound-system – the way in which these vowel-consonant combinations can be varied, using alterations in melody, loudness, speed of speaking and the like (cf. the concept of intonation on p. 131). When these features of pronunciation first came to be studied in detail, in the early forties, it was the phonemic approach which was used. Scholars distinguished 'pitch phonemes', for example; that is, minimal, functionally contrastive units of pitch. Say a word with one pitch phoneme and it would have a different meaning from the same word uttered with a different pitch phoneme. An example would be the word *yes* said with a firm tone of voice as opposed to a doubtful one. The two 'tunes' involved would be different, and the difference would be explained by saying that different combinations of pitch phonemes were being used. Contrastive units in suprasegmental phonology were sometimes called *prosodemes*, or *prosodic phonemes*. And various categories came to be distinguished within the field as a whole, also based on the emic concept. The *toneme* was one, referring to features of pitch which could cause a word to alter in meaning *completely* (not just giving it a different attitudinal nuance, as in the *yes* example). A 'tone-language' was a language in which alterations in pitch would cause the meaning of a word to be changed in this total way – many Oriental and African languages provide examples. The story is told of one missionary, engaged in the conversion of an African tribe (which spoke a tone-language), who, having made a vernacular translation of a rousing English hymn, found that the English tune caused an apparently praiseworthy harangue against sinners to come out as a diatribe against fat people. The distinction between the meanings 'fat person' and 'sinful person' was carried by a difference of pitch height only. And such a distinction would be called *tonemic*.

The most important area of 'emic expansion' was in the field of grammar. Here, Bloomfield, and other scholars in the mid thirties, attempted to impose some rigour on the description of the variety of linguistic forms which emerged when one started considering the effects of putting phonemes in sequences, or looked at the range of sentence-types which a language displayed. In particular, the question was asked whether there could not be found a fundamental unit in grammar, which could be established for the grammatical analysis of *any* language, as powerful as the phoneme had been in establishing order in apparently heterogeneous phonetic detail. The phoneme, it will be remembered, was the minimal contrastive unit of sound in a language. Could one not then establish a minimal contrastive unit of grammar in a language also? The main theme of linguistics in the early forties was debate about the status of such a unit, which was called, on analogy with the phoneme, the *morpheme*. This too turned out to be a fruitful concept, and I shall discuss it in a separate section below. But there were many other emic concepts which were devised in this first period of grammatical investigation, between 1930 and 1950. Terms such as *tagmeme*, *taxeme*, *sememe* and *episememe* are examples. They add a certain ponderousness to the literature of this period, and these days many of the definitions and debates are largely of historical interest. But the concentration on terminological precision was very beneficial in fostering a more rigorous attitude towards grammatical analysis; and in some cases the concepts involved turned out to have a lasting relevance, being the corner-stones on which whole theories of language structure came to be constructed. One example of this is the *sememic* approach to language developed by S. M. Lamb (see the remarks about this on p. 212). Another example – the most notable in its breadth of vision – is the theory of K. L. Pike, who not only attempts to apply emic ideas to phonology, grammar and vocabulary (under the heading of *tagmemics*, cf. p. 209), but also insists on applying these same principles to the analysis of other areas of human behaviour besides language. He argues that linguistic methods are able to identify the functionally important (i.e. emic) features of any aspect of behaviour out of the objective (i.e. etic) data which the analyst is presented with. In this way, minimal, contrastive units of function abound – from the general idea of a 'behavioureme' to the more particular notions of 'gusteme' (i.e. the minimal unit of taste) or 'kineme' (i.e. minimal unit of facial expression or body gesture). It has been argued, against this approach, that this is to make the originally highly specific notion of an emic contrast so broad as to empty it of meaning. The criteria which were established in the thirties which had to be borne in mind when classifying sounds into phonemes were very specific, and the units being classified, the sounds, were readily identifiable and analysable. But with phenomena such as taste or smell or movement, the units involved are by no means so self-evident, and the classificatory criteria involved are by no means clear. It is probable, in other words, that the emic concept has been stretched too far in this approach, though the question is still an open one. Applying emic notions to the more central areas of linguistic structure would seem a more important initial task, and here there is a great deal still to be done.

The presence of the -eme coloured linguistic thinking for many years, and still does – if only in the sense that we have to understand it in order to avoid using it! At least one important term, *lexeme*, has been introduced in the last few years, referring to the common, abstract element which underlies the variant forms of a word – *go*, *goes*, *going*, *gone*, *went* would all be forms of the same underlying lexeme, GO, for example (cf. p. 236). Also a number of alternative theories have been developed partly or wholly in specific opposition to the principles of traditional phonemics. I have already had cause to refer to the Jakobsonian emphasis on distinctive features above. Another example would be the theory of 'prosodic phonology' of J. R. Firth (cf. p. 253) which was to a great extent a reaction against the use of the phoneme as a general explanatory principle for phonology. In grammar, and in other areas of language structure, there were reactions too; but in order to follow more recent developments in this area, we must first look at the nature of grammatical analysis as carried on by its earliest linguistic practitioners, in the early forties.

III Morphology

The morpheme, the smallest unit of grammatical analysis, is another of those fundamental ideas in linguistics that linguists would never bother defining in the normal course of conversation; but it would be wrong to think that it has always had its current 'routine' status. During the forties and fifties there was considerable heated discussion as to what morphemes were, how they were best defined, what implications for other aspects of linguistic theory could be drawn from them, and so on. To appreciate the basis of the complexities and extent of these discussions – and these days much of it seems irrelevant to the main tasks of linguistics (which is why this section is to be a fairly short one) – we must remember to take account of the intellectual climate of the time. In the glow of achievement which was almost universally felt by scholars who had used the illuminating phoneme concept, the idea that there might be an explanatory concept as validly applicable to grammatical analysis in all languages was tantamount to the suggestion that here was a linguistic 'philosopher's stone'. If the grammar of a language *could* be analysed in terms of identifying a set of minimal units, classifying them, and describing the patterns into which these classes fell – and there was no reason to think that this would not be feasible – then this was surely a goal to which as much attention as possible should be given. The initial apparent comprehensiveness of the morpheme concept gave to it a cogency which it retained for some years, until various limitations in the idea had been demonstrated. We can only understand some of the theorizing which took place during this period if we bear this point in mind.

The original idea, then, was to postulate that all the phenomena that people talked about under the heading of grammar could ultimately be broken down into these basic units, or morphemes. One metaphor used was that of bricks, which could be fired in different shapes and sizes (*sc.* classes) and put together in different combinations to produce walls of different types (*sc.* sentences, etc.). But why morphemes? Why introduce a new and in some ways a rather fearful term, when we have the perfectly familiar idea of 'word' to play with? Why can we not simply say that the smallest unit of grammatical analysis is the word, that sentences are composed of words, and continue accordingly? Would not the concept of 'word' do to base a grammar on just as well?

These questions were early raised, and they got an early answer. The short answer to the last question was No. Whatever weaknesses the morpheme concept might have, the weaknesses in the word concept were rather worse (or so it might be argued). There were a number of reasons for this, some real, some imaginary. To begin with, there were problems over identifying words in a language. This may not strike people born and bred in a literate society as being much of a problem. For them, words are usually fairly easy to identify. In writing, a word is something which has a space on either side. But in speech, there is no exact equivalent of this; we do not pause after every word when we speak. And most linguistic communities are not literate (cf. pp. 59–60). The anthropological linguists found very early on that it was an extremely difficult matter to decide what the words were in a language which had never been written down. We all have this difficulty temporarily, of course, when we first come into contact with a foreign language. We come up against a stream of unbroken noise which for a while we are unable to organize. The sentences may stand out fairly distinctly, but inside these there is no way of telling, without much further study, how many words a sentence consists of or where the boundaries between them go. And in the case of a language which has never been studied before, placing these boundaries accurately is no easy matter.

Some techniques have of course been devised to help matters. Old views of words as 'units of sense' provide one suggestion, but this does not help very much, as there are many units of sense which consist of more than one word (*spick and span, A rolling stone gathers no moss*, etc.); and what constitutes the boundaries of any such unit is indefinable (cf. the problem of sentence definition in terms of a 'complete thought', which is often cited). A number of more formal criteria have been suggested, however. One such is the criterion of 'potential pause'. If we are asked to speak slowly, then we can and do introduce pauses at various points; and it usually turns out that these coincide with the spaces that in a literate community a written version of our utterance would impose. Anthropological linguists have had some success in asking their informants to dictate utterances slowly – as it were, 'word for word'. But this criterion by no means always clarifies the situation. Even in English it will not always work. Would you pause between the last two items of the following sentence, for instance? *The paper is on the washing-machine*. There are many units in English which we do not know whether to take as one word or two in speech – and we have corresponding difficulty over their written form (e.g. whether to use a hyphen or not in the above sentence, whether to put spaces in between the 'bits' of *insofaras*). Moreover, we cannot really define words by reference to this pause feature, as this is something which is only characteristic of abnormal speech. We surely have to be able to identify words under normal conditions, if the concept is to be really usable.

Another suggested procedure is that words are the smallest units in a language that can be used alone as a sentence. We can say *Go. Here. Men. Interesting*. We cannot use the bits of words as sentences, as with *un-*, *-ize*, *-ing*. But here too there are a few problems. Should we then call *the*, *my*, or *of* words in English, for they cannot be used on their own as sentences? Or in French, can we call *je* or *tu* words, since whenever they are used on their own as sentences (for example, in answer to a question), they adopt a different form, *moi* and *toi* respectively. These problems are not very numerous, but they involve 'words' which are of rather frequent occurrence in language, and hence they are not altogether trivial.

Yet another criterion for word identification is in terms of 'minimal unit of positional mobility' – which is simply a precise (*sic*) way of saying that the word is the smallest unit which can be moved from one position to another in a sentence – bits of words cannot be so moved. For example, taking the sentence *Little children should be seen and not heard in the early morning*, we can derive all kinds of new sentences from this by a simple process of moving the words around in certain ways or omitting to put some words in, e.g. *In the morning, little children . . .*, *Early children should be heard and not seen . . .* But we cannot, say, move the *-ren* of *children* somewhere else, or the *-ing* of *morning*. Nor, for that matter, can we move *the*, either, as this is positionally fixed, preceding the noun it modifies – and so there is still a certain problem. For the few items in language which are tied in this kind of way, their status as 'word' is still a matter for doubt, in terms of the mobility criterion.

A more reliable way of trying to 'get at' words in a language is to view them as units which have a fixed internal structure. If we take a sentence like *The policeman coughed politely*, then each of the units we would want to call a word has a fixed structure, in the sense that the bits which constitute them cannot be rearranged in any way (we cannot have *manpolice*, *edcough*, etc.), nor can they be separated by other units (we cannot have *policetheman*, *policeniceman*, etc.). Technically this characteristic is often referred to as 'internal stability'. If we want to insert fresh information into a sentence, then it is *between* the words that this information goes and not within them (e.g. *The nice policeman just coughed politely*). Words interrupt; they are not interruptable.

Other criteria have been suggested, too; for example, it is conceivable that there could be a language each word of which is marked by a distinct feature of pronunciation. No one has found one, but we get something like this in languages where words of more than one syllable usually have one of the syllables emphasized above the other or others. In Turkish for example, the emphasized syllable (or *accent*) is generally the last; in Welsh, it is generally the next-to-last. But there are numerous exceptions to these 'rules'. All in all, when we try and define the words of a language, we find that – in terms of the criteria discussed so far – it is impossible to be absolute and clear-cut. In any language, some lexical units seem to be more 'word-like' than others; and between languages, there is no necessary parallelism. For example, because of the way *the* behaves in English, it is hard to call it a 'word' in the same clear sense as *children* is a word. On the other hand, it is certainly more word-like than the *-ren* of *children*. And similarly, it is more word-like than the definite article in Rumanian, which is always added to the noun (as in *pomul* 'the tree'), but which cannot be separated from its noun by the addition of other words (unlike English *the nice policeman*, etc.).

What does all this mean? It means, in effect, that it is likely to be a very difficult matter indeed to develop a notion of 'word' which can be satisfactorily and consistently used to account for the grammatical patterning of a language, to act as the basic unit in a grammar. Not only is it difficult within any one language; it is also difficult when we are comparing different languages – and we should perhaps remember at this point the *general* aim of the whole linguistic exercise, to develop a general linguistic theory, and not one which will fit just English. For some languages, indeed, it hardly seems to make sense to talk of them having words at all. The so-called *agglutinative* languages (see p. 150) are so called because their sentences are mainly composed of strings of units, none of which have any independent, word-like status. A sentence like *He did not ask me* might be built up using a root *ask*, to which particles indicating 'he', 'not', 'did', and 'me' would be attached following certain rules. We do not, in English, generally build up words in this way; whenever we do, it can be a source of humour, as in the coinage *antidisestablishmentarianism*. The point is that in some languages most of the 'words' are of this type; they display an extremely complicated internal structure. It is not difficult to see from this how stretched the idea of a word has to be in order to cope with the ramifications of such languages. It becomes so stretched, many linguists argue, that it is a better policy to drop the notion altogether (or at least, not to try to make it the starting-point for any grammatical analysis) and look for something else.

We can thus see the morpheme as being, in a way, a reaction against the word-based grammars of the preceding two thousand years. We must also remember, as further indication of this, that the traditional model of language in terms of parts of speech was very firmly grounded in the notion of word. Indeed, the distrust of the parts of speech approach (see p. 73) was a real factor in influencing linguists to devise grammatical models based on some alternative principle of classification. The morpheme was suggested as a way around the problems of identification and classification which the word had presented. On the face of it, a unit of analysis smaller than the word seems to have many points in its favour. It was by no means a totally new idea, of course: people had dealt with word structure, in terms of prefixes, suffixes, and so on, for generations – the new concept was more general, but dealt with the same kind of thing. It also seemed to be a more readily applicable general concept on which to base grammatical investigation. The units out of which agglutinative languages built their sentences seemed to be the same sort of thing as the units which constituted words (and sentences) in English. By using the morpheme concept, then, the languages seemed more immediately comparable, and this augured well for the development of a grammatical theory. It might even be possible (it was felt, by some) to obtain a considerable simplification in a model of language by doing without the idea of a word. Once we had listed the morphemes of a language, and classified them, all larger units (such as phrases, clauses, sentences, paragraphs) could presumably be shown to be simply patterns of these – the brick wall analogy again. Instead of saying, as earlier, that words built up sentences, as in

The + taller + girls + in + the + railway + station + haven't + eaten + lunch,

we say that morphemes build up sentences, as in

The + tall + er + girl + s + in + the + rail + way + station + have + n't + eat + en + lunch.

If we can get the same results without having to use the awkward concept of the word, it was argued, then let's do so.

This is not the place to go into details. It will suffice to record and briefly illustrate that in attempting to carry out the three tasks of morpheme identification, classification and distribution, problems arose which made many of the difficulties of word identification and classification seem elementary. The problems of identification again loomed large. The original concept, as I said, was to see the morpheme as the minimal unit of grammatical analysis. In other words, if you analysed a piece of speech (of any length, but let us say a word) into its constituent grammatical elements, there would come a time when you could analyse no further. To make the term 'grammatical' clearer, the words 'contrastive' and 'meaningful' are sometimes added to the definition. A morpheme is the smallest bit of language which has a meaning – and moreover this meaning is different from (contrasts with) the meanings of all the other morphemes in the language. Two things follow from this. Firstly, if you add a morpheme to an utterance, or take one away, by definition you alter the meaning of that utterance. Thus the following words mean different things – *nation*, *national*, *nationalize*, *denationalize*, *denationalization*. (In some cases, of course, altering morphemes in this way would produce nonsense, as in *dealize*, but this does not contradict this first point.) Secondly, if you try to analyse a morpheme into its constituents, it loses its identity, and you end up with a sequence of meaningless noises, e.g. *nation* (strictly, /neɪʃn̩/) could be split up into *na-* + *-tion*, or *nati-* + *on*, and so on, but the constituents could only be described as combinations of phonemes or phonetic features. Analysing the structure of morphemes leads you straight into phonology.

A morpheme, then, can be viewed from a number of different angles, of which three stand out. Firstly, it is a formal, or physical unit; it has a phonetic shape. Secondly, it has a meaning. And thirdly, it has a syntactic role to play in the construction of larger grammatical units. So far, so good. Take a sentence like *The three girls kicked the red ball*, there would be no problem over identifying morphemes. *The*, *three*, *red* and *ball* are all minimal, meaningful, syntactically relevant units. *Girls* and *kicked* have two each: take the *s* away from *girls* and we get a distinct meaningful unit *girl* – in other words, the *s* carries the singular/plural difference – and similarly, the *ed* can be removed from *kicked* to turn the past tense into present.

Not all examples are so straightforward, however, and I will give just a few instances of the kind of difficulties we quickly run into. The process of identifying morphemes, we must remember, is a process not solely of identifying single morphemes, one at a time, but of ensuring that when the same morpheme turns up again, we can recognize it *as an example of the same morpheme*. Thus, in my example above, *the* is counted only once, though it turns up twice in the sentence. We know it is the same morpheme because its phonetic shape, its meaning, and its grammatical role have not changed from the first occurrence to the second. But what happens when one of these variables *does* change? To take the first case, of phonetic change, we very often want to count as the same morpheme forms which are slightly but explicably different in their phonetic shape. Going back to the question of noun plurals in English (originally introduced on p. 57), we find a very clear example of this. Here the morpheme which indicates plurality – the *s* of written English – has three distinct pronunciations, phonetically [s] as in *pots*, [z] as in *toes*, and [ɪz] as in *horses*. It would be silly, however, to suggest that we have here three morphemes, as clearly the meaning of the forms is identical in each case (namely, plurality), the grammatical function of the *s* is constant, and the phonetic differences are there solely because of the influence of the sound which precedes them: if a noun ends in a sibilant (an 's'-like sound, as in *bus*, *buzz*, *hatch*, *hash*, *lodge* and *rouge*), then the [ɪz] form is used; if it ends in a voiceless non-sibilant ([p], [t], [k], [f], etc.), then a voiceless [s] is used; and if it ends in a voiced non-sibilant ([b], [d], [g], [v], etc.), then a voiced [z] is used. In a despairing search for an analogy, water, steam and ice suggests itself: in different sets of environmental conditions, the same underlying substance takes on different forms. In the linguistic case, whenever the phonetic shape of a morpheme is altered because of the direct phonetic influence of the sounds around it, we tend to discount it, as being nothing to do with the morpheme itself, which preserves its essential, abstract identity. We talk of the morphemes being 'phonologically conditioned', and the resulting forms being 'variants of' the same basic morpheme. Technically, they would be called *allomorphs* of the same morpheme (the analogy is with 'allophones of a phoneme', of course, cf. p. 174). Another way of putting it would be to call them *morphemic alternants*. And this was how the linguists of the forties developed the idea of the morpheme to take account of such cases as noun plurality above.

But the question arose then, and arises now: how much phonetic variation are we going to allow in under the heading of an allomorph? Using the same reasoning as in the previous paragraph, we would presumably analyse *the bigger woman* into *the* + *big*(g) + *er* + *woman*, the *-er* being the mark of 'comparison' here. But in English, whenever an adjective is longer than two syllables, there is a dominant tendency not to use the *-er* method of forming comparatives, but to use *more* instead, as in *the more beautiful woman* (not **the beautifuller woman*). Here, *more* is the index of comparison. We are thus forced to argue that *more* and *-er* are phonologically conditioned variants of the same morpheme. But there is clearly a certain tension in doing this, and the possibility of considerable conceptual confusion, when we compare what we have done with the earlier statements of morphemic principle. There it was said (in so many words) that words were composed of morphemes – but here we have a morpheme one of whose forms is a word! It was also suggested that morphemes had to be phonetically similar, and yet here we have two instances of the same morpheme with nothing phonetically in common at all (/mɔː/ and /ə/ respectively). The situation has a hint of topsy-turvydom about it. If we allow in *this* amount of phonetic flexibility, then the floodgates are open – all sorts of forms could be called instances of the same morpheme if they were simply grammatically and semantically identical. Any two synonymous nouns, or sentences, might be labelled so. There is more than a hint here of the uncontrolled notional classifications which were slated so strongly in Chapter 2. And while this is an unpalatable development, it is very difficult to see how it might be avoided without *either* being inconsistent in our use of the morpheme concept, *or* leaving out examples such as the comparative (which rather diminishes the comprehensiveness of the supposedly 'basic' concept), *or* developing such an abstract level of discussion for morphemic analysis that we lose touch with formal reality altogether.

There is another side to this problem. If we return to the example of the noun + plural, then the question quickly arises of what to do with the irregular forms. *Cat* + *s*, *bus* + *es*, and so on, are easily handled; but what do you add to *mouse* to get *mice*, or to *man* to get *men*? It should be obvious that you do not really add anything at all – rather the vowel in the singular 'changes into' or 'is replaced by' the vowel of the plural. But how can these examples be made to fit with the morpheme principle? Such was the question which exercised a great deal of ingenuity in the forties. If *mice* consisted of two morphemes, that of 'mouse' plus that of 'plural', where were they to be found? Was the plural bit the /ai/ in /mais/? This could hardly be so, as take the /ai/ away from the word /mais/ and you are left with /m-s/, which can hardly be identified with the morpheme /maus/. Well, then, perhaps the plurality is in the process of change from the vowel /au/ to the vowel /ai/? But again, if morphemes are to be viewed as formal units at all (as was the claim), then it is hardly consistent to talk of such vague things as 'processes' as morphemes. Many such 'solutions' were proposed to this kind of problem, some in retrospect seeming to be quite bizarre. Thus, it was argued, in the two sentences *The sheep is coming* and *The sheep are coming*, the first *sheep* is singular and the second plural, therefore there must be a plural allomorph in the second sentence somewhere. Two possibilities are open, in view of the formal fact that the word *sheep* is obviously the same both times. First, it might be in the verb form, which is the only indication that there is a difference between the two sentences. But against this, we could argue that it would be conceptually odd to think of the plural of a noun being expressed by a form of the verb – and in any case the question of whether *sheep* means singular or plural applies even when the verb's influence is eliminated (by saying, for example, *The sheep came*, which could be either). The second suggestion, which was in fact favoured by many, was to talk about a 'zero morpheme' – that is, the plurality could be said to be present in principle, though not given any phonetic manifestation. Here indeed was the limiting case of phonetic identity for the morpheme! *Sheep* singular, *sheep* + zero (usually written ∅) plural.

At this point, I usually pause for laughter from any lecture audience to whom I might be trying to introduce morphological ideas, for the idea of something being expounded by nothing certainly strikes a note of incongruity. When the laughter has subsided, I try to point out that there is nothing essentially odd about an analytical concept of zero. The idea that 'nothing' has a job to do, a clear function in a network of relationships, is a common enough notion in many other areas of experience than language – for example, in the idea of a car 'not' being in gear, or a railway signal which is in its 'not raised or lowered' position, or, more generally, in the use of o in arithmetic. But what is odd, I concede, is the way in which the morpheme idea has been stretched from its original conception to something which is theoretically very different. It is easy to see what has happened. Proponents of the morpheme theory have been so convinced of its validity (or, perhaps, so desirous of displaying its validity) as a general explanation for grammatical phenomena that, when faced with features of language which were recalcitrant to analysis in terms of the theory, they were analysed in terms of it nonetheless. It seems to have been the old story of 'forcing your facts into your theory'. It is easy to see this now, looking back, and to say: What should have happened was for people to have recognized, straight away, that the morpheme concept had grave weaknesses, that there were many features of language which it could not handle, and that it is not essential to ensure the accurate phonetic identification of all the units we might want to call morphemes. At the time, however, bearing in mind what I said about the search for a linguistic philosopher's stone, such an attitude would have been laughed out of court; and one can understand why.

What is clear nowadays, however, is that the morpheme concept is only of limited value. It can certainly display the minimal units of grammatical analysis in a vast amount of language data. The irregularities of English are not, after all, very many. And when it comes to the analysis of the agglutinative languages, the morpheme concept is invaluable, as these languages are, as it were, tailor-made for it. But when we consider the difficulties of morphemic identification as a whole – and I have by no means covered them all in my illustrations so far – it is clear that the concept is not as all-embracing as it has sometimes been made out to be. When we consider other problems of identification, due to semantic variability, for instance, the situation gets even cloudier. Is *boy* in *Send the boy* (said by a shopkeeper about a part-time assistant) the same morpheme or different from *boy* in *This is my boy* (said by a parent)? A glance at any large dictionary would show how vast the problem of 'semantic overlapping' is. As a result of such problems, there is no linguistic theory these days which is based primarily on the morpheme concept; but every linguist would recognize the existence of morphemic units in language and would try to make his theory take account of them in some way. Morphemes are viewed as the units that the grammatical rules of the language have to work on – the minimal, meaningful units which it is the purpose of a grammar to organize into the various structures which it contains. Putting this another way, for many linguists the inventory of morphemes in a language is the basis of that language's dictionary, or lexicon. The role of morphemes has thus changed considerably since they were first introduced into linguistic analysis; but they are still very much with us.

In this brief look at the main principles underlying what was a very formative period in the development of linguistics, I have not had space to discuss – or even mention, so far – the attempts made to construct coherent models of linguistic behaviour using morphological data. *Item and arrangement*, items and process, and *word and paradigm* are three labels given to models of analysis which were used, particularly with reference to morphological data, during this period and afterwards. The differences between them need not concern us in this book; but it is at least important to be aware of their existence, if only to avoid making over-simple generalizations about the themes and emphases of this period. Nor have I had space to devote to the considerable amount of attention paid at this time to the discussion of methods of classification for morphemes, or of the ways in which the various types combine into larger units (the so-called 'morphotactics'). Nowadays, many linguists would establish a separate branch of study for the analysis of the particular areas of interplay between morphology and phonology – the way in which phonemes (or sets of distinctive features) vary in the context of particular morphemes, and the way in which morphemes are realized differently in particular phonological contexts. This branch is called – appropriately enough – *morphophonology* (or *morphophonemics*). Some linguistic theories tend to emphasize this interplay rather than talk separately about phonology and morphology, in fact (see p. 179, for instance). But to go into these and related matters in an introductory book would be unrepresentative of the contemporary linguistic scene, where the primary problems and interests have moved away from those of morphology into those of syntax.

IV 'Surface' Syntax

It is perhaps not so surprising that, when people found that grammatical analysis in terms of minimal units of language was not so all-powerful an approach as had been anticipated, their attention should swing over to the investigation of grammatical models in terms of maximal units. And so, after the emphasis on words, and on units smaller than the word, we find a corresponding emphasis on units larger than the word, in particular the sentence. With very few exceptions, systems of grammatical analysis proposed since the forties have been based on the notion of sentence. But there are considerable differences in theory and procedure between these various approaches, and one of these differences underlies the choice of titles for this and the next section (for its explanation, see p. 209 and subsequently). I shall be looking at work in syntax in two sections, the present one dealing with developments in the late forties and early fifties (what is sometimes, rather cynically, referred to as B.C. – viz. Before Chomsky), the next dealing with the subsequent work motivated by the transformational-generative approach.

I do not propose to digress here about the best way of defining the concept of sentence. It would be impossible to give this topic a fair treatment (bearing in mind the hundreds of definitions which have been suggested since Plato), and in any case it is important to realize that it would be a digression. It is highly unlikely that there will ever be a 'best' definition of a term like 'sentence'. We must remember that the value of terms like this is very much determined by the way in which we use them in our analysis of the language. 'Sentence' refers to certain features of language and not others.

Exactly where the boundary-line is to be drawn between what constitutes a sentence and what does not is to a very great extent a matter of definition, just as with the other terms discussed already in this chapter. In one model, there may be a distinction made between 'sentence' and 'clause', let us say; another model may decide not to talk about clauses at all, referring to them as types of sentence; a third may even try to do without the term 'sentence', talking instead of 'utterance', or some such notion. Any one of these approaches could be illuminating, and could, if developed sufficiently, produce an organized account of grammatical phenomena which is comprehensive, self-consistent, and intuitively satisfying. However, it is probably clear by now that no grammatical theory has achieved any of these aims, and so we are able to talk about evaluating the merits and demerits of various grammatical proposals only in the broadest of terms. Ideally, we can look forward to the day when evaluation measure will allow us to assess the claims of different grammatical theories – or, more specifically, to assess the various definitions of a term like 'sentence'. Meanwhile, we can only demand explicitness in people's use of the term, and take pains to understand any given definition in the light of the theory as a whole of which it constitutes a part.

When it is said that the sentence is the maximal unit of grammatical analysis – as is commonly said these days – we must be careful to see this claim in the light of the previous paragraphs. It is not saying, for instance, that there are no units larger than the sentence. Obviously there are sequences of sentences which can be viewed as forming larger constructions, which we might label as 'utterances', 'discourses', 'paragraphs', or whatever. All that is being claimed is that the sentence is the largest unit *recognized by the linguist* as being *capable* of accounting for the range of grammatical classes and structures which turn up in a language. Other notions could do this job also, as can be seen from considering alternative ways of 'handling' the following example: *Will John be here tomorrow? He will be, if his train is on time.* We can look at this piece of conversation from at least three points of view, as far as its initial grammatical analysis is concerned. We could say (a) here is a piece of discourse, consisting of two sentences, the second being dependent on the first; or (b) here are two sentences of different types, combining in a certain way, and the second consists of two clauses; or (c) here are three clauses, the last one being dependent on the second, and the latter two being jointly dependent on the first. We could formulate further alternatives, but let us stick to these three. Each account, or model, explains the data, but the starting-point is different each time: in the first case, the analysis starts off with the idea of a discourse, in the second case with a sentence, and in the third case with a clause. All other concepts in any of the accounts must be related to one or other of these basic, or 'primitive' concepts (cf. p. 114). Linguists make up their minds which model to use in a variety of half-understood ways. For example, they may see a more obvious picture emerging in terms of types of sentence than in terms of either of the other two, and this may lead them to prefer that model. It is undoubtedly partly a question of taste; but there are formal reasons too. The kinds of grammatical relationship which link sentences together into larger units are much less obvious and less general than the features which differentiate types of sentence. Few linguists accordingly have advocated a 'discourse model' of language, because so little is known about the features which operate at this level (but current research trends may well alter this situation: cf. p. 246). Most linguists take account of features of an inter-sentence type by postulating separate sentence structures and then allowing in the inter-sentence links in various ways. One brief illustration of this might be if the above example were viewed as two sentences, as follows: *Will John be here tomorrow? John will be here tomorrow, if his train is on time.* The change from *John* to *he*, and the omissibility of *here tomorrow* are features displaying inter-sentence linkage which could be sorted out and incorporated into the account *after* the initial analysis in terms of sentences had been made.

Most linguists, then, would start their grammatical study by taking the notion of a sentence and applying it to the analysis of data. They may give it a working definition to guide investigation (such as talking about it as an 'independent linguistic form', or as a 'subject-predicate' construction) and elaborate or modify this as new material emerges. There may also be clues in the data which can be used in the process of identifying sentences, such as punctuation or intonation. But these matters are ancillary to the main task of postulating a unit which will act as a satisfactory basis for a coherent and comprehensive analysis. The total definition of sentence, then, ultimately comes out of this analysis: it is one of the products of a grammar, and not something which we have available before we begin.

What I have been saying characterizes much of the modern approach to syntax. It was a considerable time, however, before these attitudes became clear. In the early days of syntactic analysis, a great deal of energy was spent arguing about the relative merits of competing definitions of sentence (and other terms), and in raising procedural questions, such as those of identification mentioned in the previous paragraph. The modern approach to syntax is very much a reaction – sometimes a quite explicit one – against the emphases and principles of this early period, which consequently must be looked at in some detail.

It begins with the development of more explicit techniques of grammatical analysis than hitherto, of which the most important was *immediate constituent* analysis. This term was introduced by Bloomfield, who illustrated the way in which it was possible to take a sentence (he chose *Poor John ran away*) and split it up into two immediate constituents (*Poor John* and *ran away*), these being in turn analysable into further constituents (*Poor* and *John*, and *ran* and *away*). In other words, a sentence is seen not as a sequence or a 'string' of elements, *Poor + John + ran + away*, but as being made up of 'layers' of constituents, each cutting point, or 'node' in the diagram being given an identifying label. This was made quite clear in the form of a 'tree diagram', such as

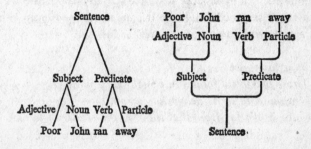

Linguistics

It is a fact, it was argued, that speakers of a language can divide up sentences in this way, and it is this kind of analysis which ought to be developed and formalized so as to take account of all possible sentences. The similarity of IC analysis (as it was called) to traditional techniques of parsing sentences used by the schools should be obvious. But IC analysis was a much more powerful method of analysing sentences than parsing. It forced the analyst to be far more explicit about his reasons for analysing the data in a given way, as opposed to the arbitrariness and overconcentration on matters of terminology as an end in itself which were the hallmarks of traditional clause analysis ('Now class, you will remember that there are eight (or was it eighteen?) kinds of adverb clause, with the following names . . .') There are clear directions as to how the analysis of any sentence should be carried out – one set is given in Fries's *The Structure of English*, for instance. Moreover, the linguist, being a person with a descriptive bent (at least, at that time), would be anxious to make the method applicable to the awkward sentence types, as opposed to the very limited range of constructions that traditional parsing was ready or able to handle ('How do you parse *Yours truly*, Miss?' 'Be quiet, Johnny!'). And the detailed analysis of specific sentences would naturally develop a clearer awareness of the basis of classification of words, morphemes, and other units (such as the need for clear distributional criteria, cf. p. 79), which would produce a more coherent account of syntax as a whole.

Or so it was felt. And it is certainly true that the techniques of IC analysis which were developed, and the detailed elaborations of some of Bloomfield's followers (such as Zellig Harris) were both illuminating and precise. A great deal of new information was accumulated in a systematic way, particularly about the way in which small sentences could be expanded to apparently infinite lengths following certain procedures, as in

> *Buns taste nice.*
> *Those delightful buns you bought taste nice.*
> *Not quite all those delightful currant buns you bought*
> *the other day from that shop on the corner taste nice.*
> etc.

The same kind of diagram as above could be used to display many of the structural relationships which exist between the words and morphemes of these complex sentences, as in the figure below. Not surprisingly, however, it was recognized in due course that there were many problems involved in IC analysis, and it is important for understanding subsequent developments to be fully aware what these were. They fell into two categories. On the one hand, it was sometimes difficult to use IC analysis in a completely consistent way; on the other, there seemed to be a number of important insights into grammar, which IC analysis was missing. And while techniques based on IC analysis are still used by most linguists, they are now viewed as a very small part of what a grammar has to do.

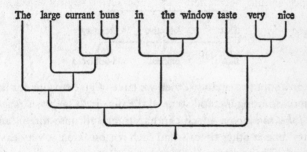

Example of unlabelled IC analysis

It is easy to illustrate these problems, and no more than a brief illustration is required to make the point. It is not always clear, for instance, where the break (or 'cut') between constituents is to come. Normally it is possible to decide intuitively, on the basis of the way in which the meaning of a sentence is organized, or, more explicitly, in terms of the way in which the parts of the sentence distribute themselves and function, where to draw the dividing line between constituents. No one in their right mind would divide our earlier sentence into *Poor* and *John ran away*, for instance. But sometimes two linguists, both in their right minds, will not agree about the place of a cut. Consider the problems raised by the kind of structure discussed in the Interlude above (p. 126 ff.). *That nice, efficient, old-fashioned secretary is here.* After the first cut, which causes no problem (between *secretary* and *is*), what should we do? Should the noun phrase be divided into *that* and *nice, efficient, old-fashioned secretary*, or into *that nice, efficient, old-fashioned* and *secretary*, or should we somehow try to take out *that* and *secretary* together (producing a 'discontinuous' constituent), thus leaving the adjectives? Or, considering adjectives separately, should we make our first cut between *nice* and *efficient, old-fashioned*, or between *nice, efficient* and *old-fashioned*? Or should we drop the normal IC principle of cutting two at a time (as the above diagrams show), and allow a simultaneous threefold cutting process to take place here, as follows?

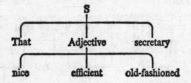

If we do adopt this analysis, then we have to give reasons for using a 'binary' splitting method some of the time in IC analysis (as with *Poor John ran away*, which can hardly be split into three), and a 'ternary' one at other times – and such reasons are not very easy to think up. The existence of so many alternative analyses, then, constitutes a major problem.

Such difficulties might of course be overcome, given time and ingenuity. What makes one not want to bother trying to overcome them is the realization that IC analysis is not worth it. It is not the key to the understanding of grammatical structure in language. It is a technique – an extremely useful technique, at times – which can organize our data in certain ways and provide a first insight into its structure. But there is too much of importance in grammar which IC analysis, by its very nature, cannot handle, to allow it to be any more than a preliminary tool for sorting and classifying. In what main ways, then, is it inadequate?

It does not take much thought to see that there are many important grammatical relationships which could never be brought to light by I C techniques, or which are taken for granted by them. The kinds and degrees of relationship which exist between sentences, for example, are obscured. There is no way of finding out about such intuitively obvious correlations as the relationship between active and passive sentences, for instance. Part of the reason is that I C analysis proceeds one sentence at a time. It can suggest one analysis for *That man saw John's mother*; it can suggest another for *John's mother was seen by that man*. But how does I C analysis tell us that these two sentences are closely related, that one sentence is 'the active of' the other – that in this case they both mean the same thing? It cannot provide this information. All the analysis tells us about is the structure of the two sentences, seen as isolates. And yet, it can be argued (and all linguists would argue) it is important for a grammar to tell us about their relationships as well. Knowing a language means, amongst other things, knowing when there are two ways of expressing the same thing grammatically. It means being able to manipulate the rules of the language, so that we do not have to learn the structure of every new sentence we wish to use from scratch, but rather apply an already-learned rule to fresh material. Once I have 'learned' that two such sentences as the above are structurally related, I can apply my knowledge and pro- duce fresh pairs of sentences. Given the sentence *Seventeen ele- phants trampled on my country house the other day*, I 'know' that it is possible to say *My country house was trampled on by seventeen elephants the other day*. And the only way in which we can explain how I know this is by postulating that I have learned a rule which tells me how to form passive sentences from active ones, and vice versa. This rule, then, is a feature of the language's structure which any grammatical analysis should make explicit. I C analysis, however, does not make it explicit. It tacitly assumes that any such information would be supplied, in an informal way, by the intuition of the native speaker. But such an assumption is very much against the requirements of a linguistic science advocated in Chapter 3.

This argument would not be so important if it were an isolated instance; but of course it is not. We can make a very strong case indeed for saying that the whole of language is a network of mutually defining structural relationships – relationships between sounds, as we have seen, between morphemes, between words, and between sentences. Similar examples in grammar to the active/passive one would be the relationship between positive and negative sentences, between statements and questions, or, less obviously, between attributive and predicative adjectives (cf. *the good man* and *the man is good*). I have already talked in earlier sections about the view of language as a functional system. IC analysis takes very limited account of this, emphasizing almost wholly a concern to identify and classify constituents of sentences, and paying next to no attention to the *functions* of any given constituent, or class of constituents – or indeed of the sentences as wholes. And it is this emphasis which is perhaps the dominant feature of the post-Bloomfieldian grammatical scene – up until the mid fifties. It was felt (as Chapter 3 has pointed out, p. 121) that linguistics was essentially a means of providing procedures for segmenting and classifying utterances, on the basis of identifying partial formal similarities between them, and for plotting the distribution of these similarities in terms of structural sequences of various kinds. To establish the 'structure' of different types of utterance in this way, using the procedures of IC analysis, was considered an adequate goal for linguistics. The whole tenor of argument in the late 1950s was to show that this is not so; but from Bloomfield until Chomsky these ideas were on the whole unquestioned. The term 'structuralism' was often used, in fact, in a narrow sense to refer to the kind of emphases which characterized post-Bloomfieldian linguistics (in a broad sense, of course, *all* linguistics is structural). Ironically, in view of the time gap which inevitably separates research and pedagogy, this kind of structuralism is often still advocated as the latest thing, in some schools, 'structural' approaches to English in the classroom being commended, or 'structural' approaches to the teaching of foreign languages. For many people, linguistics and structuralism in language are the same thing – such has been the influence of the post-Bloomfieldians. The view is about fifty years out of date.

The other major feature of the post-Bloomfieldian period in linguistics arises out of the use of the term 'formal' above: there was no theoretical reliance on the idea of 'meaning' in making or formulating a grammatical analysis. Utterances were analysed and items classified on the basis of their formal properties – their physical shape, their observed distribution and structure. The meanings of the utterances, or of their component parts, were not given a systematic place in the investigation. This attitude had a very clear origin in the markedly behaviourist principles of Bloomfield in his book *Language*, where there was fairly inflexible adherence to the demands of empirical scientific method; he placed no reliance at all on the intuitions of the analyst or native speaker, and avoided like the plague any suggestion that the constructs of linguistic analysis had a psychological status. Meaning was felt to be an 'internal' phenomenon, a mental residue not susceptible to direct investigation – and only approached in terms of distinctive configurations of behavioural stimuli and responses. The lack of any precise tools for identifying, defining, classifying and interrelating meanings added to the avoidance of meaning in grammatical study. As a result, linguists of this period attempted to carry out their descriptions without any reference to the meaning of the utterances being described. Some tried to eliminate all mention of meaning from their accounts, considering it 'extra-linguistic' in character. Others, including Bloomfield himself, recognized and emphasized that one could never really exclude meaning from questions of linguistic analysis, but considered statements about meaning to be a later task of the linguist, dependent on the prior study of the formal characteristics of language in their own terms. In any case (it was argued), syntax was already complex enough to analyse properly without letting meanings in as well. It is this kind of reasoning which underlay many of the criticisms of traditional grammar (cf. p. 73), and which led scholars to set up noun (etc.) classes by defining them formally, in terms of their position in a sentence, their morphological characteristics, and so on, and leaving questions of their meaning (either as a class, or individually) until a later, and unspecified, stage of investigation.

The most important books which tried to develop these principles were written in the early fifties. Zellig Harris's *Methods in*

Structural Linguistics, published in 1951, was the most rigorous attempt to develop formal techniques of description based upon the physical properties and distribution of units. George Trager and Henry Lee Smith Jr. published (also in 1951) *An Outline of English Structure*, in which the various 'levels' of linguistic analysis outlined so far in this chapter were presented in a strict order – phonetics, phonology, morphology, syntax – and it was argued that each level had to be studied independently of any other, and that any analysis had to start with the phonetics end and work through the others in sequence in the order stated. Both of these books exerted a great influence on linguistic thinking in the fifties, as did Charles Carpenter Fries's *The Structure of English*, published in 1952, though this dealt solely with syntax. This book was the most systematic application of the structuralist approach to a language that had been attempted, and its importance lies both in its discussion of methodological and theoretical issues and in its detailed account of many aspects of English grammar in terms of the formal arrangement of items in structures. Any of these books would put flesh on structuralist ideas about language – as would any of the textbooks which began to multiply in the mid fifties, many of which were consciously concerned to develop the positions of Trager, Fries, and others. (And while mentioning the names of important books in this period, I ought to add a reference to Archibald Hill's *Introduction to English Structures*, published in 1958, which has the significant sub-title *From Sound to Sentence in English*, that reflects the structuralists' methodology clearly. H. A. Gleason Jr.'s *Introduction to Descriptive Linguistics*, published in 1961, and Charles F. Hockett's *Course in Modern Linguistics*, published in 1958, both transcend the limitations of the structuralist account of language in many important ways, but were influenced strongly by it, and present very clear accounts of it. Martin Joos's *Readings in Linguistics* (Volume I, published in 1958) collects many of the important articles written throughout this period.)

Here ends (with apologies) this bibliographical excursus. It goes without saying that there were many differences between the various so-called structuralists: the post-Bloomfieldian 'school' is by no means as homogeneous as the word 'school' implies. But the point about treating meaning as secondary in linguistic descriptions is fundamental in much that they said. And the critical point which has to be made, and which has been made, frequently, by the generative grammarians, is that meaning is far too important and central to language to be left out or subordinated in this way. Whatever else language is, it is *meaningful* activity. What distinguishes the sounds issuing from our mouths as language from mere noise is whether they 'carry a meaning' or not. To communicate meaning successfully is the main end of linguistic behaviour. To talk about linguistic analysis without reference to meaning, would be like describing the construction of ships without any reference to the sea. Even nouns and sentences (cf. p. 73) might usefully be defined on semantic as well as formal grounds, if the terms of the semantic definition could be made precise. And we have already seen how impossible it is to rule considerations of meaning out of even the most elementary of formal notions: how we group sounds into phonemes, or where we make the cut in IC analysis, and the whole basis of morphemic analysis presupposes the importance of meaning. It would seem both stubborn and naïve not to introduce it systematically into any analysis right from the beginning, therefore.

Further consideration of IC analysis, moreover, suggests more specific areas in which the need to consider meaning is paramount. I have already pointed to the necessity for grammars to take into account the meaning-relations which exist between types of sentence, in the active/passive example. Another, equally important thing that grammars have to do is take account of ambiguity in language. If we consider one of the examples which has now become a famous illustration of this point (it comes from Chomsky), the implications of this will be clear. In response to *The police were ordered to stop drinking about midnight*, we say 'Yes, this is ambiguous' (in four ways, no less – Was the drinking taking place at midnight, or the ordering? And who was drinking, anyway? The police, or someone else?). Perceiving an ambiguity is becoming aware that any given utterance has more than one interpretation, or meaning. The means whereby we become aware of this may simply reflect the use of an ambiguous word, or an ambiguous intonation; but just as often (as in this example), it is due to the grammatical structure of the utterance being ambiguous. We can clarify the above ambiguities only by relating the different possible senses to other structures which are similar in meaning but which are unambiguous – for example, *At midnight the police were ordered to stop drinking* (which selects the interpretation that the ordering was taking place at midnight) or *The police were ordered to stop them drinking at midnight* (which eliminates the possibility that they were drinking themselves). There are many ways in which this might be done. The point is that the possibilities for doing this make use of grammatical operations, e.g. altering the position of the adverbial phrase *at midnight* in the first example, inserting a personal pronoun at a specific point in the second. Now we are constantly 'disambiguating' (as it is sometimes massively put) sentences all the time when we use and listen to language; so much so that any grammatical theory must have as one of its primary goals the means of accounting for this facility. Meaning and grammatical analysis, on this account, turn out to be two sides of the same coin.

In IC analysis, however, such disambiguation was impossible: an IC diagram either presented one meaning of a sentence only, and ignored the others; or it left us with a sentence analysis which was still ambiguous. Another of Chomsky's famous examples illustrates this last point more clearly. He takes the two sentences *John is eager to please* and *John is easy to please*, and points out that in traditional constituent terms, both sentences would get the same analysis. 'On the surface' (to introduce the metaphor most widely used in this connection) they have the same structure. But 'underneath' we all know, if we think about it for a moment, that the word *John* has two very different roles to play in the two sentences. In the first sentence he is the person who is doing the pleasing; in the second sentence, he is the person who is being pleased. Putting it in grammatical terms, *John* is the underlying 'subject' of the first sentence, and the underlying 'object' of the second. Here too, then, we can see how a traditional linguistic account of the 'surface grammar', in terms of the classification and distribution of morphemes in the sentence, would get nowhere near explaining a fundamental distinction of this kind. A concept of 'deep grammar' has to be invoked. For this reason, if none other, structuralist accounts of language would have to be drastically revised. We must now turn to some of the proposed revisions.

V 'Deep' Syntax

Before Chomsky, there had been a number of critical reactions to aspects of the structuralist approach of the post-Bloomfieldians, and these tend to be overshadowed by the contemporary concentration on generative grammar. Kenneth Pike, for example, pointed to the impossibility and undesirability of keeping the different levels of linguistic analysis as distinct as people like Trager wished. Many points such as this came to be discussed in the early fifties. Chomsky's analysis is perhaps the most comprehensive alternative proposed to structuralism, but it is by no means the only attempt to develop a more powerful explanation of linguistic structure. Pike himself was responsible for a fresh theory of language which tried to get away from the over-concentration of the Bloomfieldians on classification and distribution at the expense of function. In his *tagmemic* theory – 'tagmemics', as it is usually called – he develops the notion of the *tagmeme*, a term Bloomfield had used. The tagmeme is a Janus-faced construct: it tries to combine into one conceptual unit two ideas which had previously been quite disassociated, the ideas of class and function. When you analyse a sentence in Pike's terms, you do not end up with two independent statements, one telling you what the bits of a sentence are and the classes they belong to, the other telling you the functions they perform (such as would be illustrated by the analysis of the sentence *John kicked the ball* as 'Noun phrase + Verb + Noun phrase' and 'Subject + Predicator + Object' respectively). Rather the sentence is analysed into a sequence of tagmemes, each of which *simultaneously* provides information about an item's function in a larger structure, and about the class to which it belongs that could also fulfil that function. A metaphor that is regularly used here is to talk of a structure as a series of 'slots' into which various types of 'filler' can go: extending the above example, the Subject slot can be filled by a Noun phrase, a pronoun, a Verb phrase (as in *To err is human*), and so on. The working out of a comprehensive tagmemic theory, so as to integrate lexical, grammatical and phonological kinds of information, is something which has exercised the minds of Pike and his associates for some time – the idea having been first developed in the early fifties. To do this, Pike makes extensive use of a presentation of information in terms of *matrices* – that is, he establishes a network of intersecting dimensions, and plots significant points within it, thus expressing both structural and functional information simultaneously. Its full application is explained in Pike's massive *Language in Relation to a Unified Theory of the Structure of Human Behavior*, which had a preliminary edition in 1954. This 'unified' view makes extensive use of a model derived from physics, in which language is viewed as a complex of relationships of 'particle' (covering phonemic and morphemic systems, for instance), 'wave' (referring to the dynamic way in which these systems merge and overlap), and 'field' (referring to the functional role of language in relation to personality and culture). It is a theory which has been primarily used in the description of languages of Central and South America and West Africa – in particular in those areas in which the missionary activities of the Summer Institute of Linguistics (of which Pike was the founder) have been most noticeable.

A very similar theory in some respects, which also departed in many ways from structuralist approaches, is that associated primarily with the British Linguist Michael Halliday. This has developed considerably from its earliest formulation, when it was known as *scale and category* grammar, in the early sixties. The reason for the labels 'scale' and 'category' is that they refer to the two basic ideas underlying the theory: it was felt that the best way of accounting for language's structure was by postulating four major theoretical categories, and relating them via various scales of abstraction. A rough idea of what is involved (no more is needed in this book) can be had by illustrating the main constructs used. The categories comprised *class* (covering concepts such as 'verb' and 'noun'), *unit* (covering concepts such as 'sentence' and 'clause'), *structure* (covering concepts such as 'subject' and 'predicate'), and *system* (covering such concepts as the set of 'personal pronouns' or 'tenses'). Scales were the model's constructs which related these categories, and the linguistic features subsumed under them, to each other. For example, one scale was the means of relating the 'units'. The various units recognized (sentence, clause, group, word, and morpheme) were considered to be arranged hierarchically on a *rank* scale, and each unit was conceived of as consisting of one or more of the units below it – a sentence was considered as consisting of one or more clauses, a clause as consisting of one or more groups, a group of one or more words, and a word as one or more morphemes. Thus the utterance *The girl will kick the ball* would be analysed as one sentence, consisting of one clause, which consists of three groups (*the girl, will kick, the ball* – Halliday uses 'group' where most other linguists would talk of 'phrases'), each group consisting of two words, and each word consisting of one morpheme. Other scales would relate other observations about linguistic structure.

An account of the earlier model, outlined here, is to be found in the book by Halliday, Angus McIntosh and Peter Strevens called *The Linguistic Sciences and Language Teaching*, published in 1964. More recently, Halliday has developed out of this a concept of *systemic* grammar, and this would now be considered a quite distinct model. As its title suggests, it is based on the idea of system, which was a category of the early approach. This idea suggests that at any given place in a structure, the language allows for a choice among a small, fixed set of possibilities (we can have *the/this/my/a ... man*, for instance); and it is very similar to the Saussurean concept of paradigmatic relationships mentioned on p. 162. Language is viewed as a series of 'system networks', each network representing the choices associated with a given type of constituent (e.g. clause system network, nominal group (*sc.* noun phrase) system network, and so on); and in this approach, it is the clause system which is taken as the point of departure in analysis, not (as in most other models) the sentence. It is not important (for this book) to follow the details of this outline, or to remember the terminology: any of this may alter, as the approach is still developing. What *is* important to note is that this approach, like Pike's, tries very hard to integrate information about structure with information about classification in a single model. In the hierarchy of units, for instance, each unit has a particular structure and belongs to a particular class, and thus has a range of functions. As such, there is an important development here from previous grammatical approaches of the constituent analysis type.

Sydney Lamb's *stratificational* grammar is a third development which is appropriately mentioned at this point. In origin, it synthesizes various features of post-Bloomfieldian structuralism with features of another early theory known as *glossematics* (see p. 253). The theory is called 'stratificational' because one of its chief features is its model of linguistic structure in terms of several structural layers, or *strata*. (Halliday talked of 'levels' of structure here.) Language for Lamb – as for Halliday – is best viewed as a system of complex relationships which relates sounds (or, of course, their written counterparts) to meanings. These relationships are not all of the same kind, however, but break down into more restricted sub-systems, each of which has its own structural organization; one sub-system operates at each stratum. There are three main strata hypothesized for all languages, 'semology', 'grammar' and 'phonology'; and these are subdivided in various ways to produce further systems. The complexity of linguistic relationships is said to be due to the different structural patterns exhibited by sounds, on the one hand, and meanings, on the other – there is no clear one-for-one relationship between the two. The various strata are viewed as in a hierarchy, the structure of each stratum being represented explicitly in any adjacent stratum by means of a small set of basic relationships; and Lamb has developed a notation and method of diagrammatic presentation to try to represent these relationships adequately. The details are presented in Lamb's book, *Outline of Stratificational Grammar*, published in 1966.

At this point it is perhaps appropriate to stop and draw breath. An account of three linguistic theories in as many pages is a heavy burden to assimilate. It is not of course important, as I have said, to follow the proposals of each theory or remember all the terminology. I doubt whether there is any linguist alive capable of giving a detailed account of all three – or four, if generative grammar be included – and the complex terminology involved is alone a major deterrent to any amateur linguistic investigator. This is not by any means a problem unique to linguistics, of course. It is generally the case that a scholar, from whatever field, will have been brought up in a single intellectual stable, will tend to prefer to use some particular theory as a starting-point in day-to-day investigation, and will tend to be in closer contact with colleagues sharing the same theoretical background. Linguistics has developed its 'schools' of analysis, as any other subject, mostly geographically based on the centre where its leading proponent works (the Massachusetts Institute of Technology for generative grammar, for example – indeed, generative grammar is often referred to loosely as 'M.I.T. Linguistics', and there was a fashion a few years ago to refer to young exponents of that approach as 'mitniks'). On the other hand, it is important for linguists – as for the subject as a whole – to break out of their theoretical isolation, and to learn something of the competing claims of other theories than their own. Such awareness can be both a guard against group complacency as well as a sharp stimulus to the development of one's own ideas. And it is essential for an introductory book to broaden its scope as much as possible, as so much of everyday linguistic chit-chat and polemic is the product of the conflicting principles and practice of these various theories.

All three of the theories outlined above have attracted a great deal of interest, though they are less in the public eye than generative grammar. All three are theories of language as a whole, and not just of syntax; but they have a place at this point in the book, for it is impossible to understand their syntactic claims without reference to their overall approach. They have also a great deal in common, both terminologically and conceptually, particularly when viewed against the background of generative grammar. It is important to adopt this perspective, in fact, when studying them – at least for a few moments – as a considerable amount of criticism has been made of them by Chomsky and others, and the criticisms themselves have attracted as much attention as the original theories. The criticisms have largely been that such theories are inadequate to explain the complexity of linguistic structure, and that a generative model is more powerful. Chomsky calls such theories *taxonomic* (he uses the term pejoratively), and indeed says that his own approach was developed partly as a specific alternative to taxonomic approaches to syntax. What does he mean by 'taxonomic' here? The general sense of this word refers to any investigation which is motivated by a primary concern to systematically identify, classify and name types of phenomena within a subject-field. The clearest example of a taxonomy is in the biological classification of plants and animals on the basis of their presumed natural relationships. 'An X is a kind of Y' is the sort of statement produced by this approach. Chomsky's use of the term is narrower than this. He defines taxonomic syntactic theory as the view that a representation of a sentence in terms of surface structure only is all that is necessary for a syntactic analysis – in other words, this is an analysis of a sentence in terms of the temporal sequence of its elements and their category names, to produce the labelled bracketing of the type illustrated on p. 199. Putting this another way, Chomsky is saying that such approaches fail to distinguish surface structure from underlying, or deep structures of meaning; and as the latter is an essential and basic feature of linguistic structure (as the examples of the type *John is eager to please* argue), such failure is tantamount to denying the validity of any such theory as a whole. Only transformational-generative grammar, he claims, incorporates the fundamental insight about deep structure, in addition to being able to handle surface structural relationships as well.

It is a matter of some interest whether these early criticisms of Chomsky's were totally justified, in relation to the grammars he cited at that time. Certainly these days it would be unfair, and rather naïve, to label any of the above grammars taxonomic, and expect people to understand what you mean. There are many differences between the various theories all labelled taxonomic; and these days the original grounds of Chomsky's criticisms do not in many cases apply, recent developments having tried to take account of them. Halliday's systemic grammar, for instance, operates with a concept of 'depth' in grammatical analysis which is similar to Chomsky's in many respects. It still retains much of the emphasis on classification which prompted the original criticism, but it is by no means solely a taxonomic model now. It is a difficult matter to determine just how much of any such recent modifications has been original, and how much due to Chomsky's own influence; and perhaps such questions cannot be decided. The cautionary point is not to be fooled by the suggestion that the dichotomy between generative and taxonomic is inevitably an opposition of theoretical significance.

It is easy to see from the various matters raised so far in this chapter how peculiarly complex Noam Chomsky's contribution to linguistics has been. His name has occurred on many pages here and in Chapter 3, and this reflects very well the all-embracing character of his specific proposals, developed under the heading of transformational-generative (TG) grammar. Recently, the more general psychological and philosophical implications and pre-suppositions of his approach have been in the forefront of discussion. What must not be forgotten is that Chomsky's original work was purely within linguistics, and that the detailed and technical proposals in *Syntactic Structures*, published in 1957, were primarily a positive reaction to the grammatical and general linguistic predispositions of the preceding decades – in particular, to the post-Bloomfieldian and 'taxonomic' accounts of language. His early work, then, falls into two related parts: his criticisms of available linguistic approaches, and his own formulation of linguistic theory.

Many of his criticisms have been discussed already in the course of this book. His opposition to linguistic analysis based solely on a corpus, and to the idea that the task of a grammar is to account for linguistic performance only, was discussed in Chapter 3, and would nowadays receive general agreement. His views on linguistic competence, while more debatable (see p. 103), were novel and essential. His related view of language as a creative, dynamic force, capable of making infinite use of finite means, was both opportune and productive; and this too I have already had occasion to refer to. Also discussed in Chapter 3 is the need for linguistics to be as clear as possible about its goals; to be clear about what it can and should achieve. It is to Chomsky that we owe this salutary emphasis on goals and levels of achievement (he talks more specifically in terms of types of 'adequacy'), even if, as is the case, there is considerable disagreement over the nature and feasibility of these goals, as he formulates them.

Syntax, for Chomsky, is the core of a language, its organizing principle (the metaphors are endless). (This emphasis has a number of side-effects, and one of these needs to be mentioned before we go any further, as it sometimes confuses people approaching the study of TG grammar for the first time. This is that the term 'grammar' is being used here in an all-embracing sense, covering the subject-matter of phonology and semantics as well as morphology and syntax, as we shall see below. My own usage, in this book, has been the more restricted one [grammar = morphology and syntax]; but in what follows it will be necessary to use the term in its wider sense. Once the point is recognized, it generally does not cause any difficulty.) There is far more to Chomskyan syntax than an accumulation of descriptive insights about the structural principles and usage of different languages, however. What is primary is the precision and explicitness with which he *formalized*, using mathematical concepts, the properties of alternative systems of grammatical description. One of the problems over making specific evaluations of different grammars is that the metalanguage is different in each case, the criteria varyingly explicit, and the assumptions, in various degrees, unstated. It is impossible to promote clear thinking about different kinds of grammar unless some attempt is made to formulate their properties in terms of an independent yardstick – and clearly, the yardsticks which look most promising are those provided by mathematics. There has been some scepticism of late as to whether mathematical models of language can be so generally applicable and illuminating as was originally implied. It has been argued that there is so much indeterminacy and amorphousness in natural language that it is unlikely that anything other than a very restricted area will be susceptible to formalization in mathematical terms. This may well be. But the gains from getting into a mathematical state of mind have been so great as to make the problems of limitations secondary. And when Chomsky first looked at language in this way, it was clear that here was a tool for the development of linguistic conceptualizing that should not readily be foregone. His discussion of different grammatical models, then, ranging from the extremely simple ('finite-state grammars') to the more complex ('transformational') kinds, which can be found in *Syntactic Structures*, is essential reading for anyone wishing to take their knowledge of linguistics below iceberg-tip level.

I do not propose to present an account of T G grammar in detail, as it is now too vast a subject. General introductions are available in F. R. Palmer's *Grammar* (2nd edn. 1984) and (more technically) in R. Huddleston's *An Introduction to English Transformational Syntax* (1976). There is also a beautifully succinct account of the basis and background of the more important claims in John Lyons's book, *Chomsky* (second edition, 1977). But no introduction to linguistics would be complete, nor would it be possible to understand recent trends, without reference to the salient characteristics of this approach.

The obvious beginning point is to understand what, in this account, is conceived to be the purpose of a grammar. An early definition talks of a grammar as a *device which generates all and only the grammatical sentences of a language.* There are a number of terms here which need explanation. Firstly, this approach is firmly orientated towards the sentence. Concepts such as 'clause' and 'utterance', if it were felt useful to distinguish them, would be obtainable only derivatively, in relation to the prior notion of sentence. Secondly, and more importantly, the definition emphasizes that only the *grammatical* sentences of a language are to be explained in the grammar – that is, sentences which we intuitively accept as being well-formed. A grammar in this sense does not concern itself with the structure of ungrammatical sentences. This may seem to be stating the obvious, but it is not. It would, after all, be perfectly possible to write a grammar which would tell us what all the grammatical sentences of a language were, but which would in so doing tell us about a number of ungrammatical ones as well. If the grammar is to be absolutely explicit (that is, if it is to leave nothing to chance, nothing to be 'filled in' by the intuitions of the native speaker), it must tell us when a sentence is grammatical and when it is not. A boundary-line has to be drawn somewhere; and the task of a grammar is to define one. It is of course possible in principle for a grammar, once it has made the distinction between grammatical and ungrammatical sentences clear, to give explicit information about the structure of ungrammatical sentences (or at least some types of them, such as those 'deviant' sentences which occur in poetry) – and there has been some controversy over the extent to which this is desirable. But the above definition rules out such extensions by the use of the phrase *and only*.

Making a distinction between grammatical and ungrammatical does not of course mean that we can always tell with certainty what an ungrammatical sentence is. Sometimes the ungrammaticality of a sentence is unclear. There may be differences in usage, or stylistic nuances, such as those mentioned in Chapter 2 (p. 65), which would make some people consider one sentence as grammatical, others as ungrammatical. Sometimes we may not be sure ourselves about our own reaction to the grammaticality of a sentence, as we have already seen (p. 134). A sentence such as *It was the city which the army arrived in front of* would regularly produce divergent opinions on the point. The existence of such problems, however, does not make the theoretical distinction between grammatical and ungrammatical useless. On the contrary, the only way in which we can decide what to do with such problem sentences at all is by reference to the norms, or rules, dictated by the grammar. If the grammar makes quite explicit what it considers to be grammatical, then we may not agree, and we may wish to extend its rules to cover other cases, but at least we know where we are and can evaluate its claims accordingly. As Chomsky puts it, as long as the theory covers the clear cases (i.e. the sentences about whose grammaticality there is no doubt), then it can be used to decide the status of the unclear cases. Of course, a grammar which defined too few sentences as grammatical (i.e. left out too much which our intuitions would want to include) would be – speaking absolutely, for a moment – a bad grammar. This was one of the grounds on which objections to traditional grammar was based (cf. pp. 57, ff.): it defined as ungrammatical sentences which were generally felt not to be so. (In passing, I should point out, in case the similar terminology misleads, that the 'rules' which it is the aim of generative grammar to formulate are not the same as the 'rules' of traditional grammar, which I was so critical of in Chapter 2. The latter were prescriptive rules, criticized because they were prescriptions for actual usage which were unrealistic. Generative rules are not prescriptions about usage, nor are they descriptions of actual speech events: they are formulations which attempt to present the structure of a sentence in an *abstract* way, and as such are independent of any considerations of correctness in usage which may arise.)

The third point which arises out of the definition is in connection with the word *all*. As we have seen (p. 102), it is an important principle of this approach that a grammar should be able to explain not only the sentences used in any given corpus of data, but should be able to account equally well for all possible (grammatical) sentences in a language. It is assumed that the number of sentences which any grammar has in principle to account for is infinite. On the other hand, it is clear that the rules which constitute the grammar of a language must be finite – for otherwise they would be unlearnable. What has to be done is to relate the finite system of rules to the infinite set of possibilities by 'projecting' (as the term is) the former on to the latter. The most important way in which this is done is through the notion of *recursion*: some of the rules which produce sentences are capable of being used more than once in developing a particular sentence. The adjective-sequence example in the Interlude (p. 127, ff.) is an instance of a recursive rule: there is in principle no limit to the number of adjectives which may appear between the article and the noun in English. There are limitations in practice, of course (in performance, as Chomsky would say) – for example, of memory, of subject-matter, of breath; but presented with a sentence containing *n* adjectives, it is always possible to 'apply the same adjective-inserting rule again', so to say, and construct a sentence containing *n* + 1 adjectives, arguing that it is just as grammatical as the one before. Some varieties of English, in fact, make use of this property of grammar to a quite remarkable degree, as in the advertisement, *Why do you think we make Nuttall's Mintoes such a devilishly smooth cool creamy minty chewy round slow velvety fresh clean solid buttery taste?* And it is easy to see that much of the creative and dynamic potential of language is due to the flexibility we have in varying the extent to which we make use of recursive rules in our grammar.

Having said these things, I have in the process said a great deal about the most important term in the definition of grammar, the term which is used as the identifying label for this kind of approach to language as a whole, namely 'generative'. So far, I have talked about a grammar 'producing' or 'developing' or 'explaining' the structure of sentences. 'Generating' is the precise term which is used to state this function. It summarizes the two main properties of a grammar: its ability to account by its rules for the infinite sentences of a language (i.e. define them as grammatical) and its ability to be absolutely explicit about the grammaticality of sentences by precisely defining the characteristics of their internal structure. The term 'generate' itself comes from mathematics, as do many other terms Chomsky uses in his explanation of the properties and purpose of a grammar. The use of the term 'device' in the above definition is another example. These terms have struck students of language as very odd, as until recently few such students ever had any contact at all with the branches of mathematics involved which used them. What must be guarded against, of course, is the literal interpretation of these terms. To talk of a grammar as a 'device' or a 'machine' is not to imply that the best way of seeing grammar is as a piece of mechanical hardware which somehow mirrors the internal state of a speaker of a language. Rather, 'device' is a totally abstract concept, referring to the theoretical properties of any given system, not its physical manifestations.

Much of what I have been saying would be accepted by linguists, whether they called themselves generative grammarians or not. It refers to questions of general linguistic theory, which can and should be discussed independently of any particular model of syntax, phonology, etc. that one might personally advocate. And here we come to an important conceptual distinction, which the metaphor of 'schools' of thought in linguistics has quite obscured. I am sometimes asked, for instance, whether I am a generative grammarian, whether 'I follow Chomsky', and the like. The trouble is, there is no straight answer to such a question. It would be impossible *not* to follow Chomsky on many of the fundamental theoretical issues he raises. It is certainly impossible for a linguist these days to avoid being influenced by him. Even if one holds views which are in some respects radically opposed to generative grammar, one still has to take account of the generative position and argue a case partly in its terms – if only to avoid the charge of 'side-stepping the relevant issues'. But agreeing with some of the basic tenets of generative grammar would not be enough to qualify one as being a generative grammarian. It is quite possible to believe, with Chomsky, that a grammar is a device which should generate sentences, and so on; but it is also possible to disagree at the same time as to *how* this might best be done. Many linguists are in this position. They accept many of the general claims, but dispute the specific properties of the various models which Chomsky has proposed.

This last phrase, 'various models', leads me to another point. Chomsky's approach has, quite naturally, altered over the years. What people usually point to is the difference between his 1957 publication, *Syntactic Structures*, and his 1965 publication, *Aspects of the Theory of Syntax* (referred to in the trade as *Aspects*, for short). There are many differences between the two accounts, and we have to be very clear about which stages of Chomsky's thinking we are referring to in any discussion. The distinction between competence and performance raised in Chapter 3, for example, is not to be found in *Syntactic Structures*, except perhaps implicitly. But it is stated as a guiding principle of *Aspects*, where the generative rules are explicitly identified with competence, and the generally mentalistic character of the approach becomes a more dominant feature. There are also many differences of a detailed, technical nature, which it is not possible to go into here, but which it is essential to be aware of in order to appreciate the full implications of Chomsky's proposals. What I shall do now, however, is draw attention to some of the main changes in the general model between the two books, for this progression of ideas and change in emphasis is essential to an understanding of more recent work in linguistic theory.

It will be recalled that one of the criticisms made of IC analysis and related techniques was their inability and lack of desire to deal with the problem of meaning. Chomsky's examples suggested very clearly that any grammatical analysis would have to be carried on at two levels, one of which would talk about the superficial or apparent structure of sentences, the other about the sentence's underlying structure. Thus the pair of sentences *John is eager/easy to please* would have identical 'surface' structures, but different 'deep' structures. This distinction between surface and deep syntax became a major dichotomy as work in generative grammar progressed, and for many people it is the main difference between the old and the new approaches to syntax – which is why I have adopted it in my section headings above. To begin with, however, it was only implicit in the model of grammar that Chomsky proposed in *Syntactic Structures*. The first 'component' of this grammar is in many respects a familiar one (to people familiar with the earlier history of linguistics): Chomsky adopts an IC analysis to provide information about the constituent structure of sentences. The difference with the earlier technique, though, is that he does not just draw a diagram to illustrate the structures involved; he formalizes the analytic divisions into a system of ordered rules. This he refers to as a *phrase structure grammar*. For example, instead of analysing the sentence *The boy saw the girl* as

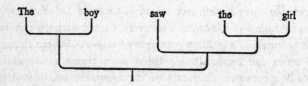

in which the order of decisions which produced the analysis is not explicit (where was the second cut made?), and the relationship between the various cutting points is unclear, Chomsky develops a notation which both orders the analytical decisions and formally relates them to each other by *deriving* each decision from some previous one. A simplified example, similar to the one used by Chomsky in *Syntactic Structures*, is as follows:

```
Sentence (S) → Noun phrase (NP) + Verb phrase (VP)
VP          → Verb + NP
NP          → T + Noun (N)
T           → the ...
N           → boy, girl ...
V           → saw ...
```

Here, the first rule takes as a primitive the concept of sentence and makes an initial statement about its internal structure. The arrow is an 'instruction' to replace (or 'rewrite') the element on the left into the 'string' of elements on the right. We are told, at the end of the first rule, in other words, that sentences in language basically consist of two elements, noun phrases and verb phrases. We have not yet, however, been told what noun phrases and verb phrases are, and so the next rules make these concepts more explicit. The verb phrase consists of two elements, a verb and a noun phrase. So this means, referring back to the first rule, that our underlying sentence now consists of three basic elements, namely NP + V + NP. The third rule adds more information about what a NP can be analysed into, namely, a 'determiner' or 'article', here labelled simply as T, to avoid having to choose, and a noun. Our underlying sentence now has the form T + N + V + T + N. And this is as far as the abstract side of our classification of sentence elements goes. The remaining rules translate these abstract elements into more concrete vocabulary items. In this absurdly simple grammar, the only T element there is *the*, only two nouns are given and only one verb. Replacing each element in the string T + N + V + T + N by one of these, we can get *The boy saw the girl* or *The girl saw the boy*. Both are possible English sentences, and thus the grammar has some generative capacity – though not very much! By increasing the number of vocabulary items in the last three rules, we of course increase the number of sentences these rules can generate quite a lot. Adding *woman* and *asked*, we can now get *The boy saw the woman, The woman asked the girl*, and many others. Other rules would now be added to account for the complexity of noun and verb phrase that the above example omitted to mention. There would have to be rules to introduce adjectives, auxiliary verbs, pronouns, and many other things. And such rules have, of course, been introduced and argued about in more extensive grammars since.

This was the first component of a generative grammar, as conceptualized in *Syntactic Structures*. It consisted of rules which took an initial element (S, standing for any sentence) and assigned to it a particular phrase structure; these rules would then produce strings of elements which represented the underlying structure of a sentence (a 'kernel' sentence). The second component consisted of *transformational* rules – rules which operated on the strings produced by the phrase structure component, and altered them in various ways (e.g. by turning 'active' strings into 'passive' ones, by altering word order, by adding inflections, and so on), making the various relationships between different types of sentence explicit. The passive transformation, for example, altered the order of elements in the active sentence and added three further elements (a form of the verb *be*, in the appropriate tense; a particle, *by*, to indicate the agent following; and a past participial affix, symbolized as *en*, attached to the main verb, V). One formulation of this rule could be as follows: $NP_1 + Aux + V + NP_2 \rightarrow NP_2 + Aux + be + en + V + by + NP_1$. NP_1 stands for the first noun phrase in an active sentence: NP_2 for the second. Aux stands for auxiliary verb. The rules says in effect: 'to form a passive sentence, reverse the positions of NP_1 and NP_2, and introduce the verb *be* in one of its forms, a past participial affix, and a particle *by* between V and the NP_1'. (Exactly which form of *be* is required, and how the affix gets transferred from its place in front of the verb to its place at the end of the verb, would be the subject-matter of later rules in the grammar.) As it stands, however, this rule goes a long way towards formally relating such sentences as *The boy will kick the ball* and *The ball will be kicked by the boy*. The way in which these transformations were understood and formalized was a major contribution to linguistics – ironically it is one which I have to skip over almost in silence here, but it is impossible to explain the transformational component of a generative grammar fairly and accurately except at length. The third and final component of this grammar consisted of a set of *morphophonemic* rules (cf. p. 196), which converted the string of words and morphemes produced into a string of phonological units – in other words, told you how the sentence as a whole was to be pronounced. We can diagram this model as follows:

Initial element (S)
↓
Phrase structure component
↓
Transformational component
↓
Morphophonemic component
↓
Phonological representation of sentence

In *Aspects*, the components of the grammar alter in number, status and name. The main reason for this was the increased role that the meaning of sentences had come to have in Chomsky's thinking. In *Syntactic Structures*, semantic considerations were not felt to be directly relevant to syntactic description: syntax was to be described independently of, and prior to, the actual meaning of the structures in the language. In this respect, the book faithfully reflected post-Bloomfieldian priorities. But it quickly came to be realized, in the light of such examples as on p. 208, that it was not possible to grant meaning its due recognition in a half-hearted way. Meaning could not be allowed in 'through the back door of the grammar', as it were: it was an integral part of grammatical analysis. After all, it might be argued, if we are paying more than lip-service to the notion that language is, above all, meaningful activity, then this priority should be reflected in the model used for the analysis of language. In this way, we obtain a new model, in which syntax is seen as a system of rules which relates sounds to meanings, as follows:

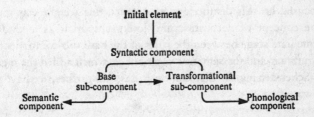

The syntactic component consists of two sub-components, the base sub-component and the transformational sub-component. The base corresponds to the earlier phrase structure component, though it is rather different in character: its function is to generate the underlying representations of sentences, which is what provides the deep-structural information. These deep structures are then interpreted in two ways: they are converted into pronounceable strings, via the transformational sub-component and the phonological component; and their meaning is specified, via the semantic component. Putting this simply, the syntax gives you information about the structure of a sentence; the transformations and the phonology tell you how to pronounce it; and the semantics tells you what it means. The phonological and semantic components are sometimes called 'interpretative', accordingly, because they 'interpret' the output of the central, syntactic component into meaningful, pronounceable utterance. Grammar, on this account, is the relationship between sounds and meaning: this is the fundamental insight of the model – it is of course a very old insight, but its formalization is new and illuminating.

Since *Aspects*, generative grammar has continued to develop, and several other models of the theory have been proposed. To see the way in which these models relate to each other requires a more detailed and technical investigation than it is possible to enter into here (see further, F. R. Palmer's *Grammar* (2nd edn. 1984)). But some general remarks will indicate the direction of recent thinking. Most of the developments have arisen from a further consideration of the relationship between grammar and meaning (see p. 231), and one of the first alternatives to the *Aspects* model (the 'Standard' Theory, as Chomsky came to call it) focused on this distinction. In *Aspects*, due weight was given to the concept of deep structure, looking upon it as a kind of intermediate stage between the rules of the base sub-component of the grammar and the semantic component, which added the meanings. Schematizing the diagram on p. 225 still further, we have the following:

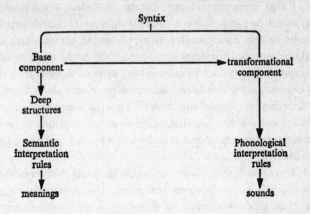

Several changes have occurred in the conceptualizing of this model since this time, and both involve considerations of the status and boundaries of semantics in relation to the rest of linguistic theory. One arose in the suggestions of such generative linguists as James McCawley, who pointed to the 'extra level' of structure posited on the left side of the diagram. No one, he argues, would want to do without the base, transformational, semantic and phonological components in some shape or form. But surely the need to posit a separate level of deep structure is unnecessary? Why should not a grammar consist of a base component which goes directly to the semantics, as follows?

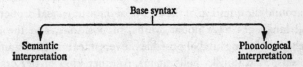

If the whole point about talking about deep structures at all in the first place was to take account of meaning, and the structural ambiguity problems arising therefrom, then why should not these 'meaning-problems' be incorporated as part of the study of other meaning-problems which the semantics component has to face anyway? McCawley, in a 1968 paper, alludes to the generative argument in connection with the phoneme (cf. p. 178). There it is argued that there is no need for the phoneme, if phonological analysis can be carried on successfully without it, and the structural patterns in the data handled without setting up an extra level. Similarly, no need for deep structure ... What he suggests is that the traditional approach to syntax, both by generative grammarians and others, and which leaves semantic problems until 'later', has led linguists to ignore the overall view of linguistic structure, and thus not ask the question, without preconceptions, whether a twofold splitting up of the area between syntax and semantics is justifiable.

This proposal was taken up enthusiastically by a number of scholars, and its implications still attract discussion. At the same time, close study of the nature of deep structural information was leading to attack on another front. A point which I did not make clear in my earlier discussion of Chomsky's approach concerns the status of the deep structures posited by the grammar. It was in fact claimed that the underlying and irreducible propositions into which a sentence could be analysed, and which constituted its deep structure, were *universal* in character. This concept, of linguistic universals, is very important in generative theory. We must remember that Chomsky's view of linguistic theory (and one which most linguists share) is seeing it as 'an hypothesis about linguistic universals' – in other words, the job of linguistics is to establish the universal design-characteristics which define human languages. And much of the discussion in linguistics over recent years has been around the question of the nature of these universal properties. Do all languages have nouns, verbs, prepositions, and the like? These would be one kind of possible universal feature ('substantive' universals, as Chomsky calls them). Another kind of universal is illustrated by the question as to whether the base component of a grammar, in the sense outlined above, is universal, and if so what its properties are (this would be a 'formal' universal). In particular, it is asked, What kind of categories should be introduced into the deep structures generated by the base component, and how far are *these* universal?

An early radical suggestion about the nature of the base component of a grammar was made by Charles Fillmore, in a theory of transformational grammar which he called *case* grammar. The extent to which his modifications were fundamental is a source of some dispute: some proponents of case grammar called it a fresh theory, embodying a whole new set of insights; others, such as Chomsky himself, suggested that Fillmore's proposals (and other proposals of a similar nature) were little more than notational variations of the generative theory as presented in *Aspects*. The issue is of some importance. By 'case', Fillmore did not mean the inflectional variations in nouns, which is the traditional sense of the term. Rather he was referring to a set of concepts which identify types of judgements which human beings are capable of making about the events going on around them (who did something, who did it happen to, what got changed, where did it happen, and so on). For example, in the sentences which follow, it is intuitively obvious that basically the same meaning is being expressed in each sentence, but that the surface-structure relations are extremely variable. (I have extended Fillmore's examples a little.)

(a) *John opened the door with the key.*
(b) *The key opened the door.*
(c) *The door opened.*
(d) *John used the key to open the door.*
(e) *It was the key that opened the door.*
(f) *It was John who opened the door with the key.*

In (a)–(c), *the key, John*, and *the door* are all surface subjects of the verb *open*; but their deep relationship to the verb is by no means the same in each sentence. In (a), the subject position is occupied by the 'agent', or 'actor', *John*; in (b), it is occupied by the 'instrument' whereby the action was performed, *the key*; and in (c), it is occupied by the 'goal' of the action, the 'thing which was opened', namely, *the door*. Putting this another way, the function of the underlying meanings in relation to the verb does not change from sentence to sentence, despite the surface differences; and it is this fundamental, semantic identity which is the important thing to recognize about these sentences, and the central fact which a system of grammatical analysis should explain. It is always the key which is opening the door, and never the door which is opening the key, for instance. It is always John who is performing the action (whenever he is mentioned). And so on. The phrase containing *key*, that is to say, has the same underlying function in each sentence – Fillmore would call it an 'instrumental' function – despite the variant surface realizations this notion has (in sentence (b) it is 'subject', in (d) it is 'object', in (e) it is 'complement', in (a) it is in an adverbial phrase). In the same way, one could argue that *John* was 'agentive' in each sentence in which it occurred. These 'meaning-relations', of agentive, instrumental, and the like, are what Fillmore called his *cases*, and he hypothesized that they constitute a universal system in deep structure. (He specified six cases in all in his early paper, but their number increased in the work of others using his system, and the number of cases that might be established is a matter of dispute.) In other words, the sentences of all languages, it is argued, can be reduced to a set of propositions, the main features of which would be a configuration of cases around a verb. Moreover, the sequence of these cases in relation to the verb and to each other, as realized in the surface structure, is not relevant to their description. For example, in English, the agentive characteristically comes before the verb, whereas in Welsh it comes afterwards (cf. *Mae Sion yn* . . . and *John is* . . .); but it is the *same* underlying case in both languages. The suggestion that cases have no ordering corresponding to the order of elements in surface structure was one major difference between Fillmore's proposals and most other suggestions about the nature of deep grammar. But there is a second implication, namely, that the meaning-relations specified by the cases are somehow 'deeper' than the categories normally established in deep grammar – that is, they seem to be constructs more of a *semantic* (or perhaps even of a logical) nature than of a syntactic type. In other words, the form of a grammar has now become one in which semantic information is considered prior to the syntatic, as the following diagram shows. Meanings (that is, semantic representations) are generated first, and these are then correlated with sentence structures via syntactic and other rules.

Initial element

↓

Semantic component (including the set of cases)

↓

Transformational component

↓

Surface structures

It is this fundamental implication of the 'reversal' of the organization of the components in a grammar which was so important.

Case grammar is no longer as popular as it was in the early 1970s, and other models have become fashionable. In the early 1970s, Chomsky developed the approach found in *Aspects* to produce what was called the 'Extended Standard Theory'. The 'extension' is primarily due to the range of the semantic rules, some of which were to be allowed to operate with surface structure as input. In other words, it was no longer the case that the deep structure alone would determine the semantic representation of a sentence. It seemed that there were several features of surface structure which had to be taken into account, if a satisfactory semantic representation was to be reached. For instance, there is the way in which intonation and stress are used to alter the meaning of a sentence, or the way the speaker can focus on a particular part of the sentence and so alter the presuppositions that govern the way in which that sentence should be interpreted. In a sentence such as *It was John who came to dinner*, the focus is on *John*, and this word would usually be made prominent by intonation. In such a form, the sentence could be the answer to the question *Who came to dinner?* but not to the question *What did John do?* Semantic interpretation is plainly involved. But as the feature of intonational prominence is a feature of surface structure, some kind of theoretical relationship evidently needs to be allowed between this level and the level of meaning.

In a later development of this view, it is argued that perhaps the whole concept of deep structure in relation to the semantics can be dispensed with, it being replaced by an extended conception of surface structure. The basic idea is that the surface structure representation of sentences should be developed to allow in certain kinds of information that relate to the meaning. This information takes the form of 'empty' elements – abstract markers which are not physically realized in speech, but which give information about the underlying structure of the sentence. One type of empty element is called a *trace*. When a sentence element (such as a noun phrase) is moved by a rule from one part of the sentence to another, it is said to leave a 'trace' behind, to mark the place in the structure where it was originally found. This trace is symbolized by *t*. For example, at one stage in the derivation of the sentence *The man is certain to arrive*, the structure would be specified as *It is certain [the man to arrive]*. To generate the correct surface structure, there has to be a rule which moves the subject of the embedded clause (*the man*) so that it becomes the subject of the main clause. This produces *The man is certain t to arrive*, the *t* indicating that *the man* is the subject of *to arrive*, as well as of *is certain*. In other words, the *t* gives information about the semantic interpretation of this sentence. But it is a part of the surface structure (often now referred to as *S-structure*, to avoid confusion with the earlier notion of surface structure, where no reference to meaning was involved).

Traces are not the only empty elements in this approach, but they will suffice to illustrate the point of principle involved. However, if this is accepted, what is there left for deep structure to do in a grammar? It no longer has a role to play in determining the meaning of a sentence. But it is of course still needed, in order to initiate and constrain the transformations that the grammar requires, so that ungrammatical sentences are not generated. (This revised notion of deep structure is often referred to as *D-structure*.) In fact, a major theme in grammatical theory in recent years has been to determine the best ways of controlling the operation of the various transformations recognized by the grammar. One way is to restrict the D-structure rules in such a way that only permissible surface structures will be generated. This is accomplished by devising restrictions upon transformations known as *constraints*. For example, there is a constraint which stops certain types of noun phrase from being moved out of a relative clause, in order to be the focus of a question. Normally, a noun phrase can be focused in this way, as when *I asked the question* becomes *Which question did I ask?*. But the sentence *I saw the girl who asked the question* does not permit the same transformation: **Which question did I see the girl who asked?* Determining the nature of constraints of this kind has been a major focus of recent research in this area.

However, there is an alternative way of preventing the grammar from generating ungrammatical sentences, and that is by leaving the underlying rules alone, letting them generate unacceptable surface structures, and then controlling the range of permissible surface structures by using devices which have come to be called *filters*. For example, the passive sentence *That house has been sold* has no corresponding active sentence *Sold the house. But if we are to derive all passive sentences from active ones by a single, simple rule (see p. 224), we *need* to specify a subject in the deep structure of this sentence. One proposal was to specify a 'dummy' subject for sentences of this kind – an abstract notion (symbolized by Δ), which would make the deep structure look regular, and thus permit the application of the passive rule. Thus (ignoring tense forms), Δ *sell the house by PASSIVE* would transform into *The house sell by* Δ. But we cannot permit sentences with a Δ symbol inside them to be generated by the grammar. These symbols (or the phrases they are part of) have to be deleted, and one way of doing this would be to filter them out, by having a general condition which says that 'any surface structure containing a Δ should be eliminated'.

These are but some of the notions which have emerged in grammatical theory in recent years, as grammarians have wrestled with ways of preserving the insights and strengths of the generative approach. The true complexity of the exercise can be appreciated only by studying the matter in greater detail than it has been possible to present here: Andrew Radford's *Transformational Syntax* (1981) provides a good general guide, and for those who wish to go into the matter further, Chomsky's thinking of the early 1980s is to be found in his *Lectures on Government and Binding* (1982). At the same time, more radical alternatives to Chomsky's approach have been proposed – models, for example, in which the whole notion of transformation is dispensed with – and other ways of handling structural relationships introduced. The significance of these alternatives for the future development of grammatical thought is not yet clear, but they do at least show the way in which the complex field of syntax continues to be a fascinating focus of research, within linguistic theory.

This is the position in the early 1980s. But before moving on to look at some recent trends in areas other than syntax, I have two apologies to make. I must apologize to those readers who expected to see more in this book on Chomsky. I must also apologize to those readers who expected to see less. In a field as theoretically fragmented as linguistics is, it is difficult to deal rough introductory justice to any side without offence. What makes the exercise defensible is the alternative – to present an introduction which makes no reference to the 'other' side at all. This, it should by now be clear, is an approach with which I have very little sympathy, though it is all too common these days.

VI *Semantics*

'If meaning is as important as all that,' a harsh reader might say, 'then it is about time that he got to semantics.' It might indeed seem odd that linguistics should take over fifty years to get its priorities right, and attempt systematic analyses of meaning. It is not so odd when we find 'late developers' a characteristic of other sciences too. And, to be fair, linguists and earlier scholars of language often had very clear ideas about the importance of meaning and the need for study of it. It was simply not the kind of subject which it proved easy to study. There were, to begin with, numerous preconceptions and false ideas about the nature of meaning which hindered clear thinking, but which it was difficult to get rid of because of their respectable ancestry. One was the tendency (illustrated by many of the beliefs cited in Chapter 2) to identify words and things, to think that meanings were somehow concrete entities – words would be called 'dirty', 'dangerous', 'beautiful', and so on, instead of the objects or events being referred to. This conception we have seen goes back to Plato and before, and is still with us. Another was the attempt to see meaning wholly in terms of behavioural stimulus and response, as in Bloomfield – but here too, such clearly semantic considerations as personal connotations or abstract ideas show that it is not possible to determine the meaning of a linguistic event solely by observation of the environment and behaviour. Simplifications of the idea of meaning, for example by defining it as 'the relationship between words and things', or as 'the use of language', were common in the early part of this century. And when more sophisticated accounts of meaning developed, there was a tendency to talk about the philosophical or rhetorical implications of the questions, and to skate over the theoretical questions presupposed by any systematic analysis. This point can be illustrated from a number of sources – for instance, from the educational doctrines of 'general semantics', associated with the name of Alfred Korzybski in particular, which aimed at the general improvement of human beings by better training in the use of words and other symbols; or from the semantic analysis practised by the logical positivists; or by the rhetorical and literary discussion of the concept by C. K. Ogden and I. A. Richards in *The Meaning of Meaning*, published in 1923. Another example of this very general theorizing was in the debates about the relationship between language and thought, and language and reality, carried on by psychologists, philosophers, anthropologists and linguists alike. In particular, there was the question of whether there are universal concepts existing independently of language, or whether language imposes a conceptual framework on our thinking, without our noticing it. 'We dissect nature along lines laid down by our native languages,' said Benjamin Lee Whorf; and his arguments, along with those of Edward Sapir, led to the development of a position known as the Sapir–Whorf hypothesis, which distracted attention from more central and testable aspects of semantics for a number of years. The history of semantics is a peculiarly complex one, because so many fields of study are involved: it is well surveyed by John Lyons in his book *Semantics*, published in 1977. It is clear from this that the subject of meaning is by no means a discovery of modern linguistics; but at the same time, little of the early work has proved to be of permanent value.

There was, then, much theorizing, but little strict theory. There was little attempt to actually analyse the structure of a language to determine in detail the way in which it 'parcelled out' reality, or to see how words (and other units) defined each other's meaning in various ways. More recently, all these points have received systematic investigation within linguistics. One of the first things to happen was an attack on the word *word*, as a means of studying a language's semantic system. Traditionally, it is assumed that 'words' are the units which carry the meaning in a language – an impression which is reinforced by the way vocabulary is listed in a dictionary. But this assumption is wrong, on two counts. First, meaning is carried by sentences (and larger units), not words. Presented with a single word (such as *table*), there is little that can be said about what is meant: it is not even clear what kind of table is in question (a piece of furniture? part of a printed page?). To understand what is meant, we have to put the word in a context – which usually means, put it into a sentence. If the sentence were *She sat down at the table*, it is plain that the furniture sense is involved; *She corrected the table* makes it clear that the printing sense is involved; and so on. Secondly, there is a problem over the ambiguous way in which the word *word* is used. *Walk, walks, walking* and *walked* are all 'words', in one sense. In another sense, we want to say that they are all different forms of the same 'word'. The solution to this problem was to invent fresh terminology, and the terms *lexeme* or *lexical item* have come to be widely used to refer to the latter. *Lexeme* was devised as an analogy with *phoneme*, *morpheme*, and other such terms: a lexeme is the minimal distinctive unit in the semantic system of a language. We can thus talk about the lexeme W A L K (small capitals are often used to identify a lexeme) and the various grammatical realizations of the lexeme – that is, the words *walk*, *walks*, etc. This distinction also allows us to talk without paradox about semantic units which contain more than one word, such as *switch on*, *kick the bucket* (in the sense of 'die'), and so on.

Early on, in any semantic analysis, we will want to plot the relationships of meaning which obtain between the various lexemes in the language. This is a perspective which differs markedly from most traditional views of meaning, where words were thought of as referring directly to 'things' in the world or 'percepts' in our minds. The meaning of language cannot be explained in this way.

There are few lexemes which label the world directly (proper names are the main category of items which do), and there are few occasions where it proves possible to explain the meaning of a lexeme by referring directly to the world (it would be an impossible situation if, whenever we wanted to talk about something, we had to wait for the appropriate object to come into view in order for our meaning to be clear!). For the most part, we convey our meaning by relying on the network of sense relationships which the lexemes of the language have built up between them. Lexemes are identified and defined by using other lexemes. Look up any lexeme in a dictionary, and its senses will be given – by using other lexemes. In a bad dictionary, the circularity is vicious: X is defined by referring to Y, and Y is defined by referring back to X. In a good dictionary, it is never like this. X refers us to Y, which refers us to Z, which refers us to P ... In due course we may return to X, but in the process we have picked up a great deal about the way the lexeme is used, and developed a sense of what it means. In one dictionary, for example, *benefit* was defined with reference to *advantage* and *profit* (amongst other senses); *advantage* was defined with reference to *gain* (as well as *benefit* and *profit*); *gain* was defined with reference to *increase* and *obtain*; *increase* led to *rise* and *large*, and so on. With sentences used in each case to illustrate usage, it does not take long to see that there is a network of sense relationships linking the various lexemes in a language. It is a gigantic system, and it is the job of the semanticist to explicate it.

An early technique for investigating this system was based on the notion of *semantic fields*. A language's vocabulary is said to be organized into areas of meaning, within which the lexemes relate to each other in specific ways. One well-studied field was that of colour: the precise meaning of a colour term can be understood only by placing it in relation to the other terms which occur with it in demarcating the colour spectrum. Languages do not all have the same number of colour lexemes, nor do the lexemes always correspond. In Welsh, for example, the lexeme *glas* is used to correspond to *blue*, and also to some of the uses of *green* and *grey* (grass, for example, can be described as *glas*, as well as the sky and the sea). Semantic fields are a convenient way of comparing sets of lexemes in different languages, or sets of lexemes in two different historical periods in the same language, or sets of lexemes within different thematic areas of the same language. It is possible, for example, to study the vocabulary a language uses for such areas as vehicles, kinship or cooking, and to see what range of lexemes is involved and how they relate to each other. Semantic fields are not always easy to identify, however, and there are many problems facing anyone who wishes to use the notion consistently in a large-scale study. But the conception has an intuitive plausibility, relating as it does to the major conceptual classifications found in such works as *Roget's Thesaurus*, and it is quite widely encountered.

The analysis of lexemic relations can be made more precise by applying the distinction between *paradigmatic* and *syntagmatic*, which was introduced on p. 162. Paradigmatic relationships obtain between lexemes at a particular point in a sentence; syntagmatic relationships obtain between lexemes at different points in a sentence. The study of the whole network of semantic relationships which can be identified through the use of these dimensions is generally carried on under the heading of *structural semantics*. Of the two dimensions, the paradigmatic has been the more fully studied, as part of the explication of a language's *sense-relations*. A sense-relation, as its name suggests, is a relationship between sentences such that we perceive their lexemes to be in some kind of systematic correspondence. We intuitively see a connection between them. Not all lexemes can be related in this way. There is no obvious connection between the lexemes in roman type in the following two sentences, for instance:

> *I've just bought a new* car.
> *I've just bought a new* pencil.

In contrast, the lexemes in roman in the following sentence pairs *do* seem to be connected in some way:

I've just bought a new car.	*I've just bought a new* bike.
I've just bought a new *car.*	*I've just bought an* old *car.*
I've just bought a new car.	*I've just bought a new* automobile.
I've just bought a new car.	*I've just bought a new* vehicle.

It is possible to analyse these relationships in detail, and show that there are several different types. Some of them are known by traditional names. The relationship between *car* and *automobile*, for example, would traditionally be called *synonymy*, and the two lexemes would be said to be *synonyms*. The relationship between *new* and *old* would be called *antonymy*, with the lexemes being referred to as *antonyms*. But what is the relationship between *car* and *bike*? or between *car* and *vehicle*? In the structural semantic approach to these matters, the aim is to study and classify all possible sense-relations. Thus, the relationship between *car* and *vehicle* is referred to as *hyponymy* – a relationship of inclusion (a car is a kind of vehicle). *Car* and *bike* are both within the field of vehicles, but are *incompatible* terms within that field – an entity cannot both be a car and a bike at the same time. Several other such relationships have been identified.

It is then possible to take a particular sense-relation, and study the semantic differences between the lexemes in greater detail. What exactly is it which constitutes the 'oppositeness' of *new* and *old*? In what specific respects do *car* and *bike* differ? To take this last example, both cars and bikes have wheels, so it would not be possible to say that the difference between them was due to one having wheels and the other not (though this difference *would* be relevant for the contrast in meaning between, say, *car* and *sleigh*). Would 'number of wheels' be a criterion? Not always, because some bikes and some cars have three wheels. What about 'having an engine', then? Again, there is the problem of bicycles with engines. 'Number of seats' seems more promising. And so we might continue, in search of those features, or *components* of meaning, which satisfactorily discriminate the two lexemes. This kind of approach, when it is systematically applied to sets of lexemes in a language, is known as *componential analysis*. It has been especially used by anthropologists in analysing the vocabulary of kinship and other important social areas within a community, and linguists have found it a helpful way of focusing attention on important points of semantic similarity and contrast. Some linguists have tried to construct an entire theoretical framework for semantic analysis using it, but here the approach has been less successful. Small fragments of vocabulary can be usefully analysed in this way, but it is not so easy to work out universal principles which can be applied consistently to whole languages or different languages.

The study of the syntagmatic relationships between lexemes is less advanced. Here, we are concerned to establish the nature of any linguistic patterns which relate lexemes occurring in sequence. One way of doing this is to look at the way lexemes 'keep company', or *collocate*, with each other. It is possible to make predictions about the range of lexemes which can occur at a certain point in a sentence. If a sentence began *It was an auspicious—*, we would know that the blank is likely to be filled by one of a very small range of words, such as *occasion, event* or *omen*. Such expectancies between lexemes have been referred to as *collocations*. Different degrees of mutual expectancy exist. *Auspicious* predicts the occurrence of *occasion* more definitely than does *occasion* the presence of *auspicious*. It is theoretically possible to study all lexemes in a language to determine these expectancies. *Rancid* is another tightly constrained lexeme, collocating especially with *butter* and *bacon*. *Amok* is even more tightly controlled, collocating only with *run*. On the other hand, *flock* allows a wider range of collocates – such as *sheep, birds, goats*, and even *people* (*the people flocked to the sales*). *Letter* allows far more – *box, post, write, envelope, head . . .* and *alphabet, spelling, law* (cf. *the letter of the law*) . . . Here, of course, the two main meanings of *letter* are being identified by the different collocates. A similar distinction was used above (p. 236), in distinguishing the two senses of *table* (one co-occurring with *sit*, the other with *correct*). And, at the opposite extreme from *amok*, there are lexemes which have no clear expectancies, because they collocate with an enormous range of other lexemes in the language – items such as *have, go, get, put* and *big*.

No one has ever worked out a scale of collocability, because the enterprise would be so vast, but the general idea is clear enough. It is important to appreciate, also, that these co-occurrence relationships can be stated formally, without relying on our knowledge of the reference of the lexemes. This is especially important in the case of lexemes where no literal sense is involved, as in the idiomatic use of colour lexemes. In English, *green* collocates with *jealousy*, and *passages* (in a book) collocates with *purple*, even though people are not literally green, nor books literally printed in purple. There is no guarantee (or even likelihood) that other languages would express these notions using the same collocates. Some collocations, of course, are found because the real world is the way it is: in British English, *bacon* collocates with *eggs*, because that is a popular meal; in American English, the Briton has to learn an additional set of collocations, in answer to the question 'How would you like your eggs?' (*sunny side up*, *once over easy*, etc.). Putting this another way: once we know what goes on in a culture, we have a reasonable chance of getting the collocations right; but it does not necessarily follow that we can deduce from what we see how the language talks about it (we do not say *white milk*, for example, and we have to learn that, unlike butter, milk which goes off is *sour*, and eggs which go off are *addled* or *rotten*).

These are just some of the issues which arise when we study the lexicon of a language from a structural semantic point of view. There are several other lexical topics which also require investigation, such as the problem of how to analyse words which have more than one meaning; the problem of defining idioms accurately; the problem of deciding how much detail to allow into the definition of a word; the problem of styles of usage affecting the meanings of words. These are all questions which have received no satisfactory explanation, and an adequate semantic theory, which would have to account for such things, is accordingly a long way off. The existence of large dictionaries listing the meanings of words in a language should not blind us to this fact. There is nothing infallible about a dictionary (or a grammar, for that matter). All dictionaries are artefacts; they have principles about what words they will include and what they will leave out, about how to define meanings, about the order in which meanings should be defined and how they should be grouped, about ways of presenting pronunciation and spelling, about ways of dealing with etymologies, about how much information to introduce concerning stylistic or idiomatic information, and so on. It is extremely instructive to take two dictionaries and compare their treatment of any set of words. The differences are remarkable; and for intelligent use, they should be evaluated.

But much of this is fringe linguistics. Lexicography (dictionary-

Linguistics

writing) is one of the applications of language study, putting semantic information over in a certain way. Obtaining that information in the first place is independent of any particular dictionary format. And semantics, for the linguist, must be primarily concerned with the problems of how the semantic system hypothesized for a language is organized, and what kind of model might most usefully be constructed in order to facilitate analysis.

So far, we have considered only the lexical side of the subject. But semantics is involved in other aspects of language too. It could come into the study of phonetics (p. 164), for example, as when we talk about the symbolism conveyed by sounds in poetry. It is always implicit in the study of phonology (p. 170), for here sounds are being used to differentiate meanings. And these days it is felt to be especially important in the study of grammar. For many years, the study of meaning was considered to be an irrelevance, as far as grammar was concerned (cf. p. 205). Today, it is recognized that it is possible, and desirable, to study the meaning of a sentence, and of the grammatical categories and relationships it contains. We have already seen, in fact, that much of the debate in recent generative grammar has arisen in relation to the way we should draw a boundary between syntax and semantics (see p. 227), and whether it is possible to set up a basic set of semantic relations from which grammatical patterns can be derived (actor, action, location, etc. – see p. 229).

But these are not the only issues in the study of sentence meaning. It is possible, for example, to make very general statements of meaning about a sentence – distinguishing, for example, 'what we are talking about' from 'what we are saying about it' (what is sometimes referred to as the *topic* and the *comment* respectively). It is possible to analyse the semantic properties of sentences, using as a starting-point the techniques of logic to determine the truth or falsity of sentences. To know the meaning of a sentence, it is argued, is to know the conditions under which the sentence is true or false. To study the logical form of sentences, in relation to conditions which govern its use, is to engage in *truth-conditional* (or simply *formal*) semantics. This is one of the most fruitful areas of overlap between linguistics and philosophy at the present time.

But we can broaden our perspective still further, and look at sentences in terms of the function or action they perform in the whole domain of social interaction, as when someone says *I name this ship* . . ., *I baptize* . . . or *I promise* . . . J. L. Austin referred to these as *performative* utterances, and the study of the properties of these and other utterances has become a major field within semantics, as part of the study of *speech acts*. It has led to several related topics – such as the study of the *felicity conditions* under which speech acts can take place and be acceptable. To be in a position to say *I baptize* . . ., certain conditions must be met – in particular, there must be some kind of authority invested in the speaker, the speaker must want to perform the action sincerely, and the listener must want it to be done. The conditions governing other kinds of speech act can be analysed in the same way.

As we begin to study speech acts, and the contexts in which they occur, we move away from the meaning of single sentences and towards the meaning of stretches of text or discourse – even, whole conversations. At this point, it becomes difficult to define the boundaries of the study of semantics, so as to distinguish it clearly from the most recent development which has taken place within linguistics – the emergence of the field of pragmatics.

VII Pragmatics

Pragmatics studies the factors which govern someone's choice of language, when they speak or write. If we choose to say something, there are all kinds of factors which constrain what we will say, and how we will say it. In theory, we can say anything we like. In practice, we follow a large number of social rules (most of them unconsciously) which govern the way we speak. There is no law which says that people must not crack jokes at funerals, but it is generally 'not done'. Less obviously, there are norms of formality and politeness which everyone has intuitively assimilated, which we follow when talking to older people, people of the opposite sex, people of special rank, and so on. These norms affect the way in which we select sounds, grammatical constructions and lexemes from the resources of the language. We would not say *How's tricks, Your Majesty?* for example. And children from an early age are taught 'not to talk like that to – your mother, your sister, the vicar . . .'. In many languages, pragmatic distinctions of formality, politeness and intimacy are spread throughout the grammatical system. Several oriental languages have different grammatical patterns, depending on whether one is talking to an equal, a superior, or an inferior. Japanese is a well-studied instance. Nearer home, pragmatic distinctions of a grammatical kind face those who wish to assimilate the force of the difference between *tu* and *vous* in French – a pronoun contrast which is found in many languages of the world.

But even if we are talking to someone who is a social equal, there are many rules which we tacitly accept – such as the turn-taking conventions which are found in conversation. We cannot simply interrupt someone, without risk of being considered rude. Nor can we hog a conversation, or keep talking on topics which other members of the group do not want to hear about – unless we want to be considered a bore. There are manoeuvres which we all have to carry out when we enter a conversation and take our leave of it. Certain topics are widely expected at the beginning – the weather and health are common in English. Certain topics are expected at the end – a reference to the next time of meeting, or a formula expressing farewell. Some of the strategies which govern behaviour are extremely subtle – such as when, at a dinner party, guests say that it is time for them to leave. It would not normally be considered polite for the host to react positively to the first comment to this effect by the guests. It is normally denied or ignored. A few minutes later, the guest will repeat the comment, and this time it may be taken up by the host, and the leave-taking procedures begun in earnest. If the host ignores the comment a second time, then it will need to be repeated in due course, with additional emphasis, until both parties are agreed on the course of action to follow.

The study of the rules governing our use of language in social interaction is part of pragmatics, and is often referred to as *conversation analysis*. In this field, we are concerned to establish why language works, or fails to work, in maintaining a satisfactory conversation, from the viewpoint of those who participate in it. It is a difficult field to study, because naturalistic samples of data are never easy to obtain, and even when the data are available, the pragmatic rules are never easy to observe. If we enjoyed the last conversation we had with someone, or achieved what we set out to achieve, the rules have worked (for us, at least). If we left the conversation feeling dissatisfied (either because we felt we did not handle our end well, or because someone else handled their end badly), the rules have been broken.

H. P. Grice has classified the factors which affect the success of a conversation in terms of *cooperative principles* between speaker and hearer. These principles control the way a conversation proceeds. These include such 'maxims' as 'Do not say what you believe to be false', 'Be relevant', 'Be brief' and 'Avoid ambiguity'. These maxims, of course, are easier to state than to follow, partly because there may not be a correspondence between what the speaker feels is false, relevant, ambiguous, or whatever, and what the hearer feels to be the case. Often, a speaker may assume information to be known by the hearer when this is not the case, as when the sentence *I've just seen John* is followed by *Who's John?*. Alternatively, the speaker may make the wrong assumptions about a situation, as when the sentence *Would you shut the door?* is followed by *But it's already shut*.

The information people assume when they speak is generally referred to under the heading of *presuppositions*, and the implications for the way a conversation proceeds which can be deduced from the form of the sentences used are known as *conversational implicatures*. To say *I need some fresh bread* presupposes (for example) that I am hungry, and implies that my hearer can do something to solve my problem (otherwise why should I have said it?). This, at least, would be the case in a conversation where the cooperative principles were being followed by both participants. What is always interesting are the cases where the principles are violated – as when the person addressed might reply *There's a bread shop on the corner*, knowing full well that it is closed. In real-life conversations, problems of communication of this kind are always present – and provide much of the motivation for pragmatic analysis. Problems too are always to be found in the field of foreign language learning and contact, where the conventions of greeting or leave-taking may be very different from ours, or where politeness norms may vary. In some countries, it is polite, when invited for a meal, to remark to our host that we are enjoying the food; in other countries, it is polite not to. Foreigners in Britain who fail to make this remark can easily insult their hosts, or at least cause them concern ('Do you think they liked it?'); conversely, English-speakers in a foreign country can cause insult by making what to them is an unnecessary comment ('Did they think it would be otherwise?').

Concepts such as presupposition and implicature are an important part of the study of pragmatics, but they are of relevance for the study of semantics also, especially in connection with such classical problems as how to analyse the truth or falsity of sentences like *The King of the USA is ill* – a sentence which can be evaluated in this way only by considering the presupposition that there is a King of the USA. Indeed, several of the textbooks on semantics and pragmatics which have appeared in recent years display a considerable overlap. Several of the topics to be found in S. C. Levinson's *Pragmatics* or G. N. Leech's *The Principles of Pragmatics* are also treated in J. Lyons's *Semantics* or F. R. Palmer's *Semantics*. The problem with the field of pragmatics at present is that it is so wide. It is sometimes treated as something of a dustbin – anything in language that cannot be handled using the traditional levels of phonology, grammar and semantics can be called 'pragmatics'! At one extreme, the field makes contact with semantics and grammar, through such notions as presupposition, topic and comment. At the other extreme, it makes contact with sociolinguistics and psycholinguistics (see p. 260), through such notions as appropriateness and acceptability. There is little agreement, currently, over what a core syllabus in pragmatics should consist of. Some semanticists exclude pragmatic concerns from their remit, dealing only with referential meaning, truth, falsity, and the like; others broaden the field to include most of what we have discussed above. Some sociolinguists see pragmatics as a part of their domain; others try to draw a boundary between the two. Some grammarians see the search for patterns of language larger than the sentence as a separate branch of study, sometimes referred to as *discourse analy-*

sis or (in the context of written language) *text linguistics*; others see a relationship with pragmatics and semantics. The next few years will doubtless see a considerable theoretical refinement of the field of pragmatics, and it is to be hoped that in due course a consensus will emerge about its central concerns, and about its relationship to other areas of linguistics.

Language?

The definition of linguistics at the very beginning of this book used this term, and I have still not defined it explicitly. Perhaps it is not possible to frame any adequate definition, in view of its complexity of structure and function? At least we can now say that anyone who did try to frame such a definition would have to bear in mind all of what has been said in this chapter. And they would have to add a further perspective, namely, that of language's function. This final section looks briefly at the implications of this remark.

What is language's main function? The answer is clear, and generally agreed: language is the most frequently used and most highly developed form of human communication we possess. The point was made many pages ago (cf. p. 107), but its implications are very interesting. An act of communication is basically the transmission of information of some kind – a 'message' – from a source to a receiver. In the case of language, both source and receiver are human, and the message is transmitted either vocally, through the air, or graphically, by marks on a surface, usually paper. Language is one form of communication. There are of course others, not necessarily connected with human behaviour; for example, the instinctive noises which animals of a given species use to communicate with each other. This is communication, as language is, but there is little in common between human and animal forms of communication. And if we insist on talking about the 'language' of the birds and bees, then we must remember that this is a different, and strictly analogical sense of the word 'language'. There has been a great deal of interest in the properties of animal communication systems recently, often under the heading of *zoö-semiotics*, and this has shown very clearly the extent of the difference between this and human language. No animal signalling system displays the creative potential and complexity of structure which we have noted in human language. Linguists, accordingly, consider language as a distinctively human phenomenon. They would also refrain from using the word to refer to metaphorical senses of communication: for instance, when we say that a 'bond of communication' exists between musicians, conductor and composer, so that all three 'speak the same language'.

But even if we restrict the term 'language' to human communication, it is still the case that not everything which would fall under this heading is language, in the linguist's sense. We can see the reason for this if we consider all the other possibilities of human communication. We may communicate with our mouths, or with other parts of our face, or indeed by making use of any of our senses. Only the visual and vocal/auditory senses are frequently used, but there is nothing to stop us using other methods if we find them appropriate to our purpose. Some secret societies have a system of communication by touch, and I have come across advertisements which have had the scent of the product they display impregnating the paper. But on the whole the use of the senses of taste, touch and smell is extremely restricted as far as human communication is concerned.

The study of all these 'modalities' of human communication is carried on under the heading of *semiotics*. The two most highly structured modalities are the visual (or *kinesic*), and of course the vocal/auditory (the linguistic). The visual system is well-established in human beings: we need only think of all the facial expressions and bodily gestures we make use of in our day-to-day activity – hand-signals, winks, raised eyebrows, and so on – which communicate a great deal of information. Often, we pay more attention to the way people look than the way they speak – 'the expression on his face told me he was lying', or 'it wasn't so much what she said, as the way she looked when she said it'. And we are all familiar with the kinds of ambiguity which arise when we cannot see the person we are speaking or listening to – in a telephone conversation, for example, or when watching television with the picture temporarily missing. But despite its importance, the visual system of communication in humans does not have by any means the same structure or potential as the vocal – there is nothing really like grammar, for instance, and there is a very finite 'vocabulary' of gestures indeed in any culture – and linguists do not therefore call it language. They restrict the term 'language' yet further to a *vocal* system of human communication. They allow the visual a place in language only in the cases of signing (by the deaf, for example) and of writing, which differs from other visual communicative activity in that it is usually an attempt to directly transcribe our speech in a one-to-one way. All modern writing systems are designed to copy speech, to turn sounds into letters, thereby making our message more permanent; other visual signs do not do this. And lastly, in discussing human communicational activity other than language, we must mention those noises which human beings can produce other than from their mouths, which can communicate information; an example would be finger-snapping. These too linguists would exclude in their attempts to make the notion of language more precise.

But there are still other restrictions which we must place on the term 'language'. So far we have called it a system of human vocal communication. But even here, not all of this is linguistic. There are many sounds, or aspects of sounds, which we utter that are not linguistic – that is, we cannot or do not deliberately make use of them in order to communicate a message. For example, a sneeze, or snore, or our breathing are audible vocal noises which do not communicate a message in the same sense as when we speak words or sentences. A sneeze may communicate the fact that we have a cold, of course, but this is a very different sense of the word 'communication'. It is communication 'despite oneself'. It directly reflects a particular physiological state on our part, and has no meaning other than this. Words, sentences, and the like, on the other hand, are not tied down to our bodily state: we may speak or not speak (but we have no similar option in breathing or snoring), and we may use a particular word whenever we wish, regardless of the physical state we happen to be in (but we cannot sneeze at will). Uncontrolled or uncontrollable vocal noises of this kind, lacking any clear internal structure or conventional meaning, are not part of language.

Another set of vocal effects which we would exclude from language is that commonly referred to by the label 'voice quality'. While we speak, apart from the actual message we are trying to put across, we also communicate information of a quite different kind, operating at an entirely different level. This is information about our personalities. Whenever we speak, we make known our identity to the outside world; there are features of everyone's voice which allow those who know them to recognize them without seeing them. These features are difficult to pin down precisely, but they clearly exist, and they are very different from the rest of our utterance. Voice quality is a relatively permanent feature of our speech; it only alters with age or physiological change (as with a hoarse throat, for instance). Mimics (people who deliberately imitate another's voice quality) are the exception in society rather than the rule. Normally, people can do nothing about their voice quality, nor do they usually *want* to change it – unless they have some professional interest in mimicry or acting. Similarly, in writing: a person's handwriting is the factor which allows us to recognize anyone for who they are, and we only alter this on very exceptional occasions.

To exclude voice quality from language is not thereby to exclude 'accent', of course. 'Accent', as we have already seen (p. 33), is a more general phenomenon, which is used to refer to the *totality* of phonetic and phonological features a person has (including voice quality), and in particular to those non-idiosyncratic features of pronunciation. In other words, it refers to those sounds which could also be used by a number of other people and which inform us that someone comes from a particular region or social group. Voice quality tells us who someone is; accent where they are from.

Accent, then, is capable of linguistic analysis, whereas idiosyncratic facets of vocal communication are not considered as language. Language, as has been implied often in this book, is essentially a controlled behaviour, *shared* in various degrees by all the people in a given speech-community. Language transcends idiosyncrasy. Unless we all shared basically the same set of vocal conventions, we would not be able to communicate with each other. It is true, as we have seen (p. 171), that no two people ever speak exactly alike all the time; but the differences between speakers of the same language are *far* outweighed by the similarities. Society does not tolerate too much idiosyncrasy, too much originality, in language. The person who deviates too markedly from the standard forms of the language in an idiosyncratic way is either hailed as a great poet or classified as belonging to one of a very small number of categories, e.g. someone with a speech disorder, an uneducated foreigner, a lunatic.

I began by looking at the central function of language, and in developing this point I have been able to characterize language by reference to a number of factors. The discussion may be summarized by referring to language as human vocal noise (or the graphic representation of this noise in writing) used systematically and conventionally by a community for purposes of communication. Occasionally, language is used for purposes other than communication – for example, to let off steam (as in our vocal reaction to hitting our fingers with a hammer), or to give delight to ourselves purely because of the sonic effect which language has upon the ear (as in children's word-play), or as a vehicle for our own thoughts when no one else is present. But such uses of language are secondary.

Envoi

This has been very much a skeleton study of the history and present state of major linguistic themes. I think it has, however, been possible to see a steady progression of linguistic interest from phonetics to phonology, thence to morphology, surface syntax, deep syntax, semantics and ultimately to pragmatics. These are the seven 'ages' I spoke about at the beginning of the chapter. The many different approaches which I have had to refer to in the course of the chapter should not, however, obscure the existence of a considerable area of agreement within linguistics as a whole. Everyone, whether they talk in terms of levels, strata, branches, components, or whatever, agrees that we need to distinguish phonology, syntax and semantics in the structure of language, even though the relationships existing between them and the subject-matter constituting them may differ. We are also now much clearer as to what the goals of linguistics are, and have much more positive suggestions as to how these goals might best be achieved. The distinctive characteristics of language, as a uniquely human rule-governed behaviour, are now fairly well understood, and their properties formalized, and the place of language in relation to other forms of human and non-human communication fairly well established. The existence of controversy over fundamental issues is a fact, of course, and cannot be denied. But who should want to deny it? It would be a dull science about which there was nothing left to disagree. In linguistics, as in much else, it is precisely this controversy, and the challenge which it embodies, which is the basis of its appeal.

Appendix to Chapter 4:
Some other names

In a two-dimensional chapter, in which I have tried to develop a coherent progression of basic themes, it has not been possible to sketch in all the simultaneously developing strands of linguistic thought, as these would have destroyed my line of argument. But an introductory book without any mention at all of some of the names below would be seriously weakened, as some of them are of frequent occurrence in everyday linguistic conversation (accompanied by varying degrees of polemical and pejorative overtones), and are comparably basic – though perhaps less influential – to the names discussed at length in the body of the chapter. For more about these and other issues, one might look at the *Short History of Linguistics* by R. H. Robins, referred to earlier (p. 41), or G. C. Lepschy's *A Survey of Structural Linguistics*, 2nd edn. 1982.

Firthian. Refers to someone who follows the linguistic principles of J. R. Firth, Professor of General Linguistics in the University of London from 1944 to 1956. These principles, as subsequently developed, were largely in the field of phonology (where his views of 'prosodic phonology' were in opposition to traditional American phonemics), and in the study of meaning, where he developed a complex view of all levels of linguistic structure simultaneously contributing to the total statement of an utterance's meaning. The 'neo-Firthian' approach to linguistics is that primarily associated with the work of Halliday (p. 210 above). Firth's own work is well illustrated in his *Papers in Linguistics* 1934–51, published in 1957.

Glossematics. An approach to language developed primarily by L. Hjelmslev and associates at the Linguistic Circle of Copenhagen in the mid thirties. The novel name was a reflection of the originality of the school's intention to develop a theory which would be applicable, not just for language, but for general study of the humanities ('semiology', the study of symbolic systems in general). Under the influence of Brøndal, it developed a more philosophical and logical basis than is usual in linguistic theories – before Chomsky, at least – and the precision with which Hjelmslev formulated glossematic theory, in his *Prolegomena to a Theory of Language*, published in 1943, presenting language as a purely deductive system (cf. p. 114–15), is its most distinctive feature. The approach uses a forbidding terminology, and there is little real-language illustration, which is perhaps why it has been so little studied. But it has exercised considerable influence on some contemporary linguists, such as Lamb (cf. p. 212); and its exposition of theoretical postulates and categories for linguistic analysis is both cautionary and stimulating for anyone attempting theoretical formulation in linguistics.

Montague grammar. A linguistic theory which developed in the mid 1970s out of the work of the American logician Richard Montague. The approach uses a conceptual apparatus derived from the study of the semantics of logical languages, in which the focus of attention is on the nature of the relationship between syntactic and semantic components of a grammar.

Prague School. As we have seen in the discussion on phonology, this was the name given to a group of scholars working in or around Prague in the late twenties and early thirties. The Linguistic Circle of Prague was founded in 1926, and published an important journal (*Travaux du Cercle Linguistique de Prague*). Much of the inspiration for its work came from Saussure, but two of its most important scholars, Roman Jakobson and Nikolai Trubetskoy, were Russian, the Austrian psychologist Karl Bühler was very influential, and many specifically linguistic features of their work are thus not to be found in Saussure at all. Their contribution to linguistics was primarily in connection with the formulation of a phonological theory (see p. 176), based on the Saussurean notion of a functional system; but they made important contributions to our understanding of other areas of language too. They (in particular, Vilém Mathesius) developed an approach to syntactic analysis using the Saussurean notion of functionally contrastive constituents of sentences (it is known as the theory of *functional sentence perspective*), and this has been developed in Prague (by Josef Vachek, Jan Firbas, and others) in the work of a 'neo' Prague school. This was intended partly as a contribution to a theory of style, and the Prague scholars did a great deal of work into the formal properties of literary language and the expressive properties of language in general. A convenient collection of articles is *A Prague School Reader in Linguistics*, edited by J. Vachek in 1964.

Jakobson, an original member of the group, was later to move to the United States, where he further developed notions of the various functions of language, and of diachronic linguistics, and had an influential role in the development of generative phonology (see p. 177).

Journals. Some widely used linguistics journals which publish in English are *Language*, the publication of the Linguistic Society of America; *Journal of Linguistics*, the publication of the Linguistics Association of Great Britain; and *Lingua*, published in Amsterdam. An abstracting journal, *Linguistics Abstracts*, commenced publication in 1985.

5. Linguistics and Other Fields

The last chapter very clearly demonstrates that the hunt for a satisfactory linguistic theory is still on: there are still a large number of fundamental issues which have not yet been resolved. The main merit of research over the past few years is that people now have a much clearer idea as to what the important questions of linguistic theory are: over the next few years, we may go some way towards solving some of them. It should be clear from this attitude, then, that those who clamour for applications of linguistics – myself included – are not likely to be satisfied for a while. Too much of the subject is in an unformulated state to be able to be applied in any useful way to the study of some other field – though, as we shall see, some restricted areas have come to be fairly well investigated and introduced. The absence of any complete grammar of English (which has been the most analysed of all languages) is one of the most obvious limitations of the applicability of linguistics at the present time. The presence of so much fundamental theoretical disagreement, which has to be gone into before one can adopt a particular 'applied' line, is another. However, it would be wrong to criticize linguistics for failing to come up to expectations, or for being too negative (in its criticisms of earlier work), or for being too complicated and abstract – such criticisms are not uncommon. The negative flavour of early linguistics was, as we have seen, an essential preliminary to the development of a more constructive and open-minded state of mind on the part of language scholars. Understanding the weaknesses of early accounts of language helped them to reach an understanding of the fact that it *was* complex, and to appreciate the nature and extent of its complexity. It was this awareness which promoted the careful analysis of data and the development of the necessary (albeit abstract) distinctions of phonetics, morphology, and the other levels. It is in fact this very complexity which is the reason why linguistics has not developed further than it has. It would be perfectly possible for any competent linguist to sit down and write a linguistic grammar of English, in the light of available knowledge, for the purpose of language teaching; but it is unlikely that it would be a wholly satisfying job. There is still too much dispute about the theoretical principles on which such a grammar should be based, too much dispute over terminology, and too much uncertainty over the facts of the language, to produce a sound, comprehensible and comprehensive grammar. And bearing in mind that linguistics has been with us such a short time, this inadequacy is perhaps not surprising. A great deal has nonetheless been achieved.

Awareness of this inadequacy has not of course stopped people from trying to write such grammars; nor should it. The more attempts there are to formulate adequate grammars for particular applications in teaching and elsewhere, the more quickly the difficulties will be appreciated, and the sooner they will be overcome. What is important is that the potential users of these books should not make premature demands for their production (rushed research is regretted research), and that the authors of these books – or their publishers – should not make premature claims for their product. This prematurity can be possible in two ways. First, a linguistic introduction to the structure of English, let us say, can be premature in the sense that the kind of model in which it presents its rules and facts has been outdated by new ideas about the nature of the model, or about the formalization of the rules, or even about the nature of the facts (e.g. new statistical information about usage having become available). This has often happened, particularly in generative grammar, where the development of ideas has been so rapid that a grammar book is liable to find itself dismissed as old-hat by linguists, even when it is hot off the press. Naturally, teachers who are trying to get to grips with generative grammar are disturbed by this reaction; but they should not be, if they appreciate the inevitable movement in the progression of scientific theory. They should use a grammar book, for the time being, not as an authoritative account of linguistic structure, that has to be taught to the letter; but as a set of suggestions about ways of looking at language which they are likely to find illuminating and applicable to specific problems. This can be done even though there is a likelihood of further developments in the subject which will make some of the specific features of the approach redundant. This critical attitude is also helpful, I believe, in that it helps to reduce the difficulties inherent in the second cause of prematurity mentioned above, namely, that not enough is known about the psychological and other demands linguistics makes upon the student, or about the methodological difficulties involved in grading linguistic material for presentation pedagogically. One book may be suitable for pedagogical context A (e.g. language teaching to immigrants from the West Indies), but not for context B (e.g. language teaching to immigrants from India and Pakistan). Teachers, however, who are eclectic in their use of linguistic material, who build up, in a personal but informed way, their own 'theory' of language and their own description of English, bearing in mind the specific needs of the situation in which they are working, are likely to avoid the more serious of these pragmatic difficulties. This of course is what many teachers already try to do, if they are in the unfortunate position of not having an applied linguistics research project trying to do the job for them (and there are more and more such projects producing materials in a variety of fields these days). It is good to see an increasing number of centres in Britain and the United States organizing courses, conferences, in-service training, and the like, in order to try to bridge the gap between theory/research and pedagogy, and to develop a positive and selective state of mind of this kind.

For such a gap does exist, and there is no point in trying to deny it. There is a considerable gap in this book, for instance, between the practical claims and suggestions of Chapter 1 (which show the potential applicability of the subject) and the academic discussions of Chapter 4. There might almost seem to be two subjects involved, the study of language, on the one hand, and the study of linguistics, on the other – and there are those who make this distinction in their work. But ultimately there is and can be no such distinction: whether or not we commit ourselves to the detail of a specific linguistic approach, when we commence the study of language, on no matter how small a scale, we are necessarily committed to the demands for clarity, consistency and accuracy, which it is the ultimate purpose of linguistic study to fulfil. As soon as we ask ourselves how we are using terms, as soon as we impose a certain grading or selection on material, we are committing ourselves to a particular linguistic view of the world. Whether we realize it is another matter. Naturally, one hopes that intelligent people will take pains to realize what they are doing – linguists included. But developing this awareness of principles of analysis is at once to do linguistics. There is no natural gap between theory and practice in language study; but there is a very real psychological and practical gap, due to the apparent complexity of many linguistic ideas, and the lack of time and material for people outside the subject to get into it. Indeed, the bridging of this gap is the whole purpose of the present book.

But there is another way in which this gap can be bridged, through the development of the relationship between linguistics and other fields of study. A cardinal principle underlying the whole linguistic approach is that language is not an isolated phenomenon (cf. p. 35); it is a part of society, and a part of ourselves. It is a distinctive feature of human nature (some, who talk of 'homo loquens', say it is *the* distinctive feature); and it is a prerequisite – or so it would appear – for the development of any society or social group. Also, as Chapter 1 suggested, it enters into a very large number of specialized fields. Consequently, it is not possible to study language, using the methods of linguistics or any other, without to some extent studying – or at least presupposing the study of – other aspects of society, behaviour, and experience. The way in which linguistics overlaps in its subject-matter with other academic studies has become well appreciated over the last few years, and in the past decade we have seen the development of quite distinct interdisciplinary subjects, such as sociolinguistics, psycholinguistics, philosophical linguistics, biological linguistics, and mathematical linguistics. These, as their titles suggest, refer to aspects of language which are relevant and susceptible to study from two points of view (sociology and linguistics, psychology and linguistics and so on), and which thus require awareness and development of concepts and techniques derived from both. And as many of the points of contact refer to issues which are obviously of everyday concern, these marginal branches of the subject stand a much better chance of avoiding the charges of irrelevance levelled at its 'purer' aspects. This can be seen by looking briefly at the kind of topic covered by the two most important branches to have developed so far, sociolinguistics and psycholinguistics.

Sociolinguistics studies the ways in which language interacts with society. It is the study of the way in which language's structure changes in response to its different social functions, and the definition of what these functions are. 'Society' here is used in its broadest sense, to cover a spectrum of phenomena to do with race, nationality, more restricted regional, social and political groups, and the interactions of individuals within groups. Different labels have sometimes been applied to various parts of this spectrum. 'Ethnolinguistics' is sometimes distinguished from the rest, referring to the linguistic correlates and problems of ethnic groups – illustrated at a practical level by the linguistic consequences of immigration; there is a language side to race relations, as anyone working in this field is all too readily aware. The term 'anthropological linguistics' is sometimes distinguished from 'sociological linguistics', depending on one's particular views as to the validity or otherwise of a distinction between anthropology and sociology in the first place (e.g. the former studying primitive cultures, the latter studying more 'advanced' political units). Usage of British and American scholars differs considerably in this respect. 'Stylistics' is another label which is sometimes distinguished, referring to the study of the distinctive linguistic characteristics of smaller social groupings (such as those due to occupational or class differences). More usually, however, stylistics refers to the study of the literary expression of a community, using linguistic methods. None of these labels has any absolute basis: the subject-matter of ethnolinguistics gradually merges into that of anthropological linguistics, that into sociological linguistics, and that into stylistics, and the subject-matter of social psychology. The kinds of problem which turn up are many and various, and some have been illustrated in Chapter 1, which was very much concerned with the role of language in society. They include: the problems of communities which develop a standard language, and the reactions of minority groups to this (as in Belgium, India, or Wales); the problems of people who have to be educated to a linguistic level where they can cope with the demands of a variety of social situations; the problems of communication which exist between nations or groups using a different language, which affects their 'world-view'; the problems caused by linguistic change in response to social factors; the problems caused (and solved) by bilingualism or multilingualism; the problems caused by the need for individuals to interact with others in specific linguistic ways (language as an index of intimacy or distance, of solidarity, of prestige or power, of pathology, and so on). I am not arguing that sociolinguistics by itself can solve problems such as these; but it can identify precisely what the problems are (this is sometimes a major task in itself), and obtain information about the particular manifestation of a problem in a given area, so that possible solutions can thereby be hastened.

One thing is clear. There is little chance of solving any of these problems until certain basic principles about the relationship of language to society have been established, and accurate techniques of study developed. And so far, there are many basic issues about which there is much controversy – for example, the extent to which our social background determines our linguistic abilities, or the rationale on which multilingual individuals use their different languages for different social purposes. There are of course innumerable facts to be discovered, even about a language as well investigated as English, concerning the nature of the different kinds of English we use in different situations – when we are talking to equals, superiors or subordinates; when we are 'on the job'; when we are old or young, upper class or lower class, male or female; when we are trying to persuade, inform or bargain; and so on. An informal definition of sociolinguistics highlights this concern to get even the most elementary of descriptive information down on paper: 'Who can say what, how, using what means, to whom, when, and why?' If we knew all these factors, we would know a great deal about social problems. These days sociolinguistics has progressed far in accumulating its own data in order to answer these questions.

To analyse a problem sociolinguistically implies being able to analyse it linguistically. Sociolinguistics makes use of the findings of linguistic theory and description in its work; and in one sense its success is dependent on success in 'pure linguistics'. On the other hand, the nature of its subject-matter means that there will arise a great deal which will be both theoretically and methodologically novel – explanatory constructs of one kind or another which are not constructs of either linguistics or sociology, but a derivative of both. One example of this is the notion of 'interference', that is, linguistic disturbance which results from two languages (or dialects) coming into contact in a specific situation. The problem of inter-ference is not something which linguistics, or any other subject, on its own, could handle. There has been some debate as to whether the existence of uniquely sociolinguistic problems of this kind requires the establishment of a quite independent discipline, with a theoretical identity and methodology of its own, or whether the dependence on linguistics in its general sense is so fundamental that such a prospect is impossible. This is an issue which will doubtless continue to be discussed for some time. Meanwhile, it is the case that for practical purposes (as in teaching linguistics) most courses would not make a clear-cut distinction, but would consider the study of sociolinguistics to be an essential part of the explana-tion of the subject as a whole.

An even stronger link is argued these days for my second example of interdisciplinary overlap, *psycholinguistics*. The relation of lin-guistics to psychology has been the source of some heated discus-sion of late, largely due to Chomsky's particular emphasis on this question. His view of linguistics, as outlined for instance in his book *Language and Mind*, is that the most important contribution linguistics can make is to the study of the human mind; and that linguistics is accordingly best seen as a branch of cognitive psy-chology. This is not an altogether surprising thing in view of the mentalistic claims of parts of his theory (cf. p. 103) and his par-ticular views on the nature of language acquisition in children (see below). But it is an extreme view, which most linguists at the present time do not share. On the other hand, no one would want to deny the existence of strong mutual bonds of interest operating between psychology and linguistics. The extent to which language mediates or structures thinking, the extent to which talk about language 'simplicity' or 'complexity' can be given any meaningful psychological basis, the extent to which language is influenced by and itself influences such things as memory, attention, recall and constraints on perception, and the extent to which language has a central role to play in the understanding of human development are broad illustrations of such bonds.

Psycholinguistics as a distinct area of interest developed in the early sixties, and in its early form covered the psychological implications of an extremely broad area, from acoustic phonetics to language pathology. Nowadays, certain areas of language and linguistic theory tend to be concentrated on by those who call themselves psycholinguists, and most of them have been influenced by the development of generative theory. The most important area is the investigation of the acquisition of language by children. Here, there have been many studies of both a theoretical and a descriptive kind. The descriptive need is prompted by the fact that until recently hardly anything was known about the actual facts of language acquisition in children, in particular about the order in which grammatical structures were acquired. Even elementary questions such as when and how children develop their ability to ask questions syntactically, or when they learn the inflectional systems of their language, went unanswered. And a great deal of work has gone on recently into the methodological and descriptive problems involved in obtaining and analysing information of this kind.

The theoretical questions have focused on the issue of how we can account for the phenomenon of language development in children at all. Normal children have mastered most of the structure of their language by the age of five. The generative approach argued against the earlier behaviourist assumptions that it was possible to explain language development largely in terms of imitation and selective reinforcement. It asserted that it was impossible to explain the rapidity or the complexity of language development solely in terms of children imitating the language used by the people around them. And as a result of the arguments supporting this assertion, it would now be generally agreed that imitation alone is not enough. Imitation is an important factor in the development of language (cf. p. 46), but it cannot be the major one, and thus the basis of any theory of language acquisition, because there is too much of central importance in language which is not amenable to direct observation, and thus not imitatable – the various meaning-relations between sentences or parts of sentences, for instance, or, more generally, the abstract knowledge of the grammatical rules of their language which adults have as part of their competence. All normal children come to develop this abstract knowledge for themselves; and the generative approach argues that such a process is only explicable if one postulates that certain features of this competence are present in the brains of children right from the beginning. In other words, what is being claimed is that children's brains contain certain *innate* characteristics which 'pre-structure' them in the direction of language learning. To enable these innate features to develop into adult competence, children must be exposed to human language, i.e. they must be stimulated in order to respond. But the basis on which they develop their linguistic abilities is not describable in behaviourist terms.

What we have here, then, is a hypothesis about the nature of language acquisition. So far, it has not been tested in any convincing way (and it may not be possible to test it, in the usual sense); but it has provoked a great deal of speculation. In particular, it raises the question of how far the innate features could be identified with the primitive meaning-relations of grammatical theory – that is, the linguistic universals talked about at the end of Chapter 4. Are all children born with an ability to discriminate 'subjects' from 'objects', let us say, in some sense? How many such basic relations might one plausibly ascribe to the child? And how specific is its innateness? Clearly, it is not possible to suggest that the child has any features of a *particular* language innate, for instance a particular feature of English syntax which does not occur in French or German. To suggest this would be tantamount to saying that children of any race would find it easier to learn English than to learn other languages (that is, their brains would pre-dispose them towards English); and all available evidence points to the implausibility of this conclusion. A Zulu child learns Zulu just as rapidly as an English child learns English, it seems. No, the innate features must be sufficiently general, sufficiently 'deep', to be capable of equally readily underlying the structure of *any* language. And on this point, the identity of interests between linguistic and psycholinguistic theory (at least, in this field) should be clear. There have of course been a number of objections raised to the innateness hypothesis – for example, on the grounds that what is innate is not so much deep structural information, but rather learning principles of a more general kind. Some people would like to see what would happen if the hypothesis were formulated in terms other than those provided by Chomsky's later work. As someone put it once, 'Why *should* we see the child as if it were born with a copy of *Aspects of the Theory of Syntax* tucked inside its head!' Unkind, perhaps; for without *Aspects*, and the work which followed it, many interesting questions might never have been raised. The issue, however, is by no means determined.

In the 1980s, the interest in the innateness hypothesis has been largely replaced by a focus on the relationship between language development and a child's cognitive skills, following on the influential work of Jean Piaget and other psychologists. There has been renewed interest in the strategies which children use in acquiring language, and the significance of such topics as imitation has come to be reconsidered in this light. Above all, there has been a concern to study the factors which characterize children's learning environment – in particular, the nature of the input language they receive from mothers and other caretakers (*motherese*). The *Journal of Child Language*, which commenced publication in 1975, is now the best source of information on current trends in the subject. Its contributors span the disciplines of psychology and linguistics, and their work illustrates a wide range of experimental and naturalistic approaches to the subject. Without doubt, the field of language acquisition remains one of the most intriguing areas of linguistics study, at the present time, and one which will certainly remain in the forefront of linguists' attention over the next few years.

There are many other applications of linguistics in fields not so far mentioned, which tend to be grouped together anonymously as 'applied linguistics'. Foreign language teaching and learning is the major application, as suggested in Chapter 1; but there is also native language teaching, translation (either individually, or using machines), the many facets of telecommunications, lexicography . . . The list could go on for some time. Each of these fields selects its basic information and theoretical framework from the overall perspective which linguistics provides, and applies it to the clarification of some general area of human experience. And it is surely the many branches of applied linguistics that will ultimately provide the main link between Chapters 1 and 4, if such a link be needed. But, as always, we must remember that an application is but the tip of a theoretical iceberg: many hours of research and discussion, much of it highly specialized, abstract, and quite unpractical, will have taken place in order to provide the basic knowledge which can be implemented in a specific application. Indeed, in many cases it is only through the illuminating models developed in linguistic theory, and the demonstration of a coherent system underlying apparently disorganized data, that applications and approaches to a problem have been thought of at all.

And it is in this way that an answer can be provided to the superficial criticisms which are sometimes made to the kind of topic discussed at length in Chapter 4. 'What does it matter', such queries run, 'whether the basic phonological unit is the phoneme or the distinctive feature? or whether the morpheme concept fits all cases? or whether there is a boundary-line between syntax and semantics?' If these questions are still being asked, then the arguments underlying my Chapter 3 about the scientific aims of linguistics have not been appreciated. The kinds of distinction drawn there are essential if we hope to build up a general theory of language; we have to appreciate the kinds of reasoning relevant to this task, even if we do not always agree with the conclusions reached. If we are adopting a rational approach to our study of (or interest in) language, then we cannot just blindly analyse and describe in a random, arbitrary way. Whatever our purpose, whether 'pure' or 'applied', we must know *why* we are doing what we are doing, if we hope to be clear and consistent and wish to convince others (or even ourselves) of its validity. It *does* matter about these questions, and many others like them, because the answers constitute our world-view of language. Choosing to work with distinctive features is one choice we make, along with many others, which ultimately builds up a coherent and self-consistent picture of language structure that intuitively satisfies us. We sit back and say, 'Yes, that makes sense.' To a certain extent, then, our final decisions about which concepts to work with are a matter of taste. But the more we understand the relative merits and demerits of the various theories, descriptions and procedures which the subject provides, the more likely we will be to reach a view of language that is reasonable and convincing, as well as personally satisfying.

Further Reading

Some introductory material has already been mentioned in the course of exposition, on pp. 41, 49, 86, 101, 135, 152, 205–6, 217, 233, 235, 246 and 253.
In addition, the following general introductions are available:

Aitchison, J., *The Articulate Mammal*, Hutchinson, 1976.

Bolinger, D. L., *Aspects of Language*, Harcourt Brace Jovanovich, 3rd edn 1981.

Brown, K., *Linguistics Today*, Fontana, 1984.

Clark, H. H. and Clark, E. V., *Psychology and Language*, Harcourt Brace Jovanovich, 1977.

Crystal, D., *Introduction to Language Pathology*, Edward Arnold, 1980.

Crystal, D., *A First Dictionary of Linguistics and Phonetics*, Blackwell, 2nd edn 1985.

Hudson, R., *Invitation to Linguistics*, Blackwell, 1984.

Leech, G. N., *Semantics*, Pelican, 2nd edn 1981.

Lyons, J., *Language and Linguistics*, Cambridge University Press, 1981.

O'Connor, J. D., *Phonetics*, Pelican, 1971.

Palmer, F. R. *Grammar*, Pelican, 2nd edn 1984.

Palmer, F. R., *Semantics*, Cambridge University Press, 2nd edn 1981.

Petyt, K. M., *Dialectology*, Blackwell, 1980.

Quirk, R. *The Use of English*, Longman, 2nd edn 1968.

Robins, R. H., *General Linguistics: an Introductory Survey*, Longman, 3rd edn 1980.

Smith, N. and Wilson, D., *Modern Linguistics*, Pelican, 1979.

Trudgill, P., *Sociolinguistics*, Pelican, 2nd edn 1983.

Subject Index

Person Index

Person Index

READ MORE IN PENGUIN

In every corner of the world, on every subject under the sun, Penguin represents quality and variety – the very best in publishing today.

For complete information about books available from Penguin – including Puffins, Penguin Classics and Arkana – and how to order them, write to us at the appropriate address below. Please note that for copyright reasons the selection of books varies from country to country.

In the United Kingdom: Please write to *Dept. EP, Penguin Books Ltd, Bath Road, Harmondsworth, West Drayton, Middlesex UB7 ODA*

In the United States: Please write to *Consumer Sales, Penguin USA, P.O. Box 999, Dept. 17109, Bergenfield, New Jersey 07621-0120*. VISA and MasterCard holders call 1-800-253-6476 to order Penguin titles

In Canada: Please write to *Penguin Books Canada Ltd, 10 Alcorn Avenue, Suite 300, Toronto, Ontario M4V 3B2*

In Australia: Please write to *Penguin Books Australia Ltd, P.O. Box 257, Ringwood, Victoria 3134*

In New Zealand: Please write to *Penguin Books (NZ) Ltd, Private Bag 102902, North Shore Mail Centre, Auckland 10*

In India: Please write to *Penguin Books India Pvt Ltd, 706 Eros Apartments, 56 Nehru Place, New Delhi 110 019*

In the Netherlands: Please write to *Penguin Books Netherlands bv, Postbus 3507, NL-1001 AH Amsterdam*

In Germany: Please write to *Penguin Books Deutschland GmbH, Metzlerstrasse 26, 60594 Frankfurt am Main*

In Spain: Please write to *Penguin Books S. A., Bravo Murillo 19, 1° B, 28015 Madrid*

In Italy: Please write to *Penguin Italia s.r.l., Via Felice Casati 20, I–20124 Milano*

In France: Please write to *Penguin France S. A., 17 rue Lejeune, F–31000 Toulouse*

In Japan: Please write to *Penguin Books Japan, Ishikiribashi Building, 2–5–4, Suido, Bunkyo-ku, Tokyo 112*

In South Africa: Please write to *Longman Penguin Southern Africa (Pty) Ltd, Private Bag X08, Bertsham 2013*

READ MORE IN PENGUIN

LANGUAGE/LINGUISTICS

Sociolinguistics Peter Trudgill

Women speak 'better' English than men. The Eskimo language has several words for snow. 1001 factors influence the way we speak. Professor Trudgill draws on languages from Afrikaans to Yiddish to illuminate this fascinating topic and provide a painless introduction to sociolinguistics.

Bad Language Lars-Gunnar Andersson and Peter Trudgill

As this witty and incisive book makes clear, the prophets of gloom who claim that our language is getting worse are guided by emotion far more than by hard facts. The real truth, as Andersson and Trudgill illuminate in fascinating detail, is that change has always been inherent in language.

Multilingualism John Edwards

This superb survey explores all the contentious topics about language: links between gender and speech styles, and the attitudes, aptitudes and brains of bilinguals. In its wit, scholarship and rich supply of unusual facts, *Multilingualism* is a book of compelling interest to anyone who cares about the role of language in society.

Grammar Frank Palmer

In modern linguistics grammar means far more than cases, tenses and declensions – it means precise and scientific description of the structure of language. This concise guide takes the reader simply and clearly through the concepts of traditional grammar, morphology, sentence structure and transformational-generative grammar.

Longman Guide to English Usage
Sidney Greenbaum and Janet Whitcut

Containing 5000 entries compiled by leading authorities on modern English, this invaluable reference work clarifies every kind of usage problem, giving expert advice on points of grammar, meaning, style, spelling, pronunciation and punctuation.

READ MORE IN PENGUIN

REFERENCE

The Penguin Dictionary of Literary Terms and Literary Theory
J. A. Cuddon

'Scholarly, succinct, comprehensive and entertaining, this is an important book, an indispensable work of reference. It draws on the literature of many languages and quotes aptly and freshly from our own' – *The Times Educational Supplement*

The Penguin Spelling Dictionary

What are the plurals of *octopus* and *rhinoceros*? What is the difference between *stationery* and *stationary*? And how about *annex* and *annexe*, *agape* and *Agape*? This comprehensive new book, the fullest spelling dictionary now available, provides the answers.

The Roget's Thesaurus of English Words and Phrases
Betty Kirkpatrick (ed.)

This new edition of Roget's classic work, now brought up to date for the nineties, will increase anyone's command of the English language. Fully cross-referenced, it includes synonyms of every kind (formal or colloquial, idiomatic and figurative) for almost 900 headings. It is a must for writers and utterly fascinating for any English speaker.

The Penguin Dictionary of English Idioms
Daphne M. Gulland and David G. Hinds-Howell

The English language is full of pitfalls for the foreign student – but the most common problem lies in understanding and using the vast array of idioms. *The Penguin Dictionary of English Idioms* is uniquely designed to stimulate understanding and familiarity by explaining the meanings and origins of idioms and giving examples of typical usage.

The Penguin Wordmaster Dictionary
Martin H. Manser and Nigel D. Turton

This dictionary puts the pleasure back into word-seeking. Every time you look at a page you get a bonus – a panel telling you everything about a particular word or expression. It is, therefore, a dictionary to be read as well as used for its concise and up-to-date definitions.

READ MORE IN PENGUIN

REFERENCE

Medicines: A Guide for Everybody Peter Parish

Now in its seventh edition and completely revised and updated, this bestselling guide is written in ordinary language for the ordinary reader yet will prove indispensable to anyone involved in health care – nurses, pharmacists, opticians, social workers and doctors.

Media Law Geoffrey Robertson, QC, and Andrew Nichol

Crisp and authoritative surveys explain the up-to-date position on defamation, obscenity, official secrecy, copyright and confidentiality, contempt of court, the protection of privacy and much more.

The Slang Thesaurus

Do you make the public bar sound like a gentleman's club? The miraculous *Slang Thesaurus* will liven up your language in no time. You won't Adam and Eve it! A mine of funny, witty, acid and vulgar synonyms for the words you use every day.

The Penguin Dictionary of Troublesome Words Bill Bryson

Why should you avoid discussing the *weather conditions*? Can a married woman be celibate? Why is it eccentric to talk about the aroma of a cowshed? A straightforward guide to the pitfalls and hotly disputed issues in standard written English.

The Penguin Dictionary of Musical Performers Arthur Jacobs

In this invaluable companion volume to *The Penguin Dictionary of Music* Arthur Jacobs has brought together the names of over 2,500 performers. Music is written by composers, yet it is the interpreters who bring it to life; in this comprehensive book they are at last given their due.

The Penguin Dictionary of Physical Geography John Whittow

'Dr Whittow and Penguin Reference Books have put serious students of the subject in their debt, by combining the terminology of the traditional geomorphology with that of the quantitative revolution and defining both in one large and comprehensive dictionary of physical geography ... clear and succinct' – *The Times Educational Supplement*

READ MORE IN PENGUIN

PHILOSOPHY

What Philosophy Is   Anthony O'Hear

'Argument after argument is represented, including most of the favourites
… its tidy and competent construction, as well as its straightforward style,
mean that it will serve well anyone with a serious interest in philosophy'
– *The Journal of Applied Philosophy*

Montaigne and Melancholy   M. A. Screech

'A sensitive probe into how Montaigne resolved for himself the age-old
ambiguities of melancholia and, in doing so, spoke of what he called the
"human condition"' – Roy Porter in the *London Review of Books*

Labyrinths of Reason   William Poundstone

'The world and what is in it, even what people say to you, will not seem
the same after plunging into *Labyrinths of Reason* … Poundstone's book
merits the description of *tour de force*. He holds up the deepest
philosophical questions for scrutiny and examines their relation to reality
in a way that irresistibly sweeps readers on' – *New Scientist*

I: The Philosophy and Psychology of Personal Identity
Jonathan Glover

From cases of split brains and multiple personalities to the importance of
memory and recognition by others, the author of *Causing Death and
Saving Lives* tackles the vexed questions of personal identity.

Ethics Inventing Right and Wrong   J. L. Mackie

Widely used as a text, Mackie's complete and clear treatise on moral
theory deals with the status and content of ethics, sketches a practical
moral system, and examines the frontiers at which ethics touches psychology, theology, law and politics.

The Central Questions of Philosophy   A. J. Ayer

'He writes lucidly and has a teacher's instinct for the helpful pause and
reiteration … an admirable introduction to the ways in which philosophic
issues are experienced and analysed in current Anglo-American academic
milieux' – *Sunday Times*

READ MORE IN PENGUIN

WOMEN'S INTEREST

Killing Rage: Ending Racism bell hooks

Addressing race and racism in American society from a black and a feminist standpoint, bell hooks covers a broad spectrum of issues in these twenty-three essays, including: the psychological trauma of racism; anti-Semitism; friendship between black women and white women; and the internalized racism of the media.

The New Our Bodies, Ourselves Angela Phillips and Jill Rakusen
A Health Book by and for Women

Rewritten and expanded to meet the needs of women and men in the 1990s, *The New Our Bodies, Ourselves* has influenced the thinking of a generation.

The Well Woman Handbook Suzy Hayman

Practical and informative, *The Well Woman Handbook* will enable you to learn more about your body and put the responsibility for its health back into your own hands.

Nine Parts of Desire Geraldine Brooks
The Hidden World of Islamic Women

'She takes us behind the veils and into the homes of women in every corner of the Middle East ... It is in her descriptions of her meetings – like that with Khomeini's widow Khadija, who paints him as a New Man (and one for whom she dyed her hair vamp-red) – that the book excels' – *Observer*

Banishing the Beast Lucy Bland
English Feminism and Sexual Morality 1885–1914

'Fascinating ... Her work is a timely reminder that balancing social responsibility and individual rights in sexuality and maternity is far from being a new debate ... This is scholarly history with a contemporary relevance' – Sheila Rowbotham

READ MORE IN PENGUIN

PSYCHOLOGY

Introduction to Jung's Psychology Frieda Fordham

'She has delivered a fair and simple account of the main aspects of my psychological work. I am indebted to her for this admirable piece of work' – C. G. Jung in the *Foreword*

Child Care and the Growth of Love John Bowlby

His classic 'summary of evidence of the effects upon children of lack of personal attention ... it presents to administrators, social workers, teachers and doctors a reminder of the significance of the family' – *The Times*

Recollections and Reflections Bruno Bettelheim

'A powerful thread runs through Bettelheim's message: his profound belief in the dignity of man, and the importance of seeing and judging other people from their own point of view' – William Harston in the *Independent*. 'These memoirs of a wise old child, candid, evocative, heart-warming, suggest there is hope yet for humanity' – Ray Porter in the *Evening Standard*

Sanity, Madness and the Family R. D. Laing and A. Esterson

Schizophrenia: fact or fiction? Certainly not fact, according to the authors of this controversial book. Suggesting that some forms of madness may be largely social creations, *Sanity, Madness and the Family* demands to be taken very seriously indeed.

I Am Right You Are Wrong Edward de Bono

In this book Dr Edward de Bono puts forward a direct challenge to what he calls the rock logic of Western thinking. Drawing on our understanding of the brain as a self-organizing information system, Dr de Bono shows that perception is the key to more constructive thinking and the serious creativity of design.

READ MORE IN PENGUIN

PSYCHOLOGY

Psychoanalysis and Feminism   Juliet Mitchell

'Juliet Mitchell has risked accusations of apostasy from her fellow feminists. Her book not only challenges orthodox feminism, however; it defies the conventions of social thought in the English-speaking countries ... a brave and important book' – *New York Review of Books*

The Divided Self   R. D. Laing

'A study that makes all other works I have read on schizophrenia seem fragmentary ... The author brings, through his vision and perception, that particular touch of genius which causes one to say "Yes, I have always known that, why have I never thought of it before?"' – *Journal of Analytical Psychology*

Po: Beyond Yes and No   Edward de Bono

No is the basic tool of the logic system. *Yes* is the basic tool of the belief system. Edward de Bono offers *Po* as a device for changing our ways of thinking: a method for approaching problems in a new and more creative way.

The Informed Heart   Bruno Bettelheim

Bettelheim draws on his experience in concentration camps to illuminate the dangers inherent in all mass societies in this profound and moving masterpiece.

The Care of the Self   Michel Foucault
The History of Sexuality Vol 3

Foucault examines the transformation of sexual discourse from the Hellenistic to the Roman world in an inquiry which 'bristles with provocative insights into the tangled liaison of sex and self' – *The Times Higher Education Supplement*

Mothering Psychoanalysis   Janet Sayers

'An important book ... records the immense contribution to psychoanalysis made by its founding mothers' – Julia Neuberger in the *Sunday Times*

READ MORE IN PENGUIN

POLITICS AND SOCIAL SCIENCES

National Identity Anthony D. Smith

In this stimulating new book, Anthony D. Smith asks why the first modern nation states developed in the West. He considers how ethnic origins, religion, language and shared symbols can provide a sense of nation and illuminates his argument with a wealth of detailed examples.

The Feminine Mystique Betty Friedan

'A brilliantly researched, passionately argued book – a time-bomb flung into the Mom-and-Apple-Pie image ... Out of the debris of that shattered ideal, the Women's Liberation Movement was born' – Ann Leslie

Peacemaking Among Primates Frans de Waal

'A vitally fresh analysis of the biology of aggression which deserves the serious attention of all those concerned with the nature of conflict, whether in humans or non-human animals ... De Waal delivers forcibly and clearly his interpretation of the significance of his findings ... Lucidly written' – *The Times Higher Educational Supplement*

Political Ideas David Thomson (ed.)

From Machiavelli to Marx – a stimulating and informative introduction to the last 500 years of European political thinkers and political thought.

The Raw and the Cooked Claude Lévi-Strauss

Deliberately, brilliantly and inimitably challenging, Lévi-Strauss's seminal work of structural anthropology cuts wide and deep into the mind of mankind, as he finds in the myths of the South American Indians a comprehensible psychological pattern.

The Social Construction of Reality
Peter Berger and Thomas Luckmann

The Social Construction of Reality is concerned with the sociology of 'everything that passes for knowledge in society', and particularly with that 'common-sense knowledge' that constitutes the reality of everyday life for the ordinary member of society.

READ MORE IN PENGUIN

POLITICS AND SOCIAL SCIENCES

Conservatism Ted Honderich

'It offers a powerful critique of the major beliefs of modern conservatism, and shows how much a rigorous philosopher can contribute to understanding the fashionable but deeply ruinous absurdities of his times' – *New Statesman & Society*

Karl Marx: Selected Writings in Sociology and Social Philosophy Bottomore and Rubel (eds.)

'It makes available, in coherent form and lucid English, some of Marx's most important ideas. As an introduction to Marx's thought, it has very few rivals indeed' – *British Journal of Sociology*

Post-War Britain A Political History Alan Sked and Chris Cook

Major political figures from Attlee to Thatcher, the aims and achievements of governments and the changing fortunes of Britain in the period since 1945 are thoroughly scrutinized in this stimulating history.

Inside the Third World Paul Harrison

This comprehensive book brings home a wealth of facts and analysis on the often tragic realities of life for the poor people and communities of Asia, Africa and Latin America.

Medicine, Patients and the Law Margaret Brazier

'An absorbing book which, in addition to being accessible to the general reader, should prove illuminating for practitioners – both medical and legal – and an ideal accompaniment to student courses on law and medicine' – *New Law Journal*

Bread and Circuses Paul Veyne

'Warming oneself at the fire of M. Veyne's intelligence is such a joy that any irritation at one's prejudice and ignorance being revealed and exposed vanishes with his winning ways ... *Bread and Circuses* is M. Veyne's way of explaining the philosophy of the Roman Empire, which was the most successful form of government known to mankind' – *Literary Review*

BY THE SAME AUTHOR

An Encyclopedic Dictionary of Language and Languages

With entries for every country and several hundred languages, for literary terms, grammar and word games, for phonetics, typography and speech disorders, this 'convenient one-stop source' provides clear and fully cross-referenced definitions of key linguistic terms.

The English Language

'Illuminating guided tour of our common treasure by one of its most lucid and sensible professionals' – *The Times*

Who Cares About English Usage?

To boldy split or not to split? Why is life so stressful? Is this something up with which we must put?

Aspects of these and many other questions come under entertaining scrutiny in this book on some of the common questions about English usage. Clearly and wittily presented with short quizzes to stimulate the mind and some pertinent cartoons, this book proves that it's fun as well as worthwhile thinking about our language, how it reflects ourselves and how best to feel at home with it.

Listen to Your Child
A Parent's Guide to Children's Language

Learning to talk is probably the greatest milestone in a child's development – a deeply moving, and often hilarious, experience for all parents.

It is also a process which has been intensively studied by psychologists and linguists in recent years; this charming and informative book shows us what they have discovered. In dealing with the whole period from (and before) birth to the early school years, David Crystal provides invaluable advice for parents as well as a painless introduction to a central topic of modern language study.